Let's Learn Kanji

Let's Learn Kanji

An introduction to radicals, components,
and 250 very basic kanji

Joyce Yumi Mitamura and Yasuko Kosaka Mitamura

KODANSHA INTERNATIONAL
Tokyo • New York • London

Distributed in the United States by Kodansha America, LLC, and in the United Kingdom and continental Europe by Kodansha Europe Ltd.

Published by Kodansha International Ltd., 17–14 Otowa 1-chome, Bunkyo-ku, Tokyo 112–8652.

ISBN 978-4-7700-2068-0

First Edition, 1997
18 17 16 15 14 13 12 11 10   18 17 16 15 14 13 12 11

www.kodansha-intl.com

Table of Contents

Part I   Radicals and Components

Chapter 3

Part II 250 Very Basic Kanji and Exercises

Chapter 4

Preface

In all languages, reading and writing are entirely separate skills from listening and speaking. Children, and even adults to a certain extent, can pick up the spoken language through listening to and participating in everyday conversation. But they go to school to learn to read and write because the written language cannot be "picked up." A person who can speak a foreign language quite fluently may have difficulty reading or writing it if not properly trained. Everyone, even native speakers, must make special efforts to acquire reading and writing skills, and the Japanese language is no exception. The only difference between Japanese and other languages is one of degree rather than of kind. The process of learning written Japanese may require more time because of the three writing systems, Hiragana, Katakana, and Kanji, and because the number of Kanji is rather large. Native Japanese learn Kanji during nine years of their education (elementary and junior high).

Non-native students, in contrast, cannot afford to spend so much time learning Kanji, so they need a systematic method to help them learn Kanji quickly and efficiently. The system devised in this workbook focuses on radicals and components and the way in which these radicals and components allow the Kanji to be arranged into related family groups. In other words, Kanji which contain the same radicals or components can be considered something like a family and the method of learning Kanji in this book is organized around this family relationship.

In Part I, which is devoted entirely to Kanji fundamentals, students will begin with the smallest unit of a Kanji character: the stroke. Next they will move on to radicals and components. These are the identifiable parts of Kanji and often carry intrinsic meaning or derivation. Most importantly, as mentioned above, radicals and components form the basis of Kanji family groups. By learning these various family groups, students will be able to break down new and complex Kanji into familiar components. This skill will facilitate the process of learning more complex Kanji.

In Part II, the students are ready to actually start writing Kanji. They will practice and learn 250 "very basic Kanji," most of which will appear later as components of more complex Kanji. In addition, each very basic Kanji is presented with examples of these more complex family group members, thereby enabling students not only to learn the 250 very basic Kanji but to recognize the related over 1,000 complex Kanji as well. Throughout Parts I and II, exercises are provided to help students learn the material presented in each chapter.

It is the authors' great hope that through the use of this workbook, students will develop a desire to continue and eventually master Kanji.

We would like to give special thanks to the following persons; without them, this workbook would not have been possible: former Professor Noboru Inamoto, at the University of Southern California, for his kind support and information including the historical details of Kanji; Mr. Minoru Yasunaga, Senior Specialist in the Japanese Language Division of the Ministry of Education for taking the time to provide us with invaluable information, and knowledgeable advice on all aspects of Kanji, including Ministry Standards; Mr. Steven Sumida and Mrs. Sadako Sumida for spending valuable time translating vocabulary; and Ms. Toshiko Imanari for her kind help in selecting examples. A dedicated student, Mr. Richard Covington, gave much of his time to review the manuscript from the students' point of view and offered innumerable helpful suggestions. Lastly, we would like to give sincere thanks to our dear friend Mrs. Virginia Newton for her patient assistance and valuable advice in the editing and typing of various drafts of the manuscript.

Joyce Yumi Mitamura
Yasuko Kosaka Mitamura

Standards and Format

The following standards and formatting guidelines are used throughout this workbook except as noted.

The Kanji used in this workbook follow the latest Japanese Ministry of Education standards:

1. Most Kanji are from the first to third or fourth grade Gakushū Kanji (a list of 1,006 Kanji to be learned by the sixth grade) although some are from the Jōyō Kanji (a list of 1,945 "daily use Kanji" to be learned by the ninth grade that includes the Gakushū Kanji.) The lists were revised by the Japanese Ministry of Education in 1989 and 1981 respectively.

2. Kanji forms (how they are written) are those that were prescribed by the Ministry of Education in 1949, some of which are radically simplified from the old forms.

3. The readings of Kanji, both On (pronunciations based on the Chinese words associated with the Kanji) and Kun (pronunciation of Japanese words associated with the Kanji) are also those prescribed by the Ministry of Education.

The order of the readings in this book is always Kun first, then On.

In Part I, the Kun reading is in romanized lower case letters and the On reading is in romanized upper case letters so that the students' attention is not divided by reading Kana. However, in Part II the Kun reading is shown in Hiragana and the On reading in Katakana.

Example Kanji for radicals, components, and basic Kanji have been specifically chosen to show students how these elements are used in actual characters. However, students are not expected to practice writing these example Kanji. They are expected only to recognize them. By doing so, the students will more than double the number of Kanji they can identify. Later, once radicals, other components, and basic Kanji have been firmly mastered, they can learn how to write the example Kanji more easily.

As for the pronunciations of the example Kanji, only the Kun reading is provided (because Kun indicates meaning), except for those Kanji that only have an On reading or seldom used Kun reading. However, both the Kun and On readings are provided when the On reading is frequently used or when a group of the example Kanji share the same components and therefore the same On pronunciation. In the case of verbs with both transitive and intransitive forms, the most commonly used form is shown. For example, for *a·keru* (v.t.) and *a·ku* (v.i.) only *a·keru* (open) is shown.

The definitions for the example Kanji are usually the most common translations. When two or more meanings are equally used, additional definitions may appear.

The following special symbols have specific meanings in this workbook. They are also noted in the text at appropriate places:

- O indicates the radicals whose names should be memorized.

- * indicates a Kanji from the Jōyō Kanji list which is not included in the Gakushū Kanji list.

- † indicates radicals or components that are independent Kanji but are no longer included in the Jōyō Kanji.

- †† indicates radicals or components that are independent Kanji in classical Japanese and are no longer included in the Jōyō Kanji.

- ‡ indicates a radical, component, or Kanji introduced earlier in the workbook; a page reference is given in the footnote.

- • indicates a Kanji that will be introduced later in the workbook; a page reference is given in the footnote.

- ▲ indicates a Kanji not introduced in the workbook; the translation is given in the footnote.

Okurigana (word ending or inflection written in Hiragana) is shown after a ".". For example: *aka·rui* and *hana·su*.

When showing the pronunciation of Kanji in Part II, euphonic change is not listed separately because it is considered simply a variation of the original reading. For example: ZEN for 千 in 三千 (SANZEN= three-thousand) is not listed; only the original reading, SEN, is listed.

Introduction to Kanji

The inspiration for Kanji is said to have come to a scribe in ancient China from the footprints of birds and animals. In reality, however, the origins of Kanji are attributed to the scribes of the Yin [殷] Dynasty which lasted from about 1700–1050 B.C. The earliest Kanji specimen known today is referred to as Oracle Bone Scripture [甲骨文], followed by Bronze Scripture [金文]. Oracle Bone Scripture was written on tortoise shell and animal bones, and was used by the Emperors of the Yin Dynasty for divination and important state affairs, while the more decorative Bronze Scripture was used for inscription on bronzeware, swords, etc., mainly in the next Chou [周] Dynasty (about 1050–220 B.C.).

It is generally believed that Kanji came to Japan from China through Korea sometime between the fourth and the fifth centuries A.D. Korea had come under the influence of China during the Early Han [前漢] Dynasty (206 B.C.–A.D. 8), and thereafter the Korean peninsula became a meeting place of cultures. However, cultural exchange between Korea, China, and Japan did not occur with any frequency until the late fourth and early fifth centuries, when the roles of scribes, correspondents, and translators in Japan were filled by Koreans and Chinese. No record of a written language in Japan exists before this time.

Kanji is ideographic, not phonetic, which means that each character represents a concept or an idea rather than a sound. In contrast, the Hiragana and Katakana syllabaries, created by the Japanese, have no fixed meaning, and are instead phonetic symbols that represent pronunciation. Both Hiragana and Katakana developed from Kanji; Hiragana is a cursive form of the entire character, while Katakana is derived from one portion of the original character. Today all forms of modern written Japanese use these three writing systems in combination.

The Number of Kanji

It is said that most Kanji were created during the Tang [唐] (618–907) and Sung [宋] (960–1279) Dynasties. A total of about 47,000 Kanji were recorded in the Kanji dictionary *Kōki·Jiten* [康熙字典] which was compiled in the Ching [清] Dynasty (1644–1912). In Japan, 3,000 to 4,000 characters were used until the Mombusho (Ministry of Education) made an effort to simplify the writing system in 1946. It selected 1,850 of the most important Kanji used in business, newspapers, magazines, and official government documents, and called this list the Tōyō Kanji [当用漢字] (Kanji for general use).

Then in 1981, the Mombusho chose 95 additional characters to be included among the most relevant to daily life. Today, most of what is written can be read with a knowledge of these 1,945 Kanji, which are known as the Jōyō Kanji [常用漢字] (Kanji for daily use). The Japanese learn how to <u>read</u> most of the Jōyō Kanji during nine years of compulsory education. However, learning to <u>write</u> them all comfortably is a harder task. Therefore, the Mombusho designated about half of the 1,945 Kanji as Gakushū Kanji [学習漢字] (Kanji to be learned) which are characters for students to learn how to <u>write</u> by the end of the sixth grade and to <u>use</u> <u>comfortably</u> by the end of the ninth grade. (The latest revised list includes 1,006 characters for the Gakushū Kanji.)

Two Ways to Read Kanji: On [音] and Kun [訓]

Two different readings of Kanji exist. The On reading is derived from the original Chinese pronunciation, while the Kun reading is the pronunciation of the native Japanese word which corresponds most closely to the meaning of the Chinese character. In Part I of this book, the On reading of Kanji is illustrated by the use of upper case letters and the Kun reading by the use of lower case letters. For example:

山 (mountain)　川 (river)　海 (sea)　石 (stone)　草 (grass)

yama　　　　kawa　　　　umi　　　　ishi　　　　kusa

SAN　　　　SEN　　　　KAI　　　　SEKI　　　　SŌ

Generally, when a Kanji appears by itself [...] ling is applied, while when two or more Kanj[...] he On reading is used (On + On). For exa[...]

山にのぼります。　　yama ni noborimasu. (I will climb a mountain.)

富士山にのぼります。　FUJI-SAN ni noborimasu. (I will climb Mt. Fuji.)

However, there are some exceptions: On + Kun, Kun + On, or Kun + Kun. For example:

王様　Ōsama (king)　　=　　On + Kun

手本　teHON (example)　=　　Kun + On

朝日　asahi (morning sun)　=　　Kun + Kun

Furthermore, there are also some single Kanji that only have On readings. For example:

愛 AI (love)　　　　　　茶 CHA (tea)

肉 NIKU (meat)　　　　晩 BAN (evening)

Many characters have more than one On reading. The number of pronunciations any one character possesses is an indication of the number of times it was introduced and reintroduced into Japan from China. In other words, each reading for the same character comes from a different era and/or region in China. For example, the following Kanji possess three different On readings, indicating that the Kanji were introduced into Japan in different eras and from different regions.

	呉音 GO·ON[1] (5th–6th Century A.D.)	漢音 KAN·ON[2] (7th–9th Century A.D.)	唐音 TŌ·ON[3] (10th–13th Century A.D.)
行	行列 GYŌ·RETSU (procession)	行進 KŌ·SHIN (march, parade)	行火 AN·KA (foot warmer)
明	明晩 MYŌ·BAN (tomorrow evening)	明月 MEI·GETSU (full moon)	明国 MIN·KOKU (Ming Dynasty)
京	京都 KYŌ·TO (city in Japan)	京浜 KEI·HIN (Tokyo–Yokohama area)	北京 PE·KIN (Beijing)

Four Types of Kanji Formation

Depending on their method of formation, Kanji can be classified into any one of four categories: 1) *shōkei moji* and 2) *shiji moji* are the most basic kind of characters. 3) *kaii moji* and 4) *keisei moji* are characters made from the combinations of these basic characters. There are two other classifications, *tenchū moji* [転注文字] ("transformed meaning characters") and *kasha moji* [假借文字] ("borrowed sound/meaning characters"), whose usages are different from the original meaning of the characters and depend not on how the Kanji were formed but rather on how they are used. These last two categories are not introduced in this workbook.

---

1 GO·ON is the pronunciation of Kanji introduced from the Southern province, Wu [呉]. Some examples are still found in words related to Buddhism.

2 KAN·ON is the pronunciation of Kanji which prevailed in the capital of China, Chang·an [長安], in Northern China as the standard language during the Sui [隨] (589–618) and Tang [唐] (618–907) Dynasties. It was introduced to Japan by missionaries

and students. Presently most On pronunciation belong to this group.

3 TŌ·ON is the pronunciation of Kanji used during the Sung [宋] (960–1279), Yuan [元] (1279–1368), and Ming [明] (1368–1644) Dynasties. It was introduced to Japan by Zen monks.

1. *Shōkei moji* [象形文字] (pictorial Kanji) are the most primitive characters and origi-
nated from pictures of objects or phenomena. Consequently, most *shōkei moji* are nouns
and are often used as a component of more complex Kanji. It is said that only about 3%
of Kanji ever developed in China are pictorial Kanji. For example:

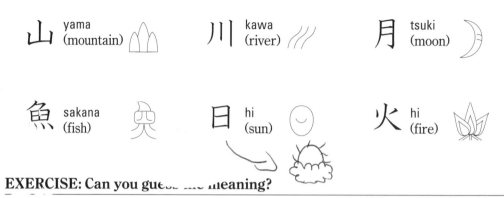

山 yama (mountain)   川 kawa (river)   月 tsuki (moon)

魚 sakana (fish)   日 hi (sun)   火 hi (fire)

EXERCISE: Can you guess the meaning?

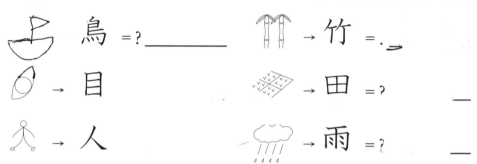

鳥 = ? _____   → 竹 = .____

→ 目   → 田 = ?   ____

→ 人   → 雨 = ?   ____

2. *Shiji moji* [指示文字] (indicative Kanji) use points and lines to express abstract con-
cepts that have no particular shape, including the notion of "in," "above," "below," etc.
The number of *shiji moji* is even less than the number of *shōkei moji*. For example:

___ 一 ICHI (one)   ─ 二 NI (two)   大 ō·kii/DAI (big)

中 naka/CHŪ (inside/middle)   小 chii·sai/SHŌ (small)

EXERCISE: Can you guess the meaning?

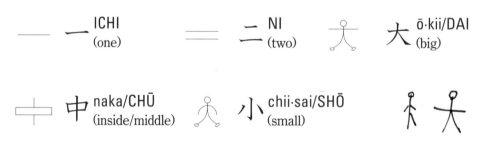

→ 三 = ? Three   → 下 = ? ____

→ 上 = ? above

3. *Kaii moji* [会意文字] (compound ideographic Kanji) are formed by combining pictorial or indicative characters to bring out a new but simple idea. The characters which are combined to form the *kaii moji* contribute to the build-up of its ultimate meaning. It is believed that there are about as many *kaii moji* as there are *shōkei* ... For ex ple

木 + 木 = 林   hayashi (woods)
(tree)   (tree)

木 木 木 = 森   mori (forest)
(three trees)

イ(人) + 木 = 休   yasu·mu (rest)
(man) person?   (tree)

田 + 力 = 男   otokc (man)
(rice field)   (power)

日 + 月 = 明   aka·rui (bright)
(sun)   (moon)

EXERCISE: Can you guess the meaning?

山 + 石 = 岩 = ? _____
(mountain)   (stone)

口 + 鳥 = 鳴 = ? _____
(mouth)   (bird)

火 + 火 = 炎* = ? to burn?
(fire)   (fire)

4. *Keisei moji* [形声文字] (phonetic-ideographic Kanji) are also combinations of two or more simple characters that have taken on a new meaning. But unlike the *kaii moji*, one component of the newly formed character represents the meaning of the entire character, while the other component represents its pronunciation. *Keisei moji* are the most advanced Kanji, evolving from more primitive characters representing only meaning to characters that are organized both phonetically and by meaning. It is said that about 90% of all Kanji fall into the category of *keisei moji*. For example:

江 KŌ (inlet)   洋 YŌ (ocean)   河 KA (river)

In the characters above, the left side [氵] (called the *sanzui* radical) indicates that the characters' meanings are related to water, while the right side represents the various pronunciations.

晴 SEI (cloudless)   清 SEI (pure)   精 SEI (spirit)

In the above characters, the left sides are quite different, which is why the meanings of these Kanji vary widely. However, because they all have the same component on the right side they share the same On pronunciation of SEI.

From these examples, you can see that by learning the basic components, it becomes possible to guess the meaning and pronunciation of many new characters.

EXERCISES

1. Can you guess what the On readings of the following are?

反 (opposite) = _HAN_

坂 (slope) = _HAN_   飯 (meal) = _HAN_   板 (board) = _HAN_

2. Circle the Kanji that is not related in meaning.

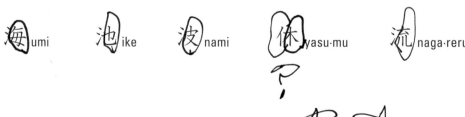

海 umi   池 ike   波 nami   体 yasu·mu   流 naga·reru

I
Radicals and Components

Chapter 1. Learning Strokes [画] (Kaku)

When learning Kanji, a solid knowledge of radicals is useful in analyzing and understanding the composition of Kanji characters. However, before you begin learning the radicals that comprise Kanji, it is important to spend some time learning about the smallest unit of a radical (and therefore of an entire character): the stroke. You will become familiar with the different types of strokes, in what order they are written, and how to count the number of strokes in a radical or a character.

Types of Strokes [一画] (Ikkaku)

Strokes can be categorized into eight major groups. These include *ten* (the abbreviated stroke), *yoko sen* (the horizontal line), *tate sen* (the vertical line), *naname sen* (the diagonal line), *kado kagi* (the corner), *naname kagi* (the sharp angle), *magari* (the curve), and *ahiru* [*ahiru* = duck] (the sharp angle-and-curve combination). There are variations of these categories which depend upon how the stroke is ended. As shown below, there are four ways to end a stroke.

Stroke Endings:

The **stop**, indicated by a period (·), requires bringing the pen to a complete stop and then lifting it off the paper.

The **jump**, indicated by a check, (✔) requires quickly flicking the pen off the paper.

The **sweep**, indicated by a dotted line with an arrow head (), requires gradually sweeping the pen off the paper in a continuous motion.

The final method, the **stop-sweep**, indicated by the stop sign (a period) followed by a dotted line (✎···), requires the pen to come to a complete stop before lifting it off the paper in a sweeping motion diagonally down and to the right.

The Eight Major Stroke Categories:
The eight major categories of strokes are shown below in example Kanji that demonstrate the stroke with its various endings. Be sure to pay careful attention to the stroke endings.

1. Abbreviated stroke (*ten*)

点	下	空	氷	鳥	冬
TEN	**shita**	**sora**	**koori**	**tori**	**fuyu**
(dot)	(underneath)	(sky)	(ice)	(bird)	(winter)

2. Horizontal line (*yoko sen*)
As a rule, the horizontal line is always written from left to right (→).

一	二	三	欠	大	天
ICHI	**NI**	**SAN**	**KETSU**	**ō·kii**	**TEN**
(one)	(two)	(three)	(lack)	(large)	(heaven, sky)

3. Vertical line (*tate sen*)
As a rule, the vertical line is always written from top to bottom (↓).

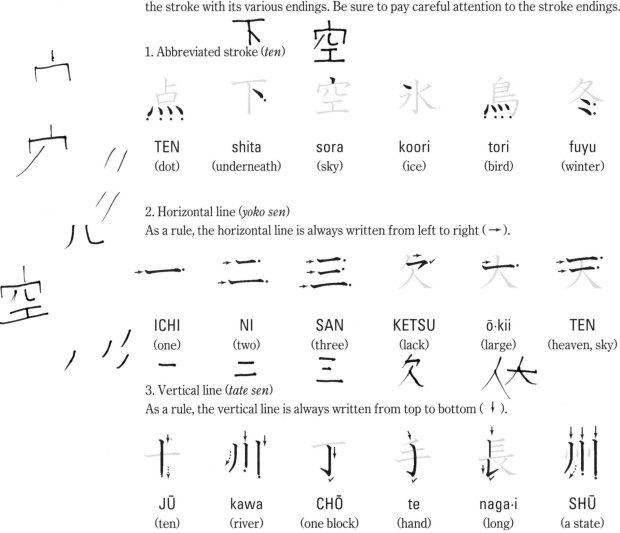

十	川	丁	手	長	州
JŪ	**kawa**	**CHŌ**	**te**	**naga·i**	**SHŪ**
(ten)	(river)	(one block)	(hand)	(long)	(a state)

4. Diagonal line (*naname sen*)

Diagonal lines that begin at the top can sweep downward to the left but those that go downward to the right end either with a stop-sweep or a jump. Those that begin at the bottom sweep upward to the right.

suku·nai	kawa	HON/moto	DAI	hito	ashi
(a few)	(river)	(book/base)	(generation)	(person)	(foot)

5. Corner (*kado kagi*)

kuchi	yama	tsuki	onna	ona·ji	KU
(mouth)	(mountain)	(moon)	(woman)	(same)	(ward)

6. Sharp angle (*nanamekagi*)

ko	yū	mizu	chikara	yumi	KŌ
(child)	(evening)	(water)	(power)	(bow)	(public)

7. Curve (*magari*)

kokoro	SHICHI	ani	ke	iro	kita
(heart)	(seven)	(older brother)	(hair)	(color)	(north)

8. Sharp angle-and-curve combination (*ahiru*)

OTSU	KU	kaze	KI	to·bu	KI
(the second)	(nine)	(wind)	(air)	(fly)	(steam)

EXERCISE

Analyze the following characters and list the types of strokes used.

1. 乙 _____

2. 七 _____ _____

3. 力 _____ _____

4. 九 _____ _____

5. 心 _____ _____

6. 手 _____ _____ _____

7. 水 _____ _____ _____

8. 月 _____ _____ _____

9. 公 _____ _____ _____

10. 女 _____ _____ _____

11. 点 _____ _____ _____ _____

12. 足 _____ _____ _____ _____

Basic Principles of Stroke Order [筆順] (Hitsujun)

Now that you have familiarized yourselves with the different types of strokes, the next step is to understand the process by which these various strokes are used to form radicals and eventually Kanji. This involves knowing the correct order in which to write the strokes. Stroke order follows a natural sequence in which each stroke flows smoothly from the previous one.

Stroke order is an integral part of Kanji that must be learned with every new radical and Kanji. Taking the time now to study the basic principles of stroke order will make learning even the most difficult Kanji much easier. Writing Kanji in their correct stroke order is also important when writing in cursive style. Cursive style Kanji written in the wrong stroke order is unreadable by anyone except the writer.

The following are some general rules for writing Kanji:

1. Kanji are written from left to right.

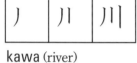

kawa (river)

SHŪ (a state)

2. Kanji are written from top to bottom.

SAN (three)

KŌ (craft)

3. Usually, horizontal lines (*yoko sen*) are written before vertical lines (*tate sen*), even if the vertical line is curved.

JŪ (ten)

SHICHI (seven)

shita (underneath)

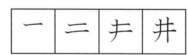

i* (well)

However, there are some exceptions. For example:

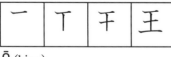

Ō (king)

ta (a field)

4. When the character is symmetric, start at the middle, then move to the left, and lastly to the right side.

]	小	小

chii·sai (small)

]	⺆	水	水

mizu (water)

5. The outside of the character except the bottom line is written before the center portion.

l	⼌	月	日

hi (sun)

l	⼌	⼌	同	同	同

ona·ji (same, p. 3)

l	⼌	⼌	冂	开	国	国	国

kuni (country)

However, there are some exceptions:

一	⼜	又	区

KU (a ward)

一	⼑	⼳	彐	矛	矢	医

I (physician)

6. A left sweep (*hidari barai*) is written before a right stop sweep (*migi barai*).

ノ	人

hito (person)

⼂	八	勺	父

chichi (father)

7. A vertical line (*tate sen*) piercing through the center of a character is written last.

⼂	⼌	口	中

naka (middle)

⼂	⼌	⼍	半	半

HAN (half)

一	厂	冂	冃	百	亘	車

kuruma (car)

8. A horizontal line (*yoko sen*) piercing through the center of the character is written last.

く	夕	女

onna (woman)

ㄥ	口	口	母	母

haha (mother)

ㄱ	了	子

ko (child)

However, there is an exception:

一	十	卄	丗	世

yo (world)

9. A <u>short</u> left sweep (*hidari barai*) precedes a horizontal line (*yoko sen*).

ノ	ナ	右	右	右

migi (right)

ノ	ナ	右	右	有	有

a·ru/YŪ (to be)

However, a <u>long</u> left sweep (*hidari barai*) follows a horizontal line (*yoko sen*).

一	ナ	左	左	左

hidari (left)

一	ナ	方	友

tomo (friend)

EXERCISES

1. Choose the correct stroke order for the following Kanji.

(1) 王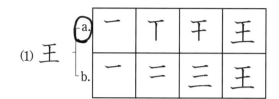

(2) 日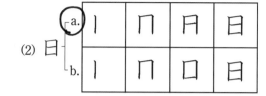

(3) 区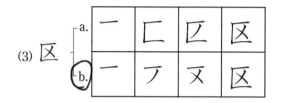

(4) 井*

(5) 右
a. 一	ナ	ナ	右	右
b. ノ	ナ	ナ	右	右

(6) 左
a. 一	ナ	ナ	左	左
b. ノ	ナ	ナ	左	左

(7) 世
a. 丨	丬	屮	山	世
b. 一	十	丗	廿	世

(8) 車
a. 一	厂	冂	戸	百	亘	車
b. 一	十	忄	市	市	車	車

2. According to the principles you have just learned, draw in the stroke orders for the Kanji you see.

(example)

1	2
ノ	人
一	十
一	七

1.

1	2	3
亅	小	小
了	子	子
丁	工	工

2.

1	2	3	4
父			父
フ	习	水	水
ノ	方	友	友

3.

1	2	3	4	5
				半
				田
				母

4.

1	2	3	4	5	6
丿	小	川	州	州	州
冂	冂	冃	同	同	同
ノ	ナ	ナ	右	有	有

Counting Strokes [画数] (Kakusū)

In the previous sections you learned the various types of strokes and the order in which they are put together to form Kanji. In this section, you will practice visually taking apart the Kanji, stroke by stroke, that is, counting the number of strokes. Knowing the correct stroke number is essential to writing Kanji properly and legibly. It is also important for beginning students of Kanji to spend some time acquiring this skill because it is an essential prerequisite for using a Kanji dictionary. When looking up Kanji in a dictionary, you should know the number of strokes in the radical(s) in order to find the page on which the Kanji is listed. Or, if you do not know the radical(s), you can also find the Kanji based on the number of strokes in the entire Kanji.

As you have seen, anything written without stopping to remove pen from paper is considered one stroke. For example, 乙 (OTSU) is an example of a single stroke Kanji. (For more examples of a single stroke, go back to the section on "Types of Strokes".)

It may sometimes be difficult for you to determine the number of strokes because what is one stroke in one radical or Kanji may be two or more in a different radical or Kanji.

For example:

└ seen in 区 KU (ward) ┌ 又 区 is one stroke,

whereas └ seen in 口 kuchi (mouth) 丨 冂 口 are two separate strokes.

However, learning the number of strokes in a Kanji is really inseparable from learning its correct stroke order. Thus, by paying attention to the stroke order of the radicals or Kanji as they are presented, you should be able to correctly count the number of strokes.

EXERCISES

1. Count the total number of strokes for the following Kanji from the section on stroke order.

1. 三 (　　) 　 2. 七 (　　) 　 3. 十 (　　) 　 4. 中 (　　)

5. 下 (　　) 　 6. 右 (　　) 　 7. 左 (　　) 　 8. 小 (　　)

9. 川 (　　) 　 10. 水 (　　) 　 11. 日 (　　) 　 12. 田 (　　)

13. 女 (　　) 　 14. 子 (　　) 　 15. 父 (　　) 　 16. 母 (　　)

17. 友 (　　) 　 18. 目 (　　) 　 19. 口 (　　) 　 20. 人 (　　)

21. 王 (　　) 　 22. 区 (　　) 　 23. 工 (　　) 　 24. 半 (　　)

25. 世 (　　) 　 26. 州 (　　) 　 27. 同 (　　) 　 28. 有 (　　)

2. Count the total number of strokes for the following familiar Kanji.

1. 手 (　　) 　2. 長 (　　) 　3. 少 (　　) 　4. 河 (　　)

5. 山 (　　) 　6. 足 (　　) 　7. 弓 (　　) 　8. 兄 (　　)

9. 毛 (　　) 　10. 月 (　　) 　11. 夕 (　　) 　12. 力 (　　)

13. 公 (　　) 　14. 乙 (　　) 　15. 九 (　　) 　16. 白 (　　)

17. 風 (　　) 　18. 点 (　　) 　19. 糸 (　　) 　20. 男 (　　)

21. 雨 (　　) 　22. 心 (　　) 　23. 本 (　　) 　24. 上 (　　)

3. From the following Kanji, choose the ones with 7 and 8 strokes. (There are two of each.)

7 strokes: (　　) and (　　)　　　8 strokes: (　　) and (　　)

1.	2.	3.	4.	5.	6.	7.
医	気	明	車	森	国	休

Chapter 2. Learning Traditional Radicals [部首] (Bushu)

You have just learned how the smallest elements of a character, strokes, are combined to form a radical. As mentioned earlier, radicals are the most basic and identifiable parts or components of Kanji. The number of radicals varies from dictionary to dictionary with some using less than 150 while others use as many as 250 radicals. Here, the 92 most common radicals are introduced as traditional radicals. In this workbook, radicals that are not traditional, either because their names are not commonly known or because they have no name at all, have been classified into one category for convenience and are introduced later in the chapter titled "Other Useful but Non-traditional Components." Finally, those radicals that are independent Kanji are included in Part II, titled "Very Basic Kanji."

The radicals presented here as traditional radicals usually indicate meaning rather than sound[4] while the radicals introduced in the next section as useful but non-traditional components often indicate sound. Knowledge of radicals also makes it possible to teach and learn characters orally. This is especially useful in Japanese daily life because there are many different possible characters for the same sounding name. For example (see Table pages 14–15 for "earth" and "hill" radicals):

"Ano Kosaka-san no saka wa tsuchi hen (earth radical) desu ka, kozato hen (hill radical) desu ka?"

("Is the 'saka' in Ms. Kosaka's name written with an earth radical, or a hill radical?")

Therefore, even though there are many radicals, it is very important to learn them by name and understand their meaning or derivation. It is also essential to be familiar with radicals when looking up new Kanji in a dictionary.

Now you are ready to actually begin studying radicals. Many can traditionally be classified into seven categories, depending on their position within the character. These include:

1. hen	2. tsukuri	3. kammuri	4. ashi	5. tare
(left side)	(right side)	(upper part)	(lower part)	(upper and left part)

6. nyō	7. kamae
(left and lower part)	(outer portion)

On pages 14–15 you will find a table listing the 92 most common traditional radicals in their respective categories which gives you an overview of what will be introduced in this chapter. Radicals with a circle (○) are the most frequently used and should be memorized by students.

---

4 See pg. xvi for *keisei moji* under Four Types of Kanji Formation.

For your convenience, the radicals have been separated into two categories. Those which are a slightly altered but recognizable form of an independent basic Kanji are shown in Category "a". Those whose forms have been completely altered or which consist of only a portion of the Kanji are shown in Category "b". These radicals no longer resemble the Kanji they were derived from and cannot stand alone as independent Kanji. The original, unaltered, or complete Kanji is shown in parentheses.

Following the table, radicals will be introduced according to their respective types. You will see the radical with its stroke number, name, and meaning or derivation, and some examples of how the radicals are used in various characters which belong to this radical's family group. Sometimes you will see a Kanji which contains more than one radical, and you may not know which family group this Kanji belongs to. For the purpose of this workbook's exercises, you may consider such a Kanji to belong to the family group of any of its constituent radicals. Then, the proper way to write it (stroke order) is introduced. Finally, you will have a chance to practice writing the radical yourself.

The Kanji that have been chosen as examples have been selected from the Gakushū Kanji, mainly from the list of first to third or fourth grade Kanji. Some characters, however, are from the Jōyō Kanji and have been marked with an asterisk (∗). Except for those Kanji for which only the On reading exists or the Kun is seldom used, the Kun pronunciation (which indicates the character's meaning) is provided. However, both the Kun and On readings are provided when the On reading is frequently used or when a group of the example Kanji share the same components and therefore the same On pronunciation. Furthermore, only the most common definitions of the Kanji are given. It is not necessary to learn to write the Kanji shown as examples here; rather, concentrate on becoming able to recognize them. This will help you increase the number of Kanji you can identify. Repetitive exercises both after each type and in a separate section of comprehensive review will help you memorize the names, especially of the most common radicals that are marked for you with a small circle (∘).

Table of Seven Types of Traditional Radicals

a: Radicals that are independent Kanji (slightly altered).
b: Radicals that are not independent Kanji (completely altered or a portion of the Kanji).

Hen 偏	**a**	口	kuchi·hen mouth	土	tsuchi·hen earth	女	onna·hen woman	子	ko·hen child	弓	yumi·hen bow
		日	hi·hen sun nichi·hen day	月	tsuki·hen moon nikuzuki flesh, meat	木	ki·hen tree	火	hi·hen fire	王	ō·hen king
		方	kata·hen direction	目	me·hen eye	石	ishi·hen stone	田	ta·hen ricefield	矢	ya·hen arrow
		矛*	hoko·hen spear	米	kome·hen rice	糸	ito·hen thread	耳	mimi·hen ear	舟	fune·hen boat
		言	gom·ben speak, word	貝	kai·hen shell, wealth	車	kuruma·hen vehicle	金	kane·hen metal	馬	uma·hen horse
	b	亻 (人)	nim·ben person	冫 (氷)	ni·sui ice	氵 (水)	san·zui water	彳 (行)	gyō·nim·ben road, go	忄 (心)	risshim·ben heart
		扌 (手)	te·hen hand	犭 (犬)	kemono·hen dog, animal	阝	kozato·hen hill, mound	巾	haba·hen width	歹	kabane·hen corpse
		礻 (示)	shimesu·hen rite, altar	牛 (牛)	ushi·hen cow	禾	nogi·hen grain	衤 (衣)	koromo·hen clothing	耒	suki·hen plow
		酉	tori·hen bird sake wine	足 (足)	ashi·hen foot, leg	食 (食)	shoku·hen eating, food				
Tsukuri 旁	**a**	力	chikara strength, power	寸	sun Japanese inch	欠	ka·keru lack akubi yawn				
	b	刂	rittō sword	卩	fushi·zukuri joint	彡	san·zukuri hair-ornament	阝	ōzato village	殳	ru·mata Katakana ル plus Kanji 又 (mata)
		斤	ono·zukuri ax	攵	boku·zukuri strike	戈	hoko·zukuri spear	隹	furutori bird	頁	ōgai big shell, head

Kammuri/Kashira 冠	a	穴 ana·kammuri hole (穴)	竹 take·kammuri bamboo (竹)	雨 ame·kammuri rain (雨)	冖 wa·kammuri Katakana wa (ワ)	宀 u·kammuri Katakana u (ウ)
	b	亠 nabe·buta lid	𠆢 hito·gashira person (人)	艹 kusa·kammuri grass (草)	耂 oi·gashira get old (老)	癶 hatsu·gashira departure (発)
		罒 ami·gashira net	虍 tora·gashira tiger (虎)			
Ashi 脚	a	心 kokoro heart	木 shita·gi tree	皿 sara·ashi plate	貝 kai·ashi shell	
	b	儿 hito·ashi human legs (人)	小 shita·gokoro heart (心)	灬 yotsu·ten 4 abbreviated strokes (火)		
Tare 垂	a	戸 to·dare door				
	b	厂 gan·dare geese (雁)	广 ma·dare linen, flax (麻)	尸 shikabane corpse (屍)	疒 yamai·dare illness (病)	
Nyō/Nyū 繞	a	走 sō·nyō run (走)				
	b	辶 shin·nyū proceed (進)	廴 en·nyō extend (延)			
Kamae 構	a	行 gyō·gamae go/road	門 mon·gamae gate			
	b	冂 dō·gamae same (同)	匸 hako·gamae box / kakushi·gamae hide	勹 tsutsumi·gamae wrap (包)	凵 uke·bako receiving box	弋 shiki·gamae ceremony (式)
		囗 kuni·gamae country (国)	气 ki·gamae air, spirit (汽)			

The Seven Types of Traditional Radicals

Hen [偏]

Radicals which appear on the left side of a Kanji are called *hen* (lit., partial, one-sided). The largest number of radicals falls into the *hen* category.

a. Radicals that are also independent Kanji.

Radical & Stroke Number	Name & Derivation	Stroke Order and Practice	Examples	
1. 口 3	kuchi·hen (mouth)	! �ㄇ 口	味	aji / MI (taste)
		口　口	呼	yo·bu (call)
			吸	su·u / KYŪ (inhale)
2. 土 (土) 3	tsuchi·hen (earth)	一　十　土	地	CHI (earth)
		土　土	場	ba (place)
			坂	saka (slope)
3. 女 (女) 3	onna·hen (woman)	巛　夊　女	好	su·ki (like)
		女　女	姉	ane (older sister)
			妹	imōto (younger sister)
4. 子 (子) 3	ko·hen (child)	了　了　子	孫	mago (grandchildren)
		子　子	孔*	KŌ (hole)
5. 弓 3	yumi·hen (bow)	乛　コ　弓	引	hi·ku (pull)
		弓　弓	強	tsuyo·i / KYŌ (strong)
			弱	yowa·i / JAKU (weak)

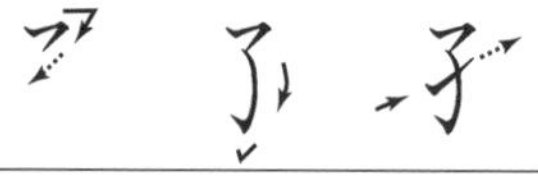

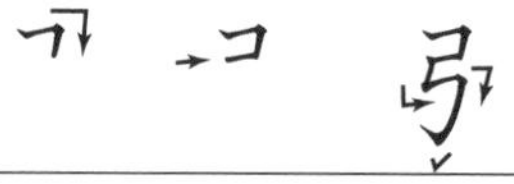

Radical & Stroke Number	Name & Derivation	Stroke Order and Practice	Examples
6. 日 4	hi·hen (sun) / nichi·hen (day)	⌐ 冂 →日 →日 / 日 日	明 aka·rui (bright, pg. xv) / 時 toki (time) / 晴 ha·reru /SEI (clear up, pg. xvi)
7. 月 4	tsuki·hen (moon) / nikuzuki (flesh, meat)	丿 刀 →月 →月 / 月 月	服 FUKU (dress) / 勝 ka·tsu (win) / 胸 mune (chest, breast)
8. 木 （木） 4	ki·hen (tree)	→一 ┼ 才 木 / 木 木	校 KŌ (school) / 村 mura (village) / 林 hayashi (woods, pg. xv)
9. 火 （火） 4	hi·hen (fire)	⺍ ⺍ 少 火 / 火 火	畑 hatake (ricefield) / 灯 hi (light) / 焼 ya·ku (burn)
10. 王 （王） 4	ō·hen (king)	→一 下 →干 王 / 王 王	理 RI (reason) / 球 KYŪ (sphere, ball) / 現 GEN (current)
11. 方 （方） 4	kata·hen (direction, way, person)	⺀ →⺀ 方 方 / 方 方	族 ZOKU (family, tribe) / 放 hana·su (release) / 旅 tabi (trip)

Radical & Stroke Number	Name & Derivation	Stroke Order and Practice	Examples
12. ° 目 5	me·hen (eye)	｜ 冂 月 月 目	眼 GAN (eye)
		目 目	眠* nemu·ru (sleep)
13. 石 5	ishi·hen (stone)	一 厂 石 石 石	研 KEN (grind, study)
		石 石	破 yabu·ru (tear)
			砂 suna (sand)
14. 田 5	ta·hen (ricefield)	｜ 冂 田 田 田	町 machi (town)
		田 田	略 RYAKU (abbreviation)
15. 矢 (矢) 5	ya·hen (arrow)	﹅ 广 二 午 矢	知 shi·ru/CHI (know)
		矢 矢	短 mijika·i/TAN (short)
16. * 矛 5	hoko·hen (spear)	乛 マ 卫 予 矛	務 tsuto·me/MU (duty)
		矛 矛	
17. ° 米 (米) 6	kome·hen (rice)	﹅ 丷 丷 半 米 米	粉 ko/kona (flour)
		米 米	料 RYŌ (fee, materials)
			精 SEI (spirit, pg. xvi)

Radical & Stroke Number	Name & Derivation	Stroke Order and Practice	Examples
18. ○ 糸 6	ito·hen (thread)	く 乡 幺 糸 糸 糸 / 糸 糸	絵 E (picture) / 紙 kami (paper) / 組 kumi (group)
19. 耳 （耳） **6**	mimi·hen (ear)	一 厂 下 F 耳 耳 / 耳 耳	取 to·ru (take) / 職 SHOKU (occupation)
20. 舟 （舟*） **6**	fune·hen (boat)	⺆ 丿 𦨒 月 舟 舟 / 舟 舟	船 fune (boat) / 航 KŌ (voyage)
21. 言 （言） 7	gom·ben (speak, word)	丶 二 亖 言 言 言 / 言 言 言	話 hana·su/WA (speak) / 読 yo·mu (read) / 語 GO (word)
22. 貝 7	kai·hen (shell, wealth)	刂 冂 月 月 目 貝 / 貝 貝 貝	貯 CHO (save, store) / 財 ZAI (wealth) / 敗 HAI (defeat)
23. 車 7	kuruma·hen (vehicle)	一 厂 冂 戸 百 車 / 車 車 車	軽 karu·i (light in weight) / 転 koro·bu/TEN (roll over) / 輪 wa (wheel)

Radical & Stroke Number	Name & Derivation	Stroke Order and Practice						Examples	
24. ○ 金 （金） 8	kane·hen (metal)	ノ	バ	스	仝	牟	舎	銀	GIN (silver)
		金	金	金	金			鉄	TETSU (iron)
								銅	DŌ (copper)
25. 馬 （馬） 10	uma·hen (horse)	!	厂	厂	开	羊	馬	駅	EKI (station)
		馬	馬	馬	馬	馬	馬	験	KEN (testing)

Hen [偏]

b. Radicals that are not independent Kanji

Radical & Stroke Number	Name & Derivation	Stroke Order and Practice				Examples	
1. 亻 (人) 2	nim·ben (man)	ノ	亻			休	yasu·mu/KYŪ (rest, pg. xv)
		亻	亻			体	karada (body)
						作	tsuku·ru/SAKU (make)
2. 冫 (氷) 2	ni·sui (ice; lit. water with two strokes)	丶	冫			冷	tsume·tai (cold)
		冫	冫			次	tsugi (next)
						凍	koo·ru/TŌ (freeze)
3. 氵 (水) 3	san·zui (water; lit. water with three strokes)	丶	冫	氵		海	umi/KAI (sea, pg. xiii)
		氵	氵			池	ike (pond, pg. xvi)
						泳	oyo·gu/EI (swim)
4. 彳 3	gyō·nim·ben from 行 (GYŌ = road, go)	ノ	彳	彳		行	i·ku/yu·ku (go)
		彳	彳			後	ushiro/ato/GO (behind, after)
						待	ma·tsu (wait)
5. 忄 (心) 3	risshim·ben (heart)	忄	忄	忄		快	KAI (pleasant)
		忄	忄			性	SEI (gender)
						情	JŌ (feelings)

Radical & Stroke Number	Name & Derivation	Stroke Order and Practice	Examples
6. 扌 （手） 3	te·hen (hand)	一 扌 扌 / 扌 扌	指 yubi/SHI (finger) 持 mo·tsu (hold) 打 u·tsu (hit)
7. 犭 （犬） 3	kemono·hen (dog, animal)	ノ 犭 犭 / 犭 犭	独 hito·ri/DOKU (alone) 犯 HAN (violate, crime)
8. 阝 3	kozato·hen (hill, mound)	⁊ 阝 阝 / 阝 阝	階 KAI (stairs) 陽 YŌ (sun) 陸 RIKU (land)
9. 巾 3	haba·hen (width)	⼁ 冂 巾 / 巾 巾	帳 CHŌ (notebook) 幅* haba (width) 帆* ho (sail)
10. 歹 4	kabane·hen from old Kanji 屍 (kabane = corpse)	一 丆 歹 歹 / 歹 歹	列 RETSU (line, row) 残 noko·su/ZAN (leave behind) 死 SHI (death)
11. 礻 （示） 4	shimesu·hen (rite, altar)	⼂ 礻 礻 礻 / 礻 礻	社 yashiro/SHA (shrine, company) 神 kami/SHIN (god) 福 FUKU (good fortune)

Radical & Stroke Number	Name & Derivation	Stroke Order and Practice	Examples	
12. 牛 （牛） 4	ushi·hen (cow)	⸍ ⸍ 二 牜 牛　　牛 牛	物	mono (thing)
			特	TOKU (special)
			牧	maki (cattle raising)
13. 禾 （禾） 5	nogi·hen (grain)	⸍ ⸍二 千 禾 禾　　禾 禾	秋	aki/SHŪ (autumn)
			和	WA (harmony)
			秒	BYŌ (second)
14. 衤 （衣） 5	koromo·hen (clothing)	⸍ ⸍ラ 衤 衤 衤　　衤 衤	初	haji·me (beginning)
			複	FUKU (multiple)
			補	ogina·u (supplement)
15. 耒 6	suki·hen (plow)	一 二 三 耂 耒 耒　　耒 耒	耕	tagaya·su (till)
16. 酉 7	tori·hen (bird; now used for *sake*)	一 丆 冂 丙 酉 酉 酉 酉 酉	配	kuba·ru/HAI (distribute)
			酸	SAN (acid)
			酢*	su (vinegar)
17. 足 （足） 7	ashi·hen (foot, leg)	⺊ 口 口 尸 昆 足 足 足 足	路	RO (road)
			跳*	to·bu (jump)

23

Radical & Stroke Number	Name & Derivation	Stroke Order and Practice						Examples	
18. 食 （飠） 8	shoku·hen (eating, food)	ノ	𠆢	𠆢	今	今	今	飲	no·mu (drink)
		食	食	食	食			飯	HAN (meal)
								館	KAN (hall, gathering place)

EXERCISES FOR HEN

1. Write in the numbers for the two Kanji that correspond to each given *hen*.

1. sanzui ___ ___

2. ito·hen ___ ___

3. risshim·ben ___ ___

4. gom·ben ___ ___

5. nim·ben ___ ___

1. 泳　2. 飲　3. 海

4. 情　5. 町　6. 行

7. 作　8. 話　9. 語

10. 快　11. 休　12. 秒

13. 組　14. 指　15. 紙

2. Give the name of the *hen* that appear in the following Kanji.

1. 輪 _____　2. 持 _____　3. 待 _____

4. 陽 _____　5. 眼 _____　6. 強 _____

7. 神 _____　8. 鉄 _____　9. 好 _____

10. 冷 _____　11. 焼 _____　12. 坂 _____

13. 和 _____　14. 初 _____　15. 村 _____

Tsukuri [旁]

Radicals that appear on the right side of a Kanji are called *tsukuri* (lit., aside).

a. Radicals that are also independent Kanji

Radical & Stroke Number	Name & Derivation	Stroke Order and Practice	Examples
1. 力 2	chikara (power, strength)	ブ 力　力 力	動 ugo·ku/DŌ (move)　功 KŌ (merit)　助 tasu·keru (help)
2. 寸 3	sun (Japanese inch)	一 寸 寸　寸 寸	対 TAI (against)　射 i·ru (shoot)　封* FŪ (seal)
3. 欠 4	ka·keru (lack) / akubi (yawn)	⺅ ⺈ ク 欠　欠 欠	歌 uta/KA (song)　欲 YOKU (desire)　次 tsugi (next, pg. 21)

25

Tsukuri [旁]

b. Radicals that are not independent Kanji

Radical & Stroke Number	Name & Derivation	Stroke Order and Practice		Examples	
1. ○ 刂 2	rittō (sword)	↓刂 刂↓ 刂 刂		別	BETSU (another, separate)
				副	FUKU (vice-)
				利	RI (profit)
2. 卩 2	fushi·zukuri from 節 (fushi = joint)	ﻉﺭ 卩 卩 卩		節	fushi/SETSU (joint)
				印	shirushi/IN (sign, seal)
				脚*	ashi (leg)
3. 彡 3	san·zukuri (hair-ornament)	ノ 彡 彡 彡 彡		形	katachi (shape)
				彩*	SAI (coloring)
4. ○‡ 阝 3	ōzato (village)	ﻨ 阝 阝 阝 阝		都	miyako/TO (capital)
				部	BU (part)
				郡	GUN (county)
5. 殳 4	ru·mata top part is similar to Kata-kana ル; bot-tom part is 又 (mata = again)	ノ 卩 殳 殳 殳 殳 殳		段	DAN (step)
				殺	koro·su (kill)

‡ 阝 is also a *hen*. See page 22.

Radical & Stroke Number	Name & Derivation	Stroke Order and Practice	Examples	
6. 斤 4	ono·zukuri (ax)	″ ʃ 斤 斤 斤 斤	新	atara·shii/SHIN (new)
			所	tokoro (place)
			折	o·ru (break, fold)
7. 攵 4	boku·zukuri (strike, attack)	ノ 攵 攵 攵 攵 攵	教	oshie·ru/KYŌ (teach)
			数	kazu (number)
			改	arata·meru (reform)
8. 戈 4	hoko·zukuri (tasseled spear)	一 戈 戈 戈 戈 戈	戦	tataka·u/SEN (fight)
			我	ware (oneself)
9. 隹 8	furutori (bird)	″ ʃ 亻 亻 亻 亻 隹 隹 隹 隹	雑	ZATSU (miscellaneous)
			難	muzuka·shii (difficult)
10. 頁 9	ōgai (big shell, indicates head or face)	一 ″ 厂 百 百 百 頁 頁 頁 頁	顔	kao (face)
			頭	atama (head)
			願	nega·u (wish)

EXERCISES FOR TSUKURI

1. Circle the Kanji which have the *tsukuri* radical.

1. 形   2. 姉   3. 対   4. 戦   5. 財

6. 印   7. 歌   8. 孫   9. 動   10. 明

11. 副   12. 数   13. 町   14. 頭   15. 次

16. 郡   17. 砂   18. 新   19. 紙   20. 船

2. Write in the numbers for the two Kanji that correspond to each given *tsukuri*.

1. rittō	__ __	1. 段 2. 別 3. 改	
2. ru·mata	__ __	4. 部 5. 顔 6. 難	
3. furutori	__ __	7. 助 8. 所 9. 利	
4. ōzato	__ __	10. 都 11. 願 12. 殺	
5. ōgai	__ __	13. 雑 14. 欲 15. 我	

Kammuri/Kashira [冠]

Radicals that appear in the top part of a Kanji are called *kammuri* or *kashira* (lit., crown or head).

a. Radicals that are independent Kanji or Katakana.

Radical & Stroke Number	Name & Derivation	Stroke Order and Practice		Examples	
1. 穴 （穴） 5	ana·kammuri (hole)	ー ヽ ヽ﹅ ̔ 宀ヽ 宀 穴. 穴 穴		究	KYŪ (study thoroughly)
				空	sora/KŪ (sky, pg. 2)
				窓	mado (window)
2. ⺮ （竹） 6	take·kammuri (bamboo)	ノ ⻑ ⺮ ⺮ ⺮ ⺮ ⺮ ⺮		答	kota·eru (answer)
				算	SAN (calculate)
				等	hito·shii (equal)
3. 雨 （雨） 8	ame·kammuri (rain)	一 ⻏ 帀 雨 雨 雨 雨 雨 雨 雨		雲	kumo (cloud)
				雪	yuki (snow)
				電	DEN (electricity)
4. 冖 （ワ） 2	wa·kammuri (Katakana ワ)	⺍ 冖 冖 冖		写	utsu·su/SHA (copy)
				軍	GUN (the military)
5. 宀 （ウ） 3	u·kammuri (Katakana ウ)	ヽ ⺍ 宀 宀 宀		宇	U (sphere)
				家	ie (house)
				安	yasu·i (cheap)

Kammuri/Kashira [冠]

b. Radicals that are not independent Kanji.

Radical & Stroke Number	Name & Derivation	Stroke Order and Practice	Examples	
1. 亠 2	nabebuta (lid)	亠 亠	京	KYŌ (capital)
			夜	yoru (night)
			高	taka·i (high)
2. 𠆢 (人) 2	hito·gashira (person)	𠆢 𠆢	今	ima/KON (now)
			会	a·u/KAI (meet, meeting)
			命	inochi (life)
3. 艹 3	kusa·kammuri from 草 (kusa = grass)	一 十 艹 艹 艹	草	kusa (grass, pg. xii)
			茶	CHA (tea, pg. xii)
			花	hana (flower)
4. 耂 4	oi·gashira from 老 (o·iru = get old)	一 十 土 耂 耂 耂	老	o·iru (to get old)
			考	kanga·eru (think)
			者	mono/SHA (person)
5. 癶 5	hatsu·gashira from 発 (HATSU = departure)	丆 フ ブ ブ 癶 癶 癶 癶	発	HATSU (departure)
			登	nobo·ru (climb)

Radical & Stroke Number	Name & Derivation	Stroke Order and Practice	Examples
6. 罒 5	ami·gashira (net)	ﾉ 冖 冖 罒 罒 罒 罒	買 ka·u (buy) 置 o·ku (to place) 罪 tsumi (sin)
7. 虍 6	tora·gashira from old Kanji 虎 (tora = tiger)	ﾉ ﾄ 广 广 卢 虍 虍 虍	膚* FU (skin) 劇 GEKI (drama)

EXERCISES FOR KAMMURI

1. Circle the Kanji which have the *kammuri* radical.

1. 等   2. 副   3. 茶   4. 次

5. 雲   6. 者   7. 物   8. 飯

9. 秋   10. 罪   11. 後   12. 軍

13. 体   14. 銀   15. 安   16. 膚*

2. Write in the numbers for the two Kanji that correspond to each given *kammuri*.

1. ami·gashira ___ ___	1. 発	2. 高	3. 考
2. hatsu·gashira ___ ___	4. 宇	5. 置	6. 老
3. hito·gashira ___ ___	7. 答	8. 買	9. 会
4. nabebuta ___ ___	10. 窓	11. 今	12. 夜
5. oi·gashira ___ ___	13. 雪	14. 登	15. 花

3. Write the name of the *kammuri* that appears in the following Kanji.

1. 空 _____   2. 家 _____   3. 電 _____

4. 京 _____   5. 算 _____   6. 写 _____

7. 草 _____   8. 命 _____   9. 窓 _____

Ashi [脚]

Radicals that appear in the lower part of the Kanji are called *ashi*. (lit., leg).

a. Radicals that are independent Kanji.

Radical & Stroke Number	Name & Derivation	Stroke Order and Practice	Examples	
1. 心 4	kokoro (heart, mind)	り 心 心 心 / 心 心	思	omo·u (think)
			息	iki (breath)
			意	I (intention)
2. ‡ 木 4	shitagi (tree)	一 十 才 木 / 木 木	楽	tano·shii/GAKU (enjoyable, music)
			集	atsu·meru (collect)
			案	AN (idea)
3. 皿 5	sara·ashi (plate)	り 冂 ㄇ 皿 皿 / 皿 皿	益	EKI (profit)
			盟	MEI (ally)
			盛	saka·n/SEI (thriving)
4. ‡ 貝 7	kai·ashi (shell)	り 冂 月 月 目 貝 / 貝 貝 貝	貨	KA (currency, freight)
			貸	ka·su (lend)
			貧	mazu·shii (poor)

‡ 木 is also a *hen*. See page 17.
‡ 貝 is also a *hen*. See page 19.

Ashi [脚] ⬜

b. Radicals that are not independent Kanji.

Radical & Stroke Number	Name & Derivation	Stroke Order and Practice				Examples	
1. 儿 （人） 2	hito·ashi (human legs)	⌣ 心				見 先 光	mi·ru (look) saki/SEN (previous, ahead) hikari (light)
2. 小 （心） 4	shita·gokoro from 心 (kokoro = heart, mind)	↓ ⺌ 小 小				恭* 慕*	KYŌ (respectful) shita·u (long for)
3. 灬 （火） 4	yotsu·ten (4 abbreviated strokes) from 火 (hi = fire)	⸍ ⺀ 灬 灬				黒 点 熱	kuro·i (black) TEN (dot, pg. 2) NETSU (heat)

EXERCISES FOR ASHI

1. Circle the Kanji which have the *ashi* radical.

1. 貨	2. 町	3. 集	4. 地	5. 息
6. 盟	7. 時	8. 恭*	9. 光	10. 校
11. 貯	12. 黒	13. 池	14. 等	15. 副
16. 楽	17. 京	18. 安	19. 究	20. 命

2. Write in the numbers for the two Kanji that correspond to each given *ashi*.

1. hito·ashi ___ ___	1. 益	2. 思	3. 服	
2. kokoro ___ ___	4. 貧	5. 点	6. 貸	
3. sara·ashi ___ ___	7. 茶	8. 見	9. 物	
4. yotsu·ten ___ ___	10. 意	11. 熱	12. 体	
5. kai·ashi ___ ___	13. 盛	14. 案	15. 先	

Tare [垂] ⌐

Radicals that appear across the top and hang from the top to the lower left side are called *tare* (lit., something hanging down).

a. Radicals that are independent Kanji.

Radical & Stroke Number	Name & Derivation	Stroke Order and Practice	Examples
1. 戸 4	to·dare (door)	一 → 丆 → 彐 → 戸 戸　戸	肩* kata (shoulder) 扇* ōgi (folding fan)

b. Radicals that are not independent Kanji.

Radical & Stroke Number	Name & Derivation	Stroke Order and Practice	Examples
1. ○ 厂 2	gan·dare from old Kanji 雁 (GAN = geese)	一 → 厂 厂　厂	原 hara/GEN (field) 厚 atsu·i (thick) 歴 REKI (successive, record)
2. ○ 广 3	ma·dare from 麻 (asa = linen, flax)	丶 → 亠 → 广 广　广	広 hiro·i/KŌ (wide) 店 mise/TEN (store) 度 DO (degree)
3. 尸 3	shikabane from old Kanji 屍 (shikabane = corpse)	彐 → 冂 → 尸 尸　尸	屋 ya (roof, shop) 局 KYOKU (bureau, office) 居 i·ru (to be)
4. 疒 5	yamai·dare from 病 (yamai = illness)	丶 → 亠 → 广 → 疒 → 疒 疒　疒	病 yamai/BYŌ (illness) 痛 ita·i (painful)

EXERCISES FOR TARE

1. Circle the Kanji which have the *tare* radical.

1. 灯	2. 局	3. 理	4. 絵	5. 歴
6. 銀	7. 放	8. 肩*	9. 吸	10. 居
11. 屋	12. 勝	13. 研	14. 度	15. 灰▲

2. Write in the numbers for the two Kanji that correspond to each given *tare*.

		1. 命	2. 原	3. 安
1. yamai·dare ___ ___		4. 路	5. 病	6. 厚
2. gan·dare ___ ___		7. 者	8. 痛	9. 折
3. ma·dare ___ ___		10. 数	11. 取	12. 広
		13. 功	14. 究	15. 店

▲ 灰 hai = ash

Nyō [繞]

Radicals that appear on the left and across the bottom of a Kanji are called *nyō* (lit., going around).

a. Radicals that are independent Kanji.

Radical & Stroke Number	Name & Derivation	Stroke Order and Practice		Examples	
1. 走 (走) 7	sō·nyō (run)	一　十　土．　走　走　走 走　走　走		起	oki·ru (get up)
				越	ko·su (exceed, pass)
				趣	SHU (taste)

b. Radicals that are not independent Kanji.

Radical & Stroke Number	Name & Derivation	Stroke Order and Practice		Examples	
1.　○ 辶 3	shin·nyū/ shin·nyō from 進 (SHIN = proceed)	⺍　辶　辶 辶　辶		進	susu·mu (proceed)
				近	chika·i (near)
				道	michi/DŌ (road)
2.　○ 爻 3	en·nyō from 延 (EN = extend)	乃　邓　爻 爻　爻		延	no·basu (extend)
				建	ta·teru (build)

EXERCISES FOR NYŌ

1. Circle the Kanji which have the *nyō* radical.

1. 味	2. 延	3. 場	4. 池	5. 進
6. 近	7. 晴	8. 起	9. 球	10. 趣
11. 建	12. 送	13. 遠	14. 電	15. 配
16. 校	17. 道	18. 地	19. 越	20. 短

2. In the blanks below, write in the numbers for the Kanji from the above list that correspond to each given *nyō*.

1. shin·nyū   _____ _____ _____ _____ _____

2. sō·nyō   _____ _____ _____

3. en·nyō   _____ _____

Kamae [構] ⬜⬜⬜⬜⬜

Radicals that appear to enclose the Kanji are called *kamae*. (lit., enclosure).

a. Radicals that are independent Kanji.

Radical & Stroke Number	Name & Derivation	Stroke Order and Practice	Examples	
1. 行 (行) 6	gyō·gamae (go, road, behavior)		街	machi (town, street)
			術	JUTSU (tactics, art)
			衛	EI (defense)
2. 門 8	mon·gamae (gate)		間	aida (between)
			聞	ki·ku (listen, hear)
			開	a·keru (open)

b. Radicals that are not independent Kanji.

Radical & Stroke Number	Name & Derivation	Stroke Order and Practice	Examples	
1. 冂 2	dō·gamae from 同 (DŌ = same)		同	ona·ji/DŌ (same, pg. 6)
			内	uchi (inside)
			円	EN (circle, yen)
2. 匚 2	kakushi·gamae/ hako·gamae (hide, enclose, putting in a box)		医	I (physician, pg. 6)
			区	KU (ward, pg. 3)

Radical & Stroke Number	Name & Derivation	Stroke Order and Practice	Examples
3. 勹 2	tsutsumi· gamae from 包 (tsutsu·mu = wrap)		包 tsutsu·mu (wrap) 句 KU (phrase)
4. 凵 2	uke·bako (receiving box)		出 de·ru/da·su (go out, put out) 画 GA (picture)
5. 囗 3	kuni·gamae from 国 (kuni = country)		国 kuni/KOKU (country, pg. 6) 図 ZU/TO (diagram) 囲 kako·mu (enclose)
6. 弋 3	shiki·gamae from 式 (SHIKI = ceremony)		式 SHIKI (ceremony) 武 BU (military)
7. 气 4	ki·gamae from 気 (KI = air, spirit)		気 KI (air, spirit, pg.3) 汽 KI (steam, pg.3)

EXERCISES FOR KAMAE

1. Circle the Kanji which have the *kamae* radical.

1. 包	2. 医	3. 銅	4. 区	5. 秋
6. 畑	7. 屋	8. 汽	9. 打	10. 特
11. 円	12. 気	13. 出	14. 発	15. 式
16. 知	17. 時	18. 画	19. 句	20. 飯
21. 同	22. 現	23. 内	24. 秒	25. 武

2. Write in the numbers for the three Kanji that correspond to each given *kamae.*

	1. 買	2. 国	3. 町
1. mon·gamae ___ ___ ___	4. 囲	5. 所	6. 聞
2. kuni·gamae ___ ___ ___	7. 街	8. 族	9. 開
3. gyō·gamae ___ ___ ___	10. 術	11. 図	12. 教
	13. 間	14. 局	15. 衛

REVIEW EXERCISES

Following are review exercises for all radicals.

1. Use the diagrams below to answer the following questions.

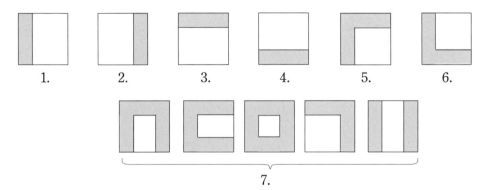

a. Write the number of the diagram that corresponds to the names of the radicals that are listed below.

1. kamae _____   2. hen _____   3. tare _____

4. kammuri _____   5. ashi _____   6. tsukuri _____

7. nyō _____

b. Write the number of the diagram that corresponds most closely to the radical found in each of the following Kanji.

1. 校 _____   2. 都 _____   3. 所 _____   4. 起 _____

5. 動 _____   6. 家 _____   7. 話 _____   8. 次 _____

9. 点 _____   10. 町 _____   11. 進 _____   12. 置 _____

13. 算 _____   14. 同 _____   15. 建 _____   16. 明 _____

17. 包 _____   18. 草 _____   19. 間 _____   20. 形 _____

21. 度 _____   22. 病 _____   23. 現 _____   24. 区 _____

25. 畑 _____   26. 原 _____   27. 見 _____   28. 屋 _____

29. 街 _____   30. 雪 _____   31. 息 _____   32. 好 _____

c. Write the number of the diagram and the stroke numbers of that radical under which you would look up the following Kanji in the dictionary.

1. 語 ____ ____   2. 道 ____ ____   3. 数 ____ ____

4. 秋 ____ ____   5. 行 ____ ____   6. 盛 ____ ____

7. 等 ____ ____   8. 電 ____ ____   9. 居 ____ ____

10. 図 ____ ____   11. 顔 ____ ____   12. 空 ____ ____

2. Write the number of the Kanji that corresponds to the following radicals.

a. kuchi·hen ____	1. 場	2. 知	3. 店
b. tsuchi·hen ____	4. 旅	5. 宇	6. 熱
c. u·kammuri ____	7. 別	8. 味	9. 料
d. kozato·hen ____	10. 飲	11. 陽	12. 越
e. kuruma·hen ____	13. 歌	14. 聞	15. 軽
f. ma·dare ____			
g. rittō ____			
h. yotsu·ten ____			
i. mon·gamae ____			
j. sō·nyō ____			

3. Match each Kanji on the right with the most appropriate radical name on the left.

_____ a. me·hen	_____ b. onna·hen
_____ c. tsuki·hen	_____ d. kai·hen
_____ e. kokoro	_____ f. uma·hen
_____ g. ono·zukuri	_____ h. yumi·hen
_____ i. shimesu·hen	_____ j. hi·hen/nichi·hen
_____ k. nabebuta	_____ l. koromo·hen
_____ m. ōzato	_____ n. rumata
_____ o. furutori	_____ p. ōgai
_____ q. wa·kammuri	_____ r. gan·dare
_____ s. ishi·hen	_____ t. kuni·gamae

1. 思　2. 眼
3. 新　4. 妹
5. 殺　6. 願
7. 京　8. 部
9. 歴　10. 研
11. 写　12. 貯
13. 験　14. 神
15. 時　16. 難
17. 国　18. 初
19. 勝　20. 強

4. The radicals contained in the following Kanji are quite common. Write their names on the lines provided for you.

a. 海 _____　b. 休 _____　c. 持 _____

d. 待 _____　e. 花 _____　f. 秒 _____

g. 開 _____　h. 近 _____　i. 雲 _____

j. 答 _____　k. 快 _____　l. 読 _____

5. The radicals in the following pairs of Kanji are similar. Write the names for each on the lines provided for you.

a. 校 _____
   秒 _____

b. 進 _____
   建 _____

c. 体 _____
   後 _____

d. 安 _____
   軍 _____

e. 福 _____
   複 _____

f. 厚 _____
   広 _____

g. 冷 _____
   池 _____

h. 陸 _____
   郡 _____

i. 指 _____
   物 _____

j. 放 _____
   歌 _____

k. 屋 _____
   肩* _____

l. 貯 _____
   顔 _____

Chapter 3. Learning Other Useful but Non-traditional Components

The radicals introduced in this section, unlike those in the previous section, either have names that are less commonly known or have no name at all. Most of them do not have clear intrinsic meanings, though if you trace their origins in dictionaries you may find obscure meanings. Instead, the components appearing in the table on the next two pages often represent sound rather than meaning. In recognizing the recurring common elements of various Kanji, learning these components is as important as learning traditional radicals because these components can form the basis of a family group just as traditional radicals do.

On the following two pages, you will see 107 useful components. These components are introduced in order of increasing stroke number. Beginner students of Kanji may choose to skip the most complex components (those with the largest number of strokes) and return to them at a more advanced level of study.

Among the components introduced in this section, some were once independent Kanji, but today none are listed in the Jōyō Kanji. Some are independent Katakana. (As you will remember, Katakana were originally parts of Kanji characters.) Exercises are provided to test your ability to analyze Kanji that contain these components. They mainly focus on recognition rather than writing and are based on the example Kanji that are introduced as members of the family group of each component. By doing these exercises carefully, you should acquire the ability to break down Kanji into familiar components or family groups. This skill will be particularly helpful when you begin writing Kanji.

Table of Other Useful but Non-traditional Components

Stroke Number					
1	し variation of 乙 (OTSU = second)				
2	十 variation of 十 (JŪ = ten)	十 variation of 十 (JŪ = ten)	几 from 机 (tsukue = desk)	⺈	匕 variation of Katakana ヒ
	ク variation of Katakana ku	コ Katakana ko	⺍ variation of Katakana so	ト Katakana to	ナ Katakana na
	マ Katakana ma	ム Katakana mu	メ Katakana me	リ variation of Katakana リ	丂
3	巾 haba width	幺 ito·gashira from 糸 (ito = thread)	⺌ variation of 小 (SHŌ = small)	夂 fuyu·gashira from 冬 (fuyu = winter)	夊 natsu·ashi from 夏 (natsu = summer)
	彳	也 †† to be	巛 variation of 川 (kawa = river)	廾 nijū·ashi (twenty)	⺍ Katakana ソ plus Kanji 一 (ICHI = one)
	厶	⺍ variation of Katakana tsu	ヨ Katakana yo	⺕ variation of Katakana ヨ	
4	圭	屮	毋 variation of 母 (haha = mother)	壬	开
	⺌ Katakana ノ plus ツ	云	勿	艮	夕
	夬				
5	牙 old Kanji † (kiba = tusk, fang)	禾 nogi Katakana ノ plus Kanji 木 (ki = tree)	夫	艮	氺 shitamizu variation of 水 (mizu = water)
	丗	乍	戊	疋 old Kanji † (hiki = counter for cloth)	疋
	旡	台	圣		

† Independent Kanji, but no longer included in Jōyō Kanji.

†† Independent Kanji (classical), but no longer included in Jōyō Kanji.

Stroke Number					
6	而 however ^{††}	聿 fude·zukuri from 筆 (fude = pen)	艮 kon·zukuri from 根 (KON = root)	西 variation of 西 (nishi = west)	羊 variation of 羊 (hitsuji = sheep)
	亥 old Kanji [†] (i = boar)	关	圭	爪	臼
	其	戋	亦 mata also ^{††}	关	戍
7	豕 buta pig	舛 mai·ashi from 舞* (mai = dance)	釆 no·gome Katakana ノ plus Kanji 米 (kome = rice)	辰 old Kanji [†] (SHIN = clam/ tatsu = dragon)	甫
	兑	鸟	呆		
8	隶 from 逮 (TAI = catch up)	坴	卓	岡 oka hill [†]	侖
	录	金	尭	釆	無
	齐	其 [†]			
9	俞	咼	咸	复	畐
	易	禺			
10	韋	臽	莫	莫	冓
	堇				
11	竟	商	隹	曾	
12	戠				

† Independent Kanji, but no longer included in Jōyō Kanji.

†† Independent Kanji (classical), but no longer included in Jōyō Kanji.

One and Two Stroke Components

Single Stroke Components

Component & Stroke Number	Derivation	Stroke Order and Practice	Examples
1. し 1	variation of 乙 (OTSU = second in order)	し　し　し	礼 REI (courtesy) 乳 NYŪ (milk) 乱 RAN (disorder)

Two Stroke Components

Component & Stroke Number	Derivation	Stroke Order and Practice	Examples
1. 十 2	variation of Kanji 十 (JŪ = ten)	一 十　十　十	協 KYŌ (cooperation) 博 HAKU (extensive)
2. 十 2	variation of Kanji 十 (JŪ = ten)	一 十　十　十	計 haka·ru/KEI (measure, plan) 針 hari (needle)
3. 几 2	from 机 (tsukue = desk)	丿 几　几　几	机 tsukue (desk) 航 KŌ (navigation, voyage, pg. 19) 凡* BON (ordinary)
4. 丿 2		丿 仁　丿　丿	毎 MAI (every) 年 toshi/NEN (year, age) 族 ZOKU (family, tribe, pg. 17)

Component & Stroke Number	Derivation	Stroke Order and Practice	Examples
5 ヒ 2	variation of Katakana ヒ	ヒ ヒ	北 kita (north, pg. 3) 化 KA (change, transform) 死 SHI (death, pg. 22)
6. ク 2	variation of Katakana ク	ク ク	色 iro (color, pg. 3) 魚 sakana (fish, pg. xiv) 急 KYŪ (sudden, urgent)
7. コ 2	Katakana コ	コ コ	己 KO (self) 弓 yumi (bow, pg. 3)
8. ソ 2	variation of Katakana ソ	ソ ソ	弟 otōto (younger brother) 半 HAN (half, pg. 6) 羊 hitsuji (sheep)
9. ト 2	Katakana ト	ト ト	外 soto (outside) 掛* ka·keru (hang) 赴* FU (go)
10. ナ 2	Katakana ナ	ナ ナ	左 hidari (left, pg. 7) 友 tomo (friend, pg.7) 在 a·ru/zai (stay, exist)

Component & Stroke Number	Derivation	Stroke Order and Practice		Examples	
11. マ 2	Katakana マ			予	YO (beforehand, previous)
				勇	isa·mashii (brave)
12. ム 2	Katakana ム			公	KŌ (public, pg. 3)
				台	DAI (platform)
				私	watakushi (I, private)
13. メ 2	Katakana メ			希	KI (hope, rare)
				殺	koro·su (kill, pg. 26)
14. リ 2	variation of Katakana リ			帰	kae·ru (return)
				班	HAN (squad, group)
15. 丂 2				号	GŌ (number, signal)
				巧*	KŌ (skill)
				朽*	ku·chiru (rot, decay)

EXERCISES FOR ONE AND TWO STROKE COMPONENTS

1. **Analyze the Kanji listed below. Write the radicals or components in the boxes. If the radical or component has a name, write it on the line. All of the Kanji in these exercises were selected from the examples shown in the prior section.**

Example:

魚 sakana (fish) = ┌ク┐ Katakana ク + ┌田┐ ta = field

\+ ┌灬┐ yotsu·ten

1. 化 ka (transform) = ☐ _____ + ☐ _____

2. 急 KYŪ (sudden) = ☐ _____ + ☐ _____

\+ ☐ _____

3. 外 soto (outside) = ☐ _____ + ☐ _____

4. 計 KEI (measure) = ☐ _____ + ☐ _____

5. 殺 koro·su (kill) = ☐ _____ + ☐ _____

\+ ☐ _____

6. 号 GŌ (number) = ☐ _____ + ☐ _____

2. Form Kanji by selecting the appropriate components on the right and writing them in the correct place in the box on the left.

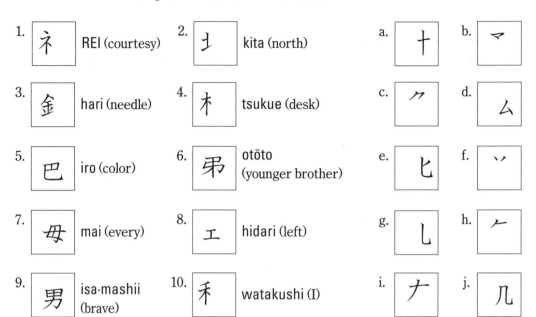

1. ネ REI (courtesy)
2. 土 kita (north)
3. 金 hari (needle)
4. 木 tsukue (desk)
5. 巴 iro (color)
6. 弔 otōto (younger brother)
7. 毋 mai (every)
8. エ hidari (left)
9. 男 isa·mashii (brave)
10. 禾 watakushi (I)

a. 十
b. マ
c. ケ
d. 厶
e. ヒ
f. ヾ
g. し
h. ⌐
i. ナ
j. 几

Three Stroke Components

Component & Stroke Number	Derivation	Stroke Order and Practice			Examples	
1. ‡ 巾 3	haba (width)	リ	口	巾	市	SHI (city)
		巾	巾		布	nuno/FU (cloth)
					帰	kae·ru (return, pg. 52)
2. 幺 3	ito·gashira from 糸 (ito = thread)	く	幺	幺	幼	YŌ (infant)
		幺	幺		率	RITSU (rate)
					磁	JI (magnet)
3. ⺌ 3	variation of 小 (SHŌ = small)	⺌	⺌	⺌	当	ata·ru (hit, success)
		⺌	⺌		常	tsune/JŌ (usual)
					賞	SHŌ (prize)
4. 夂 3	fuyu·gashira from 冬 (fuyu = winter)	ク	ク	夂	冬	fuyu (winter, pg. 2)
		夂	夂		客	KYAKU (guest)
					各	KAKU (each)
5. 夂 3	natsu·ashi from 夏 (natsu = summer)	ク	ク	夂	夏	natsu (summer)
		夂	夂		麦	mugi (barley, wheat)
					愛	AI (love, pg. xii)

‡ 巾 is also a *hen*. See page 22.

Component & Stroke Number	Derivation	Stroke Order and Practice	Examples
6. 爿 3		丬 丬 爿 / 爿 爿	状 JŌ (state or condition, letter) / 装 SHŌ/SŌ (dress, ornament) / 将 SHŌ (military general)
7. †† 也 3	(to be - classical use)	乛 丆 也 / 也 也	地 CHI (earth, pg. 16) / 他 TA (other) / 池 ike (pond, pg. xvi)
8. 巛 3	variation of 川 (kawa = river)	丿 巛 巛 / 巛 巛	流 naga·reru/RYŪ (flow, pg. xvi) / 荒* ara·i (rough)
9. 廾 3	nijū·ashi (twenty)	一 ナ 廾 / 廾 廾	算 SAN (calculate, pg. 29) / 鼻 hana (nose) / 弁 BEN (eloquence)
10. 丷 3	Katakana ソ plus Kanji 一 (ICHI = one)	丶 丷 丷 / 丷 丷	前 mae/ZEN (front, before) / 首 kubi/SHU (neck) / 益 EKI (profit, pg. 33)
11. 𠂢 3		丿 𠂢 𠂢 / 𠂢 𠂢	貿 BŌ (trade) / 留 RYŪ (stay)

†† Independent Kanji (classical), but no longer included in Jōyō Kanji.

Component & Stroke Number	Derivation	Stroke Order and Practice	Examples
12. ヽゝ 3	variation of Katakana ツ	ヽ　ヽゝ　ヽゝ	学 GAKU (study) 単 TAN (single, simple, mere) 労 RŌ (labor)
13. ヨ 3	Katakana ヨ	ㄱ → ㅋ → ヨ	雪 yuki (snow, pg.29) 婦* FU (woman) 曜 YŌ (day of the week)
14. ⺕ 3	variation of Katakana ヨ	ㄱ → ㅋ → ⺕	書 ka·ku/SHO (write, book) 君 kimi (you) 事 koto/JI (thing, matter)

EXERCISES FOR THREE STROKE COMPONENTS

1. Analyze the Kanji listed below. Write the radicals or components in the boxes. If the radical or component has a name, write it on the line.

1. 帰 kae·ru (return) = ☐ _____ + ☐ _____

    + ☐ _____ + ☐ _____

2. 賞 SHŌ (prize) = ☐ _____ + ☐ _____

    + ☐ _____ + ☐ _____

3. 客 KYAKU (guest) = ☐ _____ + ☐ _____

    + ☐ _____

4. 算 SAN (calculate) = ☐ _____ + ☐ _____

    + ☐ _____

5. 労 RŌ (labor) = ☐ _____ + ☐ _____

    + ☐ _____

6. 曜 YŌ (day of the week) = ☐ _____ + ☐ _____
+ ☐ _____

7. 前 mae (front) = ☐ _____ + ☐ _____
+ ☐ _____

8. 地 CHI (earth) = ☐ _____ + ☐ _____

2. Form Kanji by selecting the appropriate components on the right and writing them in the correct place in the box on the left.

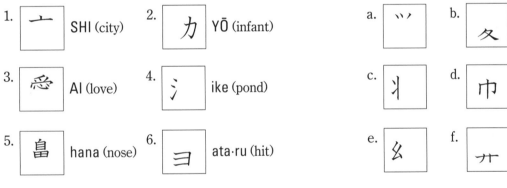

1. 亠 SHI (city)　2. 力 YŌ (infant)

3. 愛 AI (love)　4. 氵 ike (pond)

5. 畠 hana (nose)　6. ヨ ata·ru (hit)

7. 法 naga·reru (flow)　8. 字 GAKU (study)

9. 雨 yuki (snow)　10. 寽 SHŌ (military general)

a. ⺀　b. 夂

c. 丬　d. 巾

e. 幺　f. 艹

g. ヨ　h. 也

i. ⺌　j. 儿

Four Stroke Components

Component & Stroke Number	Derivation	Stroke Order and Practice	Examples
1. 圭 4		一・ 十 キ・ 圭・ 圭 圭	青 ao·i/SEI (blue, green) 表 omote/HYŌ (surface, front) 責 se·meru (blame)
2. 丗 4		一・ 十 廿 丗・ 丗 丗	共 KYŌ (common) 黄 ki (yellow) 昔 mukashi (long ago)
3. 毋 4	variation of 母 (haha = mother)	𠂉・ 𠃌 毋 毋・ 毋 毋	毎 MAI (every, pg. 50) 海 umi (sea, pg. xii) 梅 ume (plum)
4. 壬 4		ノ 二・ 千 壬・ 壬 壬	任 maka·seru (entrust) 庭 niwa (garden) 賃 CHIN (rent, wage)
5. 开 4		一・ 二・ 于 开 开 开	形 katachi (shape, pg. 26) 研 KEN (grind, study thoroughly, pg.18) 開 a·keru (open, pg. 40)

Component & Stroke Number	Derivation	Stroke Order and Practice	Examples
6. 爫 4	Katakana ノ + ツ	⌐ ⌐ ⌐ ⌐ 爫 爫	受 u·keru (receive) 暖 atata·kai (warm) 愛 AI (love, pg. xii)
7. 云 4		一 二 云 云 云 云	伝 tsuta·eru (transmit) 転 koro·bu/TEN (roll over, pg.19) 会 a·u (meet, pg. 30)
8. 勿 4		ノ ク ク 勿 勿 勿	物 mono (thing, pg. 23) 易 yasa·shii (easy)
9. 艮 4		⌐ ⼕ ⼸ 艮 艮 艮	服 FUKU (dress, pg. 17) 報 HŌ (report)
10. 夕 4		ノ ク 夕 夕 夕 夕	祭 matsu·ri (festival) 然 ZEN (suffix meaning state, condition)
11. 夬 4		⼅ ユ 尹 夬 夬 夬	快 KAI (pleasant, pg.21) 決 ki·meru (decide)

EXERCISES FOR FOUR STROKE COMPONENTS

1. **Analyze the Kanji listed below. Write the radicals or components in the boxes. If the radical or component has a name, write it on the line.**

1. 形 katachi (shape) = ☐ _____ + ☐ _____

2. 責 se·meru (blame) = ☐ _____ + ☐ _____

3. 共 KYŌ (common) = ☐ _____ + ☐ _____

4. 海 umi (sea) = ☐ _____ + ☐ _____

   + ☐ _____

5. 庭 niwa (garden) = ☐ _____ + ☐ _____

   + ☐ _____

6. 研 KEN (study thoroughly) = ☐ _____ + ☐ _____

7. 愛 AI (love) = ☐ _____ + ☐ _____

   + ☐ _____ + ☐ _____

8. 伝 tsuta·eru (transmit) = ☐ _____ + ☐ _____

9. 易 yasa·shii (easy) = ☐ _____ + ☐ _____

10. 服 FUKU (dress) = ☐ _____ + ☐ _____

11. 然 ZEN (suffix meaning state, condition) = ☐ _____ + ☐ _____

    + ☐ _____

12. 会 a·u (meet) = ☐ _____ + ☐ _____

2. Form Kanji by selecting the appropriate components on the right and writing them in the correct place in the box on the left.

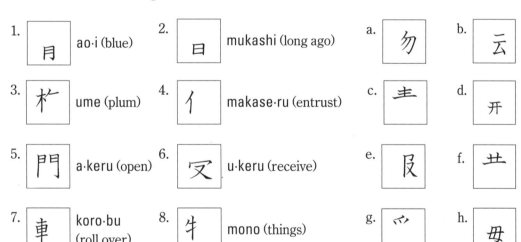

1. 月 ao·i (blue)
2. 日 mukashi (long ago)
3. 杧 ume (plum)
4. 亻 makase·ru (entrust)
5. 門 a·keru (open)
6. 又 u·keru (receive)
7. 車 koro·bu (roll over)
8. 牛 mono (things)
9. 幸 HŌ (report)
10. 氵 ki·meru (decide)

a. 勿
b. 云
c. 圭
d. 开
e. 艮
f. 廿
g. 罒
h. 毋
i. 壬
j. 夬

Five Stroke Components

Component & Stroke Number	Derivation	Stroke Order and Practice	Examples
1. † 牙 5	old Kanji (kiba = tusk, fang)	一　厂　工　牙　牙 牙　牙	芽 me/GA (sprout, bud) 雅* GA (grace) 邪* JA (evil)
2. 禾 5	no·gi Katakana ノ + Kanji 木 (ki = tree)	ノ　二　千　禾　禾 禾　禾	委 I (commit) 香* kao·ri (scent) 季 KI (season)
3. 夫 5		一　二　三　夫　夫 夫　夫	春 haru (spring) 奏 SŌ (play musical instrument) 棒 BŌ (stick)
4. 艮 5		刁　ヨ　ヨ　艮　艮 艮　艮	郷 KYŌ (native place, hometown) 即* SOKU (immediate)
5. 氺 5	shita·mizu variation of 水 (mizu = water)	亅　刂　氺　氺　氺 氺　氺	求 moto·meru (seek, request) 緑 midori (green)

† Independent Kanji, but no longer included in Jōyō Kanji.

Component & Stroke Number	Derivation	Stroke Order and Practice	Examples
6. 甚 5		一 十 廿 甘 甚	寒 samu·i (cold) 構 KŌ (structure) 講 KŌ (lecture)
7. 乍 5		ノ 一 乍 乍 乍	作 tsuku·ru/SAKU (make, pg.21) 昨 SAKU (past) 酢* su/SAKU (vinegar, pg. 23)
8. 戊 5		一 厂 戊 戊 戊	成 na·ru/SEI (become) 茂* shige·ru (thrive) 威* I (aggression, dignity)
9. 疋 5 †	old Kanji (hiki = counter for length of cloth)	一 丁 尸 疋 疋	疑 utaga·u (doubt) 礎* SO (cornerstone) 旋* SEN (whirl, revolve)
10. 疋 5		一 丁 干 疋 疋	定 TEI (fixed, regulate) 従 shitaga·u (follow, obey) 縦 tate (vertical)
11. 旡 5		一 仁 二 旡 旡	既* sude·ni (already) 慨* GAI (regret, lament)

† Independent Kanji, but no longer included in Jōyō Kanji.

Component & Stroke Number	Derivation	Stroke Order and Practice	Examples	
12. 公 5		ノ ハ ハ 公 公 公 公	沿	so·u (parallel to, along)
			船	fune (boat, pg. 19)
13. 圣 5		ブ 又 圣 圣 圣 圣 圣	径	KEI (path, diameter)
			経	KEI (elapse, via, longitude)
			軽	karu·i/KEI (light in weight, pg. 19)

EXERCISES FOR FIVE STROKE COMPONENTS

1. **Analyze the Kanji listed below. Write the radicals or components in the boxes. If the radical or component has a name, write it on the line.**

1. 芽 me (bud) = ☐ _____ + ☐ _____

2. 委 I (commit) = ☐ _____ + ☐ _____

3. 春 haru (spring) = ☐ _____ + ☐ _____

4. 船 fune (boat) = ☐ _____ + ☐ _____

5. 作 tsuku·ru (make) = ☐ _____ + ☐ _____

6. 軽 karu·i (light in weight) = ☐ _____ + ☐ _____

7. 定 TEI (determine) = ☐ _____ + ☐ _____

2. Form Kanji by selecting the appropriate components on the right and writing them in the correct place in the box on the left.

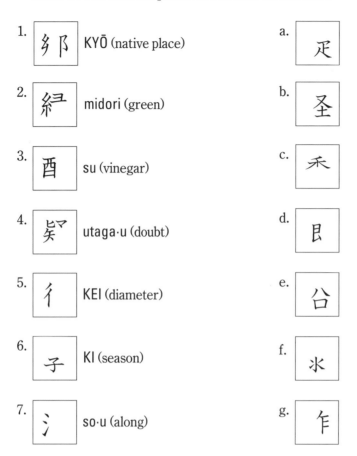

1. ⻏ 邑 KYŌ (native place)

2. 糸 midori (green)

3. 酉 su (vinegar)

4. 矣 utaga·u (doubt)

5. 彳 KEI (diameter)

6. 子 KI (season)

7. 氵 so·u (along)

a. 疋

b. 圣

c. 禾

d. 艮

e. 㕣

f. 氷

g. 乍

Six and Seven Stroke Components
Six Stroke Components

Component & Stroke Number	Derivation	Stroke Order and Practice	Examples
1. †† 而 6	(however - classical use)	一・ 丆 厅 丌 而 而 / 而 而	需* JU (demand) 耐* ta·eru (endure)
2. 聿 6	fude·zukuri from 筆 (fude = writing brush)	コ⁷ ⁊ ヨ → ヨ → 彐 → 彐 → 聿 / 聿 聿	筆 fude/HITSU (writing brush) 建 ta·teru/KEN (build, pg. 38) 健 KEN (healthy)
3. 艮 6	kon·zukuri from 根 (kon = root)	コ⁷ → ヨ → ヨ → 彐 → 艮 → 艮 / 艮 艮	根 ne/KON (root) 銀 GIN (silver, pg. 20) 限 kagi·ru/GEN (limit)
4. 西 6	variation of 西 (nishi = West)	一・ 一 冂 襾 襾 西 / 西 西	票 HYŌ (vote) 要 i·ru/YŌ (need) 価 KA (price, value)
5. 羊 6	variation of 羊 (hitsuji = sheep)	ヽ ゛゛ ゛゛・ 圤 半・ 羊・ / 羊 羊	着 ki·ru (wear) 美 utsuku·shii (beautiful) 差 SA (difference)

†† Independent Kanji (classical), but no longer included in Jōyō Kanji.

Component & Stroke Number	Derivation	Stroke Order and Practice	Examples
6. † 亥 6	old Kanji (i = boar)	亠 → 亠. 六 亥 亥 亥 / 亥 亥	刻 KOKU (time, carve) / 核* KAKU (nucleus)
7. 关 6		` `` → 兰. 兰. 半 关 / 关 关	券 KEN (ticket) / 勝 ka·tsu (win, pg. 17) / 卷 ma·ku/KAN (volume)
8. 圭 6		→ 一. 十 → 土. 壵. 圭 圭. / 圭 圭	街 machi (town, pg. 40) / 掛* ka·keru (hang, pg. 51) / 涯* GAI (end, limit)
9. 厎 6		` 丿 尸 斤 斤 厎 / 厎. 厎	脈 MYAKU (pulse) / 派 HA (faction)
10. 自 6		` 亻 丿 户 户 自 自 / 自 自	追 o·u (chase) / 師 SHI (teacher, master)
11. 其 6		→ 一 十 卄 → 廿 → 甘 甚. / 其 其	基 moto (base) / 碁* GO [the game of] Go)

† Independent Kanji, but no longer included in Jōyō Kanji.

Component & Stroke Number	Derivation	Stroke Order and Practice	Examples
12. † 戔 6		➝一・ ➝二・ ➝三・ 戋 戋 戔 戔 戔	浅 asa·i/SEN (shallow) 残 noko·su/ZAN (leave [some-thing], pg.22) 銭 * SEN (1/100th of a yen)
13. †† 亦 6	mata (also - classical use)	➝ヽ ➝亠・ 广 亦 亦 亦 亦 亦	変 kawa·ru (change) 恋 * koi (love) 湾 * WAN (bay)
14. 关 6		ヽ ソ ➝ソ・ 兰・ 关 关 关 关	送 oku·ru (send) 関 seki/KAN (checkpoint, relation)
15. 戈 6		➝一・ 十 士・ 弐 戋 戈 戈 戈	裁 ta·tsu/saba·ku/SAI (cut out [cloth], pass judgment) 栽 * SAI (planting) 載 * no·seru/SAI (place on top of)

†† Independent Kanji (classical), but no longer included in Jōyō Kanji.

Seven Stroke Components

Component & Stroke Number	Derivation	Stroke Order and Practice	Examples
1. 豕 7	buta (pig)	一 フ ブ 豕 豕 豕 / 豕 豕 豕	家 ie/KA (house, pg. 29) / 隊 TAI (troop) / 劇 GEKI (drama, pg. 31)
2. 舛 7	mai·ashi from 舞 (mai = dance)	ノ ク タ ダ 夗 夘 / 舛 舛 舛	舞* mai (dance) / 隣* tonari (next door, neighbor)
3. 釆 7	no·gome Katakana ノ + Kanji 米 (kome = rice)	ノ 丷 丷 乎 釆 釆 / 釆 釆 釆	番 BAN (number) / 釈* SHAKU (disentangle, interpret)
4. † 辰 7	old Kanji (SHIN = clam/ tatsu = dragon)	一 厂 斤 斥 辰 辰 / 辰 辰 辰	農 NŌ (agriculture) / 震* SHIN (quake) / 振* fu·ru/SHIN (shake)
5. 甫 7		一 厂 币 月 月 甫 / 甫 甫 甫	補 ogina·u/HO (supplement, pg. 23) / 捕* to·raeru/HO (capture)

† Independent Kanji, but no longer included in Jōyō Kanji.

Component & Stroke Number	Derivation	Stroke Order and Practice		Examples	
6. 兊 7		` ヽ` `ソ` `ハ` `尚` `冶` `兇` 兇 兇 兇		税	ZEI (tax)
				説	SETSU (opinion, theory)
				脱	nu·gu (take off [clothes])
7. 鳥 7		`´ノ` `ィ` `ґ` `ґ` `自` `自` 鳥 鳥 鳥		島	shima (island)
				鳥	tori (bird, pg. 2)
8. 叒 7		`ヽ` `叺` `卩` `尸` `叒` `叒` 叒 叒 叒		遠	tō·i (far)
				園	EN (garden)
				還*	KAN (return)

EXERCISES FOR SIX AND SEVEN STROKE COMPONENTS

1. **Analyze the Kanji listed below. Write the radicals or components in the boxes. If the radical or component has a name, write it on the line.**

1. 筆 fude (writing brush) = ☐ _____ + ☐ _____

2. 銀 GIN (silver) = ☐ _____ + ☐ _____

3. 要 i·ru (need) = ☐ _____ + ☐ _____

4. 需 JU (demand) = ☐ _____ + ☐ _____

5. 刻 KOKU (time) = ☐ _____ + ☐ _____

6. 美 utsuku·shii (beautiful) = ☐ _____ + ☐ _____

7. 劇 GEKI (drama) = ☐ _____ + ☐ _____
   + ☐ _____

8. 基 moto (base) = ☐ _____ + ☐ _____
   + ☐ _____

9. 根 ne (root) = ☐ _____ + ☐ _____

10. 番 BAN (number) = ☐ _____ + ☐ _____

11. 震 SHIN (quake) = ☐ _____ + ☐ _____

12. 隣 tonari (neighbor) = ☐ _____ + ☐ _____
    + ☐ _____

13. 送 oku·ru (send) = ☐ _____ + ☐ _____

14. 裁 SAI (cut out) = ☐ _____ + ☐ _____

15. 鳥 tori (bird) = ☐ _____ + ☐ _____

2. **Form Kanji by selecting the appropriate components on the right and writing them in the correct place in the box on the left.**

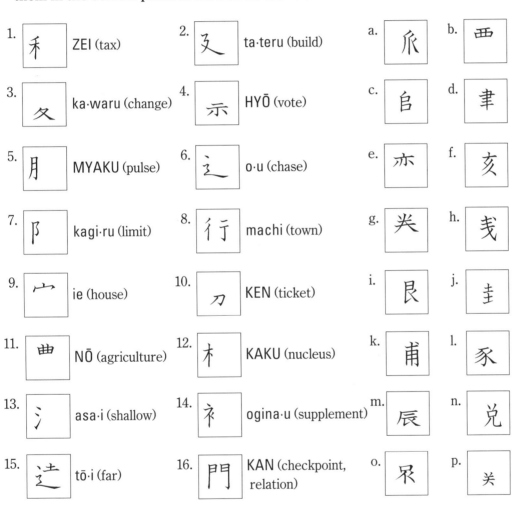

1. 禾 ZEI (tax)

2. 乀 ta·teru (build)

3. 夂 ka·waru (change)

4. 示 HYŌ (vote)

5. 月 MYAKU (pulse)

6. 辶 o·u (chase)

7. 阝 kagi·ru (limit)

8. 彳 machi (town)

9. 宀 ie (house)

10. 刀 KEN (ticket)

11. 曲 NŌ (agriculture)

12. 木 KAKU (nucleus)

13. 氵 asa·i (shallow)

14. 礻 ogina·u (supplement)

15. 辶 tō·i (far)

16. 門 KAN (checkpoint, relation)

a. 爪

b. 西

c. 自

d. 聿

e. 亦

f. 亥

g. 关

h. 戔

i. 艮

j. 圭

k. 甫

l. 豖

m. 辰

n. 兑

o. 呆

p. 关

Eight and Nine Stroke Components
Eight Stroke Components

Component & Stroke Number	Derivation	Stroke Order and Practice	Examples
1. 隶 8	from 逮* (tai = catch up)	⼆ → ㋕ → ㋕ → 聿 → 肀 → 肀 隶 隶 隶 隶	康 KŌ (calm) 逮* TAI (catch up, overtake)
2. 坴 8		一 → 十 → 土 → 𡗗 → 圥 → 圥 幸 坴 坴 坴	勢 ikio·i (vigor) 陸 RIKU (land, pg.22)
3. 卓 8		一 → 十 → 占 → 市 → 卓 → 皁 直 卓 卓 卓	朝 asa (morning) 幹 miki/KAN (tree trunk) 乾* kawa·ku/KAN (dry)
4. † 岡 8	oka (hill)	⼍ → 冂 → 冂 → 門 → 円 → 周 岡 岡 岡 岡	鋼 hagane/KŌ (steel) 剛* GŌ (hard, strong) 綱* tsuna/KŌ (rope)
5. 侖 8		ノ → 人 → 仝 → 仝 → 合 → 合 侖 侖 侖 侖	論 RON (discussion, opinion) 輪 wa/RIN (wheel, pg. 19) 倫* RIN (ethics)

† Independent Kanji, but no longer included in Jōyō Kanji.

Component & Stroke Number	Derivation	Stroke Order and Practice	Examples
6. 僉 8		ノ ヘ 今 今 令 合 合 僉 僉 僉	険 kewa·shii/KEN (steep, risky) 験 KEN (testing, pg. 20) 検 KEN (inspect)
7. 堯 8		一 十 土 坴 击 垚 声 堯 堯 堯	焼 ya·ku (burn, pg. 17) 暁* akatsuki (dawn)
8. 采 8		一 爫 爫 爫 亚 平 采 采 采 采	採 to·ru/SAI (pick, gather, adopt) 菜 na/SAI (leafy greens) 彩* SAI (color, pg. 26)
9. 無 8		ノ 仁 仁 午 冊 無 無 無 無 無	無 na·i/MU (not be) 舞* mai/BU (dance, pg. 72)
10. 斉 8		亠 亠 亠 文 斉 斉 斉 斉 斉 斉	済 su·mu/SAI (finish, save) 斎* SAI (religious purification) 剤* ZAI (medicine)
11. 其 8		一 十 卄 甘 甘 其 其 其 其 其	期 KI (period, term) 旗 hata/KI (flag)

77

Component & Stroke Number	Derivation	Stroke Order and Practice	Examples
12. 录 8		ㄱ → ㄱ → ⇒ → 彐 → 寻 → 寻 → 录 录 录 录	緑 midori/RYOKU (green, pg. 64) 録 ROKU (record)

Nine Stroke Components

Component & Stroke Number	Derivation	Stroke Order and Practice	Examples
1. 俞 9		ノ → 人 → 合 → 介 → 俞 → 俞 → 俞 → 俞 → 俞 俞 俞	輸 YU (transport) 愉* YU (delight) 諭* YU (admonish, warn)
2. 咼 9		⺆ → 冂 → 冂 → 冎 → 冎 → 咼 咼 咼 咼 咼 咼	過 su·giru/KA (exceed, excessively) 渦* uzu/KA (whirl)
3. 咸 9		一 → 厂 → 厂 → 反 → 反 → 咸 咸 咸 咸 咸 咸	感 KAN (sense, feeling) 減 he·ru/GEN (decrease) 憾* KAN (regret)
4. 复 9		ノ → 仁 → 仁 → 臽 → 旨 → 自 → 自 → 复 复 复 复 复	復 FUKU (again, repeat, restore) 複 FUKU (multiple, pg. 23) 腹 hara/FUKU (abdomen)

Component & Stroke Number	Derivation	Stroke Order and Practice						Examples	
5. 畐 9		一	仃	而	금	尸	뮤	福	FUKU (good fortune, pg. 22)
		뮤	畐	畐	畐	畐		副	FUKU (vice-, pg. 26)
								富	tomi/FU (wealth)
6. 易 9		刂	冂	日	日	旦	昌	場	ba (place, pg.16)
		易	易	易	易	易		湯	yu (hot water)
								陽	YŌ (sun, pg. 22)
7. 禺 9		刂	冂	日	日	旦	禺	偶*	GŪ (even number, unexpected)
		禺	禺	禺	禺	禺		遇*	GŪ (treatment)
								隅*	sumi/GŪ (corner)

EXERCISES FOR EIGHT AND NINE STROKE COMPONENTS

1. **Analyze the Kanji listed below. Write the radicals or components in the boxes. If the radical or component has a name, write it on the line.**

1. 朝 asa (morning) = ☐ _____ + ☐ _____

2. 菜 na (leafy greens) = ☐ _____ + ☐ _____

3. 鋼 hagane (steel) = ☐ _____ + ☐ _____

4. 輪 wa (wheel) = ☐ _____ + ☐ _____

5. 緑 midori (green) = ☐ _____ + ☐ _____

6. 旗 hata (flag) = ☐ _____ + ☐ _____
   + ☐ _____

7. 輸 YU (transport) = ☐ _____ + ☐ _____

8. 減 he·ru (decrease) = ☐ _____ + ☐ _____

9. 復 FUKU (again) = ☐ _____ + ☐ _____

10. 福 FUKU (good fortune) = ☐ _____ + ☐ _____

11. 場 ba (place) = ☐ _____ + ☐ _____

12. 焼 ya·ku (burn) = ☐ _____ + ☐ _____

2. Form Kanji by selecting the appropriate components on the right side and writing them in the correct place in the box on the left.

1. 阝 RIKU (land)
2. 言 RON (opinion)
3. 心 KAN (sense)
4. 阝 YŌ (sun)
5. 广 KŌ (calm)
6. 衤 FUKU (multiple)
7. 幹 miki (tree trunk)
8. 馬 KEN (testing)
9. 辶 sugi·ru (exceed)
10. 亻 GŪ (even number) *
11. 氵 SAI (finish, save)
12. 灬 na·i (not be)

a. 易
b. 复
c. 咼
d. 垚
e. 無
f. 禺
g. 咸
h. 隶
i. 侖
j. 僉
k. 卓
l. 斉

Ten, Eleven, and Twelve Stroke Components
Ten Stroke Components

Component & Stroke Number	Derivation	Stroke Order and Practice	Examples
1. 韋 10		リ → 卅 → 五. 卉 尚 吾 吉 吉 吉. 韋 韋 韋	違* chiga·u/I (differ) 偉* era·i/I (great) 衛 EI (defense, pg.40)
2. 臥 10		乚 丆 广 𦥑 →戶 𦥑 臣 臥 臥 臥 臥 臥	覧 RAN (look) 監* KAN (supervise)
3. 莫 10		→ 一. 十 廾 ⺾ 苪 苗 苴. 莒. 莫 莫 莫 莫	難 muzuka·shii/ NAN (difficult, pg.27) 漢 KAN (Han Dynasty, China)
4. 莫 10		→ 一. 十 廾 ⺾ 苪 苗 苗 莒. 芦 莫 莫 莫	幕 MAKU (curtain) 暮 ku·re/BO (nightfall, year-end) 墓 haka/BO (tomb)
5. 冓 10		→ 一. 十 廾 井. 並. 荓 荓 荓 荓 冓. 冓 冓	構 KŌ (structure, pg. 65) 講 KŌ (lecture, pg. 65) 溝 mizo/KŌ (ditch)

Component & Stroke Number	Derivation	Stroke Order and Practice	Examples
6. 菫 10		一　十　艹　艹　芇　苫　芇　革　革　菫　菫　菫	勤 tsuto·meru/KIN (work for, be employed) 謹* KIN (be respectful)

Eleven Stroke Components

Component & Stroke Number	Derivation	Stroke Order and Practice	Examples
1. 竟 11		�　一　十　立　立　立　音　音　竟　竟　竟	鏡 kagami/KYŌ (mirror) 境 sakai/KYŌ/KEI (border, boundary)
2. 商 11		�　一　十　艹　宀　宀　宀　商　商　商　商　商	敵 TEKI (enemy) 適 TEKI (suitable) 滴* shizuku/TEKI (a drop)
3. 隺 11		㇑　爫　亻　仁　隹　隹　隹　隹　隹　隹　隹　隹	観 KAN (view) 権 KEN (power, right)
4. 曽 11		㇑　丷　丷　㐜　㐜　曲　曲　曽　曽　曽　曽　曽	層 SŌ (a layer) 増 ma·su/ZŌ (increase) 憎* niku·mu/ZŌ (hate)

Twelve Stroke Components

Component & Stroke Number	Derivation	Stroke Order and Practice		Examples
1. 戠 12		ホー　→立・　ホー　立ノ　→立・　立ノ 立几　→音　音　戠　戠　戠 戠　戠		織　o·ru/SHOKU/ SHIKI (weave) 職　SHOKU (occupation, pg. 19) 識　SHIKI (knowledge)

EXERCISES FOR TEN, ELEVEN, AND TWELVE STROKE COMPONENTS

1. Analyze the Kanji listed below. Write the radicals or components in the boxes. If the radical or component has a name, write it on the line.

1. 違　chiga·u (differ) = ☐ _____ + ☐ _____

2. 難　muzuka·shii = ☐ _____ + ☐ _____
   (difficult)

3. 暮　ku·re (nightfall, = ☐ _____ + ☐ _____
   year-end)

4. 構　KŌ (structure) = ☐ _____ + ☐ _____

5. 権　KEN = ☐ _____ + ☐ _____
   (power, right)

6. 鏡　kagami (mirror) = ☐ _____ + ☐ _____

7. 適　TEKI (suitable) = ☐ _____ + ☐ _____

8.　増　ma·su　＝ ☐ ＿＿＿＿＿ ＋ ☐ ＿＿＿＿＿
　　　　　(increase)

9.　識　SHIKI　＝ ☐ ＿＿＿＿＿ ＋ ☐ ＿＿＿＿＿
　　　　　(knowledge)

10.　監　KAN (supervise)＝ ☐ ＿＿＿＿＿ ＋ ☐ ＿＿＿＿＿

2. Form Kanji by selecting the appropriate components on the right and writing them in the correct place in the box on the left.

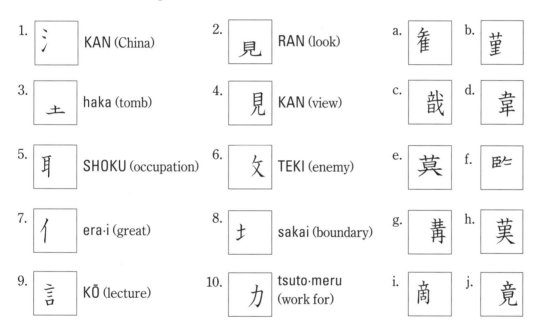

1. 氵 KAN (China)

2. 見 RAN (look)

a. 雚　b. 菫

3. 土 haka (tomb)

4. 見 KAN (view)

c. 戠　d. 韋

5. 耳 SHOKU (occupation)

6. 攵 TEKI (enemy)

e. 莫　f. 臣ム

7. 亻 era·i (great)

8. 土 sakai (boundary)

g. 菁　h. 莫

9. 言 KŌ (lecture)

10. 力 tsuto·meru (work for)

i. 商　j. 竟

PART

II
250 Very Basic Kanji and Exercises

Chapter 4. 250 Very Basic Kanji

Now that you are familiar with radicals and components of Kanji, you are going to learn actual Kanji that can also be radicals or components of more complex Kanji. The Kanji in this section are very basic, which in this workbook refers to Kanji that cannot be broken down into simpler Kanji[*5]. They are independent and can stand alone to express their original meaning and at the same time, they appear frequently as a single component that represents meaning or pronunciation in a more complex Kanji.

Knowing these very basic Kanji will help you to decipher and memorize more complex Kanji just as knowing the roots of English words can help you figure out the meaning of a word that is new to you. Sometimes the meaning of a complex Kanji may appear to have little to do with its basic Kanji components, but if you were to trace its origins you would often find that the meaning has progressively evolved from the basic Kanji over the centuries.

This section introduces 250 very basic Kanji (229 from Gakushū Kanji and 21 from Jōyō Kanji that are not Gakushū Kanji). The following diagram shows the type of information presented for each Kanji:

	Kanji and Examples		Stroke Order and Practice			
15. ⌐3 口 (mouth, pg. 16)	品 しな／ヒン (goods, refinement) 知 し・る／チ (know, pg. 18) 名 な／メイ (name)		![stroke 1] ![stroke 2] ![stroke 3] ![stroke 4] ![stroke 5]			

6 — くち　口答え（くちごたえ back talk）　出口（でぐち exit）　入り口（いりぐち entrance, pg. 92）

7 — コウ／（ク）　口論（コウロン dispute）　人口（ジンコウ population）　口調（クチョウ tone of voice）

*5 A few Kanji that can be broken down further have been classified here as very basic because they frequently appear as a single component in more complex Kanji.

1 : the number of strokes

2 : the meaning or primary meaning

3 : examples of how the basic Kanji are used in more complex Kanji. These will appear in exercises later in each section. However, some Kanji may not have examples, because they are not used in more complex Kanji.

4 : the stroke order

5 : a space to practice writing Kanji (You may also want to practice on a separate piece of paper.)

6 : the Kun reading given in Hiragana with examples of common words that will be used in the exercises later.

7 : the On reading given in Katakana with examples of common words using the On reading. These will be used in the exercises later in each section.

8 : special On and Kun readings are shown in parentheses.

Note : when the space for an On or Kun reading is blank, such reading does not exist.

The Kanji are introduced in the order of their complexity, beginning with single stroke Kanji and building to twelve stroke Kanji. Within the same stroke count, those Kanji that are conceptually related are generally grouped together. Also those that are visually similar are placed one after another so that the subtle stroke differences become more apparent.

Another aid to the student is that repeated Kanji are noted. Any later uses give the page number on which the Kanji was originally defined.

Exercises appear in each section to help you practice writing the newly introduced Kanji as they appear in words and reading them as they appear in sentences. An analyzing and reading exercise is also provided in each section for the example Kanji which are the more complex members of a basic Kanji family group. This exercise will help you increase the number of Kanji you can identify. (It may, however, be better suited to more advanced students; beginning students may wish to skip it and return to it later.)

Sometimes the English translation of a Japanese sentence in the exercises gives little clue to the meaning of the Kanji being used. In such a case, the literal translation of the Kanji is placed in parentheses ( ) after the fluent English. Additional English not present in the original Japanese sentence but which aid in fluency or comprehension are placed in square brackets [ ] where appropriate.

The following symbols appear in the charts to aid you:

* a Kanji from the Jōyō Kanji list which is not in the Gakushū Kanji list.

‡ a Kanji which appeared earlier as a radical; a cross-reference is given in a footnote.

● a Kanji appearing in a word or compound (Jukugo) which will be officially introduced (i.e., as a basic or example Kanji) later on; a cross-reference is given in a footnote.

▲ a Kanji appearing in an example Jukugo but not officially introduced in this workbook; its translation appears in a footnote; (if such a Kanji appears in an exercise, its translation follows in parentheses).

In addition, a cross-reference page number appearing by the definition of an example Kanji indicates the page on which the example was first introduced.

One and Two Stroke Kanji
Single Stroke Kanji

Kanji and Examples		Stroke Order and Practice
1. 一 (one, pg. xiv)	三 サン (three, pg. 2) 七 シチ (seven, pg.3) 土 つち (earth)	→一. 一 一
ひと・つ	一つ (ひとつ one)	一月 (ひとつき one month)
イチ／イツ	一日 (イチニチ a day)	一月 (イチガツ January)　同一 (ドウイツ identical)
2. 乙 *1 (the second in a series, pg. 3)	乾* かわ・く (dry, pg. 76)	乙 乙 乙
オツ	甲*▲乙*(コウ・オツ the first & the second in a series, A & B)	

Two Stroke Kanji

Kanji and Examples		Stroke Order and Practice
1. 二 (two, pg. xiv)	元 ゲン／ガン (origin) 示 しめ・す (to show) 仁 ジン (benevolence)	→二. →二. 二 二
ふた・つ	二つ (ふたつ two, pg. xiv)	
二	二さつ (二さつ two books, magazines)	二月(ニガツ February)　二年(ニネン two years)
2. 七 (seven, pg. 3)		一. 七. 七 七
なな／(なの)	七つ (ななつ seven, pg. 3)	七分 (なな フン seven minutes)　七日(なのか seventh day, seven days)
シチ	七月 (シチガツ July)	七時 (シチジ seven o'clock)　七人 (シチニン seven people)

　▲甲（コウ）first in a series, "A"

Kanji and Examples		Stroke Order and Practice

3. 八 [2] (eight)

Examples	
公 コウ (public, pg. 3)	
分 わけ・る／フン (divide, minute)	
穴‡ あな (hole, cave)	

Stroke order: ノ 八

| や／や・つ／やっ・つ（よう） | 八重•ざくら（やえざくら double petaled cherry blossoms） | 八つ（やっつ eight） | 八日（ようか eighth day, eight days） |
| ハチ | 八人（ハチニン eight people） | 八月（ハチガツ August） | 八さつ（ハッさつ eight books） |

4. 九 [2] (nine, pg. 3)

Examples	
究 キュウ (study thoroughly, pg. 29)	
染 そ・める (dye)	
丸 まる・い (round)	

Stroke order: ノ 九

| ここの・つ | 九つ（ここのつ nine, pg. 3） | 九日（ここのか ninth day, nine days） |
| ク／キュウ | 九時（クジ nine o'clock） | 九月（クガツ September） | 九分（キュウフン nine minutes） |

5. 十 [2] (ten, pg.2)

Examples	
針 はり (needle, pg. 50)	
古 ふる・い (old)	
早 はや・い (early)	

Stroke order: 一 十

| とお／と | 十日（とおか tenth day, ten days） | 十色（といろ ten different colors） |
| ジュウ／ジッ | 十月（ジュウガツ October） | 九十（キュウジュウ ninety） | 十分（ジップン ten minutes） |

6. 人 [2] (man, person, pg.3)

Examples	
内 うち／ナイ (inside, pg. 40)	
肉 ニク (meat, pg. xii)	

Stroke order: ノ 人

| ひと | 人手（ひとで assistance, a hand） | あの人（あのひと that person） |
| ジン／ニン | 日本人（ニホンジン Japanese people） | 八人（ハチニン eight people） |

‡穴（あな） appeared as *ana·kammuri* on pg. 29; will appear on pg. 158 .

•重（え） will appear on pg. 227.

Kanji and Examples		Stroke Order and Practice
7. ⟨2⟩ 入 (enter)	込* こ・む (be crowded)	ﾞ 入 入 入
い・る/い・れる/はい・る	入り口 (いりぐち entrance)　入れ物 (いれもの container)　入る (はいる enter)	
ニュウ	入学 (ニュウガク entering a school)　入国 (ニュウゴク entry into a country)	
8. ⟨2⟩ 刀 (sword)	切 き・る/セツ (cut)　辺 ヘン (side)　初 はじ・め (beginning, pg. 23)	ﾌﾞ 刀 刀 刀
かたな	小刀 (こがたな pocketknife)	
トウ	日本刀 (ニホントウ Japanese sword)　短刀 (タントウ dagger)	
9. ⟨2⟩ 力 (power, pg.3)	加 くわ・える/カ (add)　勉 ベン (endeavor, diligence)　男 おとこ (man, pg. xv)	ﾌﾞ 力 力 力
ちから	力持ち (ちからもち strong man)　力仕事 (ちからしごと heavy work)	
リキ/リョク	力士 (リキシ sumō wrestler)　体力 (タイリョク physical strength)	
10. ⟨2⟩ 丁 (area the size of a city block, pg.2)	打 う・つ (hit, pg. 22)　町 まち/チョウ (town, pg. 18)　頂 チョウ (summit)	一 丁 丁 丁
チョウ/テイ	一丁 (イッチョウ one city block)　銀座七丁目 (ギンザななチョウめ 7th block of Ginza St.)　丁字路 (テイジロ "T"-intersection)	

- 仕 (シ)　will appear on pg. 99.
- 士 (シ)　will appear on pg. 99.
- ▲ 座 (ザ)　seat

Kanji and Examples			Stroke Order and Practice
11. 又 *2 (again, also)	取	と・る (take, pg.19)	フ 又 又 又
	収	シュウ (collect)	
	反	ハン (opposite, pg. xvi)	
また	又（また again, also）		

EXERCISES FOR ONE AND TWO STROKE KANJI

WRITING EXERCISE
Fill in each box to make a word.

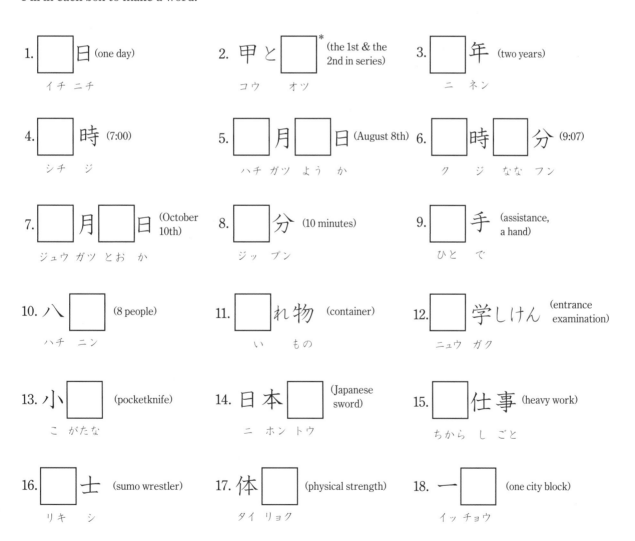

1. ☐日 (one day) — イチ ニチ
2. 甲と☐ * (the 1st & the 2nd in series) — コウ オツ
3. ☐年 (two years) — ニ ネン
4. ☐時 (7:00) — シチ ジ
5. ☐月☐日 (August 8th) — ハチ ガツ よう か
6. ☐時☐分 (9:07) — ク ジ なな フン
7. ☐月☐日 (October 10th) — ジュウ ガツ とお か
8. ☐分 (10 minutes) — ジッ プン
9. ☐手 (assistance, a hand) — ひと で
10. 八☐ (8 people) — ハチ ニン
11. ☐れ物 (container) — い もの
12. ☐学しけん (entrance examination) — ニュウ ガク
13. 小☐ (pocketknife) — こ がたな
14. 日本☐ (Japanese sword) — ニ ホン トウ
15. ☐仕事 (heavy work) — ちから し ごと
16. ☐士 (sumo wrestler) — リキ シ
17. 体☐ (physical strength) — タイ リョク
18. 一☐ (one city block) — イッ チョウ

93

READING EXERCISE

Read the following sentences, and write the correct *furigana* (pronunciation of Kanji written in Hiragana regardless of whether the reading of the Kanji is On or Kun) below the underlined Kanji.

1. りんごが一つと、オレンジが二つあります。 （There are one apple and two oranges.）

2. 本を二さつ買いました。 （I bought two books.）

3. 七月七日はたなばたまつりです。 （July 7th is the *Tanabata* [star] festival.）

4. ケーキを八つください。 （Please give me eight pieces of cake.）

5. 九月九日に学校がはじまります。 （School starts on September 9th.）
   がっこう

6. 学校まであるいて九分かかります。 （It takes nine minutes to walk to school.）

7. あの人は日本人です。 （That person is Japanese.）
   にほん

8. デパートの入り口で田中さんにあいました。 （I met Tanaka-san at the entrance of the department store.）
   たなか

9. どうぞお入りください。 （Please come in.）

10. 銀座七丁目にいいレストランがあります。 （There is a nice restaurant on the 7th block of Ginza St.）
    ぎんざ

ANALYZING AND READING EXERCISE FOR EXAMPLE KANJI

Analyze the following Kanji. Write the *furigana* below the underlined Kanji. (Some familiar Kanji are included in this exercise.)

Example:　分　＝　［八］　＋　［刀］

今　八時　十分です。　　　　　　　　　　　　(Now it is 8:10.)
いま　はちじ　じっぷん

1.　乾＝　［　　］　＋　［　　］　＋　［　　］

せんたく物が乾きました。　　　　　　　　　(The laundry has dried.)

2.　元＝　［　　］　＋　［　　］

お元気ですか。　　　　　　　　　　　　　　(How are you? (Are you in good spirits?))

3.　究＝　［　　］　＋　［　　］

なんの研究をしていますか。　　　　　　　　(What kind of research are you doing?)

4.　早＝　［　　］　＋　［　　］

私は毎朝早く起きます。　　　　　　　　　　(I get up early every morning.)

5.　肉＝　［　　］　＋　［　　］　＋　［　　］

日本では牛•肉はとても高いです。　　　　　(In Japan, beef is very expensive.)
　　　　　　ぎゅう

6.　込*＝　［　　］　＋　［　　］

あの高速道路はいつも込んでいます。　　　　(That expressway is always crowded.)
　　こうそくどうろ

7.　切＝　［　　］　＋　［　　］

この小刀はよく切れます。　　　　　　　　　(This pocketknife cuts well.)

これは大切な手紙 (letter)です。　　　　　　(This is an important letter.)
　　　　てがみ

•牛(ギュウ/うし)　　appeared as the *ushi·hen* on pg. 23; will appear on pg. 115.

8. 加＝ [　　] ＋ [　　]
　　二に七を加えると九になります。　　　　　　(If you add 7 to 2 it will become 9.)

9. 町＝ [　　] ＋ [　　]
　　妹はとなりの町にすんでいます。　　　　　　(My younger sister lives in the next town.)

10. 収＝ [　　] ＋ [　　]
　　あなたの年収はどのぐらいですか。　　　　　(About how much is your yearly income?)

Three Stroke Kanji (Numbers 1 through 14)

Kanji and Examples		Stroke Order and Practice
1. **三** ³ (three, pg. 2)		三 practice strokes

三日月 (みかづき crescent moon)　　三つ折り (みつおり fold in thirds)　　三日 (みっか third day, three days)

み / み・つ / みっ・つ

サン　三月 (サンガツ March)　　三人 (サンニン three people)　三十 (サンジュウ thirty)

| **2.** **千** ³ (a thousand) | 舌 した (tongue)
 乱 ラン (disorder, pg. 50) | 千 practice strokes |

ち　千葉 (ちば Chiba (a prefecture & city in Japan))

セン　千円 (センエン ¥1,000)　　二千人 (ニセンニン 2,000 people)　　三千ドル (サンゼンドル $3,000)

| **3.** **干** ³ (dry) | 刊 カン (publish)
 岸 きし / ガン (shore, bank)
 幹 みき / カン (trunk, pg. 76) | 干 practice strokes |

ほ・す / ひ・る　干しぶどう (ほしぶどう raisins)　　干物 (ひもの dried fish)

カン　干ばつ (カンばつ drought)

| **4.** **万** ³ (ten thousand) | | 万 practice strokes |

マン / バン　万一 (マンイチ by any chance)　　十万 (ジュウマン 100,000)　　万国 (バンコク all countries)

•葉 (は) will appear on pg. 151.

Kanji and Examples		Stroke Order and Practice
5. 大 3 (large, pg. xiv)	太 ふと・い／タイ (thick) 因 イン (cause) 美 うつく・しい／ビ (beautiful, pg. 69)	一 ナ 大 大 大
おお・きい	大きい (おおきい large, pg.xiv)　大空 (おおぞら wide-open sky)　大雨 (おおあめ heavy rain)	
ダイ／タイ	大学 (ダイガク university)　　大気 (タイキ air, atmosphere)	
6. 小 2 (small, pg. xiv)	少 すく・ない (few) 糸 いと (thread, pg. 19) 京 キョウ (capital, pg. 30)	亅 小 小 小 小
ちい・さい／ こ／お	小さい (ちいさい small, pg. xiv)　小麦 (こむぎ wheat)　　小川 (おがわ stream)	
ショウ	小学校 (ショウガッコウ elementary school)　　小説 (ショウセツ novel)	
7. 上 3 (top)	峠* とうげ (mountain pass)	丨 上 上 上 上
うえ/かみ/あ・げる/ あ・がる/のぼ・る/(うわ)	机の上 (つくえのうえ on the desk)　　上り坂 (のぼりざか uphill)　　上着 (うわぎ coat)	
ジョウ／(ショウ)	上品 (ジョウヒン elegance)　　上下 (ジョウゲ top & bottom, up & down)　　上人 (ショウニン holy priest)	
8. 下 3 (underneath, pg.2)	峠* とうげ (mountain pass)	一 下 下 下 下
した/しも/さ・げる/ く・だる/くだ・さる/お・ろす	下町 (したまち downtown)　　風下 (かざしも leeward)　　下り坂 (くだりざか downhill)	
カ／ゲ	地下鉄 (チカテツ subway)　　下水 (ゲスイ sewage)　　下車 (ゲシャ get off (a vehicle))	

• 品（ヒン）　will appear on pg. 105.

Kanji and Examples			Stroke Order and Practice
9. 3 山 (mountain, pg. xii)	岩	いわ (rock)	⌐ 山 山 山 山
	炭	すみ (charcoal)	
	島	しま (island, pg. 73)	
やま	山登り（やまのぼり mountain climbing）		山道（やまみち mountain path）
サン	山林（サンリン mountains & forest）		富士山（フジサン Mt. Fuji）　火山（カザン volcano）

10. 3 川 (river, pg. xii)	訓	クン (Kun reading of Kanji)	) 川 川 川 川
	順	ジュン (order, sequence)	
かわ	川魚（かわざかな fresh water fish）		川下（かわしも downstream）　小川（おがわ stream, pg. 98）
セン	河川（カセン river）		山川（サンセン mountain & river）

11. 3 土 (earth, pg. 90)	赤	あか・い (red)	一 十 土 土 土
	型	かた (pattern)	
	社	やしろ／シャ (shrine, company, pg. 22)	
つち	土色（つちいろ earth color）		赤土（あかつち red clay）
ド／ト	土曜日（ドヨウび Saturday）		土地（トチ land）

12. 3 士 (warrior, specialist, suffix for academic degree)	仕	シ (serve, work for)	一 十 士 士 士
	売	う・る (sell)	
	声	こえ (voice)	
シ	士道（シドウ code of conduct, way of the warrior）		会計士（カイケイシ accountant）　博士（ハクシ／ハカセ Ph.D.）

99

Kanji and Examples			Stroke Order and Practice
13. 3 **女** (woman, pg. 16)	安	やす・い (cheap, pg. 29)	
	妻	つま (wife)	
	姿	すがた (shape, figure)	

おんな / め	女の子 (おんなのこ girl)	女らしい (おんならしい ladylike)	女神 (めがみ goddess)
ジョ / ニョ / (ニョウ)	女子大 (ジョシダイ women's college)	天女 (テンニョ heavenly maiden in folklore)	女房* (ニョウボウ one's wife)

Kanji and Examples			Stroke Order and Practice
14. 3 **子** (child, pg. 3)	字	ジ (character, letter)	
	学	ガク (study, pg.57)	
	好	す・き (like, pg. 16)	

こ	子ども (こども child)	男の子 (おとこのこ boy)	
シ / ス	子女 (シジョ children)	原子 (ゲンシ atom)	扇*子 (センス folding fan)

• 房 (ボウ) will appear on pg. 124.

EXERCISES FOR THREE STROKE KANJI (NUMBERS 1 THROUGH 14)

WRITING EXERCISE
Fill in each box to make a word.

1.  ☐日月 (crescent moon)
み か づき

2.  ☐☐☐ (thirty people)
サン ジュウ ニン

3. 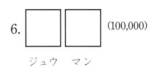 ☐円 (¥1,000)
セン エン

4.  ☐しぶどう (raisins)
ほ

5.  ☐ばつ (drought)
カン

6. 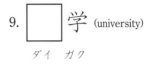 ☐☐ (100,000)
ジュウ マン

7.  ☐国 (all countries)
バン コク

8. 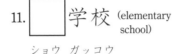 ☐空 (wide-open sky)
おお ぞら

9.  ☐学 (university)
ダイ ガク

10.  ☐麦 (wheat)
こ むぎ

11. 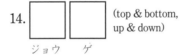 ☐学校 (elementary school)
ショウ ガッコウ

12.  ☐着 (coat)
うわ ぎ

13. 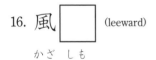 ☐り坂 (uphill)
のぼ ざか

14. 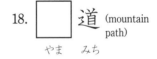 ☐☐ (top & bottom, up & down)
ジョウ ゲ

15.  ☐町 (downtown)
した まち

16. 風 (leeward)
かざ しも

17.  ☐水 (sewage)
ゲ スイ

18.  ☐道 (mountain path)
やま みち

19.  ☐林 (mountains & forest)
サン リン

20. 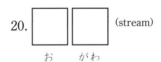 ☐☐ (stream)
お がわ

21. 河☐ (river)
カ セン

22. 赤☐ (red clay)
あか つち

23. ☐地 (land)
ト チ

24. 会計☐ (accountant)
カイケイ シ

25. ☐の☐ (girl)
おんな こ

26. 原☐ (atom)
ゲン シ

27. ☐神 (goddess)
め がみ

READING EXERCISE

Read the following sentences, and write the correct *furigana* (pronunciation of Kanji written in Hiragana regardless of whether the reading of the Kanji is On or Kun) below the underlined Kanji.

1. <u>三月</u><u>三日</u>はひなまつりです。 (March 3rd is the day of the Doll's Festival.)

2. このへやに<u>窓</u>が<u>三</u>つあります。 (There are three windows in this room.)

3. <u>田中</u>さんは<u>千葉</u>にすんでいます。 (Tanaka-san lives in Chiba.)

4. このコンピューターは<u>三千</u>ドルしました。 (This computer cost $3,000.)

5. <u>万一</u> <u>雨</u>がふったら<u>家</u>にいます。 (On the off chance that it rains, I'll stay at home; [otherwise, I'll go.])

6. あなたの<u>家</u>は<u>大</u>きいですね。 (Your house is large, isn't it?)

7. わたしは<u>小</u>さい<u>車</u>を<u>買</u>いました。 (I purchased a small car.)

8. この<u>小説</u>はとてもおもしろいです。 (This novel is very interesting.)

9. <u>机</u>の<u>上</u>になにがありますか。 (What is on the desk?)

10. この<u>洋服</u>の<u>色</u>はとても<u>上品</u>です。 (The color of this dress is very elegant.)

11. 東京の<u>地下鉄</u>はいつも<u>込</u>んでいます。 (Tōkyō's subways are always crowded.)
    とうきょう

12. わたしはよく<u>山登</u>りをします。　　　　　　　(I often go mountain climbing.)

13. <u>富士山</u>は<u>火山</u>です。　　　　　　　　　　(Mt. Fuji is a volcano.)

14. <u>土曜日</u>にはたいていゴルフをします。　　　(On Saturdays I usually play golf.)

15. よし<u>子</u>さんは<u>女子大</u>に<u>入学</u>しました。　(Yoshiko entered a women's college.)

ANALYZING AND READING EXERCISE FOR EXAMPLE KANJI

Analyze the following Kanji. Write the *furigana* below the underlined Kanji. (Some familiar Kanji are included in this exercise.)

1. 舌 = [　　] + [　　]
   <u>子</u>どもが<u>友</u>だちに<u>舌</u>を<u>出</u>しました。　(The child stuck out its tongue at his friend.)

2. 因 = [　　] + [　　] + [　　]
   円高の<u>原因</u>はなんですか。　　　　　　　(What are the causes of the strong yen?)
   えんだか

3. 少 = [　　] + [　　]
   今年は<u>雨</u>が<u>少</u>ないです。　　　　　　　(This year [we've had] little rain.)
   ことし

4. 峠* = [　　] + [　　] + [　　]
   あの<u>峠</u>を<u>越</u>えると<u>村</u>があります。　　(Beyond that mountain pass there is a village.)
   こ

5. 岩 = [　　] + [　　]
   あの<u>山</u>は<u>岩</u>ばかりです。　　　　　　　(That mountain is nothing but rocks.)

6. 島 ＝ [　] ＋ [　]
　　 日本は島国です。 　　　　　　　　　　　　　　　(Japan is an island country.)

7. 訓 ＝ [　] ＋ [　]
　　 漢字には音と訓の読みかたがあります。 　　　(Kanji has both On and Kun readings.)

8. 順 ＝ [　] ＋ [　]
　　 漢字を書く時には筆順を知ることが大切です。 (When we write Kanji, it is important to know the stroke order.)

9. 型 ＝ [　] ＋ [　] ＋ [　]
　　 小型の車を買いたいです。 　　　　　　　　　(I want to buy a small car.)

10. 社 ＝ [　] ＋ [　]
　　 毎日会社で仕事をします。 　　　　　　　　　(Everyday I work at the company.)

11. 売 ＝ [　] ＋ [　] ＋ [　]
　　 あの店ではおいしいパンを売っています。 　(At that store they sell delicious bread.)

12. 声 ＝ [　] ＋ [　]
　　 かの女の声はとてもきれいです。 　　　　　　(Her voice is very beautiful.)
　　　じょ

13. 安 ＝ [　] ＋ [　]
　　 安いブラウスを買いました。 　　　　　　　　(I bought an inexpensive blouse.)

14. 好 ＝ [　] ＋ [　]
　　 わたしはコーヒーが大好きです。 　　　　　　(I like coffee very much.)

Three Stroke Kanji (Numbers 15 through 27)

Kanji and Examples			Stroke Order and Practice					

15. 　　　　**3**
口
(mouth, pg. 16)

品	しな／ヒン (goods, refinement)
知	し・る／チ (know, pg. 18)
名	な／メイ (name)

Stroke order: 刂　冂　口　口　口

くち	口答え (くちごたえ back talk)　出口 (でぐち exit)　入り口 (いりぐち entrance, pg. 92)
コウ／(ク)	口論 (コウロン dispute)　人口 (ジンコウ population)　口調• (クチョウ tone of voice)

16. 　　　　**3**
夕
(evening, pg.3)

多	おお・い (many)
外	そと／ガイ (outside, pg. 51)
夜	よる (night, pg. 30)

Stroke order: ノ　ク　夕　夕　夕

ゆう	夕方 (ゆうがた evening)　夕日 (ゆうひ setting sun)　夕飯 (ゆうハン supper)
セキ	一朝一夕 (イッチョウイッセキ in a single day)

17. 　　　　**3**
弓
(bow, pg. 3)

弟	おとうと (younger brother, pg.51)
費	ヒ (expense)

Stroke order: 弓　弓　弓　弓　弓

ゆみ	弓矢 (ゆみや bow & arrow)
キュウ	弓道 (キュウドウ Japanese archery)

18. 　　　　**3**
工
(craft, artisan, manufacturing, pg.5)

左	ひだり (left, pg. 7)
差	サ (difference, pg. 69)
紅	べに／コウ (rouge, crimson)

Stroke order: 一　工　工　工　工

コウ／ク	工場 (コウジョウ factory)　人工 (ジンコウ artificial)　大工 (ダイク carpenter)

•調 (チョウ) will appear on pg. 219.

Kanji and Examples			Stroke Order and Practice
19. 才 **3**	財	ザイ (wealth, pg. 19)	一　寸　才　才　才
	材	ザイ (material)	
(talent; also now used for age)			
サイ	天才 (テンサイ genius)		二才 (ニサイ two years old)
20. 丸 **3**	勢	セイ (force)	ノ　九　丸　丸　丸
	熱	ネツ (heat, fever pg. 34)	
(round, globe, circle, pg. 91)	熟	う・れる／ジュク (ripen)	
まる・い／まる	丸顔 (まるがお round face)		日の丸 (ひのまる Japanese flag)
ガン	一丸 (イチガン united, roll into one)		弾*●丸 (ダンガン bullet)
21. 久 **3**	畝*	うね (ridge)	ノ　ク　久　久　久
(long time)			
ひさ・しい	久しぶり (ひさしぶり after a long time)		
キュウ／（ク）	永●久 (エイキュウ forever)		久遠 (クオン eternity)
22. 己 **3**	記	しる・す／キ (record)	�
⇁　コ　己　己　己
	改	あらた・める／カイ (reform, pg. 27))	
(self, pg. 51)	起	お・きる／キ (get up, pg. 38)	
コ／キ	自●己 (ジコ self)		知己 (チキ acquaintance)

● 弾（ダン）will appear on pg. 228.
● 永（エイ）will appear on pg. 158.
● 自（ジ）　will appear on pg. 182.

Kanji and Examples			Stroke Order and Practice
23. 3 寸 (Japanese unit of measure, about 1 in. or 2.5 cm.)	守	まも・る (protect)	一　寸　寸　寸　寸
	寺	てら (temple)	
	導	みち・びく／ドウ (guide)	
スン	一寸 (イッスン about an inch) 　　寸法 (スンポウ measure, size)		

24. 3 亡 (lost, gone)	忘	わす・れる／ボウ (forget)	亡　亡　亡　亡　亡
	忙*	いそが・しい／ボウ (busy)	
	盲*	モウ (blind)	
な・い	亡くなる (なくなる pass away, die)		
ボウ／(モウ)	亡命 (ボウメイ to defect) 　　死亡 (シボウ death) 　　亡者 (モウジャ the dead, restless spirit)		

25. 3 勺 (about 0.6 fl. oz. or 18 ml.)	約	ヤク (approximately)	勹　勺　勺　勺　勺
	酌*	シャク (serving a person sake)	
シャク	一勺* (イッシャク about 0.6 fluid ounces)		

26. 3 与 (give, take part in)	写	うつ・す／シャ (photograph, duplicate)	与　与　与　与　与
あた・える	与える (あた・える give, bestow)		
ヨ	与党 (ヨトウ party in power) 　　給与 (キュウヨ wages, allowance)		

• 法 (ホウ／ポウ) will appear on pg. 151.

Kanji and Examples			Stroke Order and Practice								
27. *3 及 (reach, amount to, match, and, exert)	扱	あつか・う (treat, deal with)	㇗	乃	及	及	及				
	吸	す・う／キュウ (breathe in, inhale)									
	級	キュウ (class, a grade)									
およ・ぶ／およ・び／およ・ぼす	及ぶ（およぶ reach, amount to, match）			及び（および and, as well as）				及ぼす（およぼす exert）			
キュウ	及第（キュウダイ passing examination）										

EXERCISES FOR THREE STROKE KANJI (NUMBERS 15 THROUGH 27)

WRITING EXERCISE

Fill in each box to make a word.

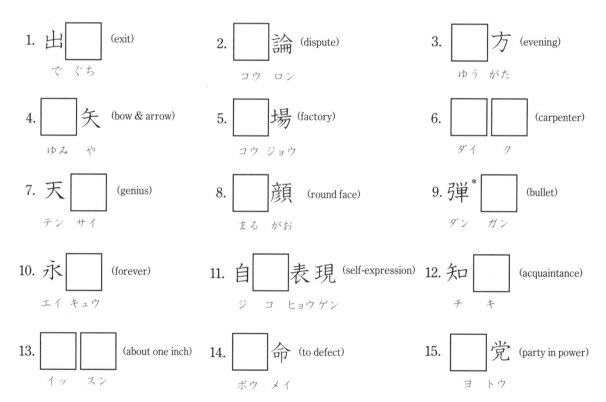

1. 出☐ (exit)
   で ぐち

2. ☐論 (dispute)
   コウ ロン

3. ☐方 (evening)
   ゆう がた

4. ☐矢 (bow & arrow)
   ゆみ や

5. ☐場 (factory)
   コウ ジョウ

6. ☐☐ (carpenter)
   ダイ ク

7. 天☐ (genius)
   テン サイ

8. ☐顔 (round face)
   まる がお

9. 弾* ☐ (bullet)
   ダン ガン

10. 永☐ (forever)
    エイ キュウ

11. 自☐表現 (self-expression)
    ジ コ ヒョウゲン

12. 知☐ (acquaintance)
    チ キ

13. ☐☐ (about one inch)
    イッ スン

14. ☐命 (to defect)
    ボウ メイ

15. ☐党 (party in power)
    ヨ トウ

READING EXERCISE

Read the following sentences and write the correct *furigana* (pronunciation of Kanji written in Hiragana regardless of whether the reading of the Kanji is On or Kun) below the underlined Kanji.

1. あの<u>子</u>はよく<u>口答</u>えをします。 (That child often talks back.)

2. ロス・アンジェルスの<u>人口</u>はどのぐらいですか。 (What is the population of Los Angeles?)

3. <u>今晩</u>いっしょに<u>夕飯</u>を<u>食</u>べませんか。 (Would you like to (Won't you) eat supper together tonight?)

4. これは<u>一朝一夕</u>に<u>解決</u>できる<u>問題</u>ではありません。 (This is not a problem that can be solved in a single day.)

5. <u>今</u>、いろいろな<u>国</u>が<u>人工衛星</u>(satellite)を<u>打ち上</u>げています。 (Now, various countries are launching artificial satellites.)
   えいせい

6. わたしは<u>今</u><u>三十二</u><u>才</u>です。 (I am now 32 years old.)

7. <u>日</u>の<u>丸</u>は<u>日本</u>の<u>旗</u>です。 (The Hinomaru is the [national] flag of Japan.)

8. <u>久</u>しぶりですね。お<u>元気</u>ですか。 (It has been a long time. How have you been?)

9. <u>洋服</u>の<u>寸法</u>をとりましょう。 (Let's get the measurements for your [new] clothes.)

10. <u>父</u>は<u>二年</u><u>前</u>に<u>亡</u>くなりました。 (My father died two years ago.)

11. <u>子</u>どもにはあまりお<u>金</u>を<u>与</u>えないほうがいいです。 (It's better not to give children too much money.)

12. 走ることでは<u>彼</u>に<u>及</u>ぶものはありません。
    はし

(No one can match him at runnning.)

ANALYZING AND READING EXERCISE FOR EXAMPLE KANJI

Analyze the following Kanji. Write the *furigana* below the underlined Kanji. (Some familiar Kanji are included in this exercise.)

1. 名 = [　] + [　]
   わたしの<u>名前</u>はジョイスです。

(My name is Joyce.)

2. 多 = [　] + [　]
   <u>東京</u>の<u>人口</u>は<u>多</u>いです。

(Tokyo's population is very large.)

3. 外 = [　] + [　]
   <u>夕方</u>、<u>外</u>はすずしいです。

(It's cool outside in the evening.)

4. 左 = [　] + [˙]
   <u>日本</u>では<u>車</u>は<u>道</u>の<u>左</u>がわを<u>走</u>ります。
   　　　　くるま

(In Japan cars drive on the left hand side of the road.)

5. 紅 = [　] + [　]
   どんな<u>色</u>の<u>口紅</u>が<u>好</u>きですか。

(What color of lipstick do you like?)

6. 財 = [　] + [　]
   かれは<u>子</u>どもにたくさんの<u>財産</u>を<u>残</u>しました。
   　　　　　　　　　　　　　さん

(He left his child a big inheritance.)

7. 材 = [　] + [　]
   いい<u>料理</u>にはいい<u>材料</u>がひつようです。

(Good ingredients are necessary for good cooking.)

8. 熱 = [ ] + [ ] + [ ]
　　きょうはかぜで少し熱があります。　　　　(Today I have a slight fever due to a cold.)

9. 熟 = [ ] + [ ] + [ ] + [ ] + [ ]
　　たまごは半熟が好きです。　　　　　　　　(I like soft (half) boiled eggs.)

10. 刊 = [ ] + [ ]
　　きょうの夕刊はもうきましたか。　　　　　(Has today's evening newspaper come yet?)

11. 岸 = [ ] + [ ] + [ ]
　　きのう海岸をドライヴしました。　　　　　(Yesterday I drove along the coast.)

12. 記 = [ ] + [ ]
　　毎日日記を書いています。　　　　　　　　(I write in my diary every day.)

13. 起 = [ ] + [ ]
　　毎朝なん時に起きますか。　　　　　　　　(What time do you get up every morning?)

14. 寺 = [ ] + [ ]
　　お寺のにわをさんぽしました。　　　　　　(I took a stroll in the temple garden.)

15. 忘 = [ ] + [ ]
　　かれはよく宿題を忘れてきます。　　　　　(He often forgets to bring his homework.)
　　　　　しゅくだい

16. 忙* = [ ] + [ ]
　　近ごろとても忙しいです。　　　　　　　　(I have been very busy recently.)

17. 約 ＝ ［　］＋［　］
　　　　うちから<u>会社</u>まで<u>約</u><u>二十分</u>かかります。　(From my home to the company it takes about 20 minutes.)

18. 写 ＝ ［　］＋［　］
　　　　これは<u>先週</u>　<u>写</u>した<u>写真</u>(photograph)です。　(This is a photo that was taken last week.)
　　　　　せんしゅう　　　　しん

19. 級 ＝ ［　］＋［　］
　　　　<u>山田</u>さんとわたしは<u>同級生</u>です。　(Yamada-san and I are classmates.)
　　　　やまだ

20. 吸 ＝ ［　］＋［　］
　　　　<u>近</u>ごろたばこを<u>吸</u>う<u>人</u>が<u>少</u>なくなったようです。(Recently there seem to be fewer people who smoke.)

Four Stroke Kanji (Numbers 1 through 15)

Kanji and Examples			Stroke Order and Practice
1. 五 ⁴ (five)	語 ゴ (word) 悟* さと・る／ゴ (become aware)		二・ 丆 丒 →五・ 五 五
いつ・つ	五つ (いつつ five)	五日 (いつか fifth day, five days)	
ゴ	五月 (ゴガツ May)	五分 (ゴフン five minutes)　五輪 (ゴリン five rings, Olympic)	
2. 六 ⁴ (six)			⼽ 亠・ 六 六・ 六 六
む／むっ・つ／ （むい）	六つ (むっつ six)	六日 (むいか sixth day, six days)	
ロク	六人 (ロクニン six people)	六才 (ロクサイ six years old)　六月 (ロクガツ June)	
3. 日 ⁴ (sun, day, pg. xiv)	春 はる (spring, pg. 64) 星 ほし (star) 早 はや・い (early, pg. 91)		⼅ 冂・ →月 →日・ 日 日
ひ／か	日の出 (ひので sunrise)	夕日 (ゆうひ setting sun, pg. 105)　九日 (ここのか ninth day, nine days, pg. 91)	
ニチ／ジツ／（ニ）	日曜日 (ニチヨウび Sunday)	先日 (センジツ the other day)　日本 (ニホン Japan)	
4. 月 ⁴ (moon, month, pg. xiv)	青 あお・い (blue, green, pg. 60) 朝 あさ (morning, pg.76) 明 あか・るい (bright, pg. xv)		⼃ 冂・ →月 →月・ 月 月
つき	月日 (つきひ time, days)	毎月 (マイつき every month)	
ゲツ／ガツ	月曜日 (ゲツヨウび Monday)	十二月 (ジュウニガツ December)	

Kanji and Examples		Stroke Order and Practice
5. 火 4 (fire, pg. xiv)	炭 すみ (charcoal, pg.99) 秋 あき (autumn, pg. 23) 談 ダン (conversation)	＾ ＼＾ ＼少 火 火 火
ひ／（ほ）	火花 (ひばな spark)	花火 (はなび fireworks)　　火かげ (ほかげ flicker of light)
カ	火曜日 (カヨウび Tuesday)	火山 (カザン volcano)　　火事 (カジ fire)
5. 水 4 (water, pg. 3)	泉 いずみ／セン (fountain, spring) 線 セン (line)	〕 刁 水 水 水 水
みず	水着 (みずぎ swim suit)	水色 (みずいろ light blue)
スイ	水曜日 (スイヨウび Wednesday) 水泳 (スイエイ swimming)	
7. 木 4 (tree)	本 ホン (book, pg. xii) 森 もり (forest, pg. xv) 栄 さか・える (prosper)	一 十 オ 木 木 木
き／（こ）	丸木 (まるき log)	木かげ (こかげ tree shade)
ボク／モク	大木 (タイボク big tree)	木曜日 (モクヨウび Thursday)
8. 天 4 (heaven, pg. 2)	蚕 かいこ (silkworm)	一 二 チ 天 天 天
（あめ／あま）	天地 (あめつち heaven & earth, universe)	天の川 (あまのがわ the Milky Way)
テン	天気 (テンキ weather)	天才 (テンサイ genius, pg. 106)　　天文学 (テンモンガク astronomy)

Kanji and Examples			Stroke Order and Practice

9. 夫 **4**

(husband)

規 キ (standard, measure)

賛 サン (praise, agreement)

二・ ニ・ 夫・ 夫 夫 夫

おっと	夫 (おっと husband)
フ／(フウ)	夫人 (フジン wife, Mrs.) 夫婦 (フウフ husband & wife) 工夫 (クフウ device, contrivance)

10. 午 **4**

(noon)

許 ゆる・す (forgive)

ノ・ ┌・ 上・ 午

ゴ	午前 (ゴゼン a.m.) 午後 (ゴゴ p.m.) 正午 (ショウゴ noon)

11. 牛 **4**

(cow)

件 ケン (case, matter)

解 と・く／カイ (solve, untie)

ノ・ ┌・ 上・ 牛 牛 牛

うし	牛小屋 (うしごや cowshed) 子牛 (こうし calf)
ギュウ	牛肉 (ギュウニク beef) 牛乳 (ギュウニュウ milk)

12. 中 **4**

(middle, inside, pg. xiv)

仲 なか (relation)

忠 チュウ (royalty)

丨・ 冂・ 口・ 中 中 中

なか	中指 (なかゆび middle finger) まん中 (まんなか center)
チュウ	中心 (チュウシン center) 中学 (チュウガク middle school) 中立 (チュウリツ neutrality)

• 正 (ショウ) will appear on pg. 141.
• 立 (リツ) will appear on pg. 141.

Kanji and Examples			Stroke Order and Practice								
13. 内 **4** (inside, pg. 40)	肉	ニク (meat, pg. xii)	!	门	内	内	内	内			
	納	おさ・める／ ノウ／トウ (to store, pay, supply)									
うち		内気 (うちキ shyness)	内金 (うちキン deposit, down payment)								
ナイ／ダイ		内容 (ナイヨウ contents)	家内 (カナイ one's wife, family)		境内 (ケイダイ precincts, grounds)						
14. 手 **4** (hand, pg. xii)	挙	あ・げる／キョ (raise, hold)	⌒	二	三	手	手	手			
	撃*	ゲキ (shoot, attack)									
て／(た)		手紙 (てがみ letter)	右手 (みぎて right hand)		手づな (たづな reins)						
シュ		手術 (シュジュツ surgical operation)	入手 (ニュウシュ obtain)		歌手 (カシュ singer)						
15. 毛 **4** (hair, pg. 3)	尾*	お (tail)	⌒	二	三	毛	毛	毛			
	耗*	モウ (lessen, diminish)									
け		毛糸 (けいと woolen yarn)	毛皮 (けがわ fur)								
モウ		毛布 (モウフ blanket)	羊毛 (ヨウモウ wool)								

● 容 (ヨウ) will appear on pg. 197.
● 皮 (かわ) will appear on pg. 150.

EXERCISES FOR FOUR STROKE KANJI (NUMBERS 1 THROUGH 15)

WRITING EXERCISE

Fill in each box to make a word.

1.  輪 (five rings, Olympic)
ゴ　リン

2. (6 people)
ロク　ニン

3.  の 出 (sunrise)
ひ　　で

4.  曜 (Monday)
ゲツ　ヨウ　び

5. 毎 (every month)
マイ　つき

6. 花 (fireworks)
はな　び

7.  曜 (Tuesday)
カ　ヨウ　び

8.  着 (swimsuit)
みず　ぎ

9.  曜 (Wednesday)
スイ　ヨウ　び

10. 丸 (log)
まる　き

11.  曜 (Thursday)
モク　ヨウ　び

12.  文学 (astronomy)
テン　モンガク

13.  の 川 (Milky Way)
あま　　がわ

14.  婦 (husband & wife)
フウ　フ

15.  前 (a.m.)
ゴ　ゼン

16.  乳 (milk)
ギュウ ニュウ

17. 子 (calf)
こ　うし

18.  学校 (middle school)
チュウ ガッコウ

19.  指 (middle finger)
なか　ゆび

20. 気 (shyness)
うち　キ

21.  容 (contents)
ナイ　ヨウ

22.  紙 (letter)
て　がみ

23. 歌 (singer)
カ　シュ

24. 糸 (woolen yarn)
け　いと

READING EXERCISE

Read the following sentences, and write the correct *furigana* (pronunciation of Kanji written in Hiragana regardless of whether the reading of the Kanji is On or Kun) below the underlined Kanji.

1. このへやにつくえが<u>五</u>つといすが<u>六</u>つあります。 (There are five tables and six chairs in this room.)

2. <u>五月</u> <u>五日</u>は<u>休日</u>です。 (May 5th is a holiday.)

3. <u>六月</u> <u>六日</u>に<u>日本</u>へ<u>行</u>きます。 (I will go to Japan on June 6th.)

4. <u>今度</u>の<u>日曜日</u>にテニスをします。 (This Sunday I am going to play tennis.)

5. <u>先日</u>はおじゃましました。 (I had a nice time visiting your home (I imposed on you) the other day.)

6. <u>月日</u>のたつのは<u>早</u>いです。 (Time passes quickly.)

7. <u>十二月</u> <u>二十五日</u>はクリスマスです。 (December 25th is Christmas Day.)

8. <u>日本</u>は<u>火山</u>が<u>多</u>い<u>国</u>です。 (Japan is a country of many volcanoes.)

9. その<u>水色</u>の<u>服</u>はあなたによくにあいます。 (That light blue dress suits you well.)

10. かれは<u>水泳</u>のせん<u>手</u>です。 (He is an expert swimmer.)

11. きょうはいいお<u>天気</u>ですね。 (Today is a nice day (weather), isn't it?)

12. わたしの<u>夫</u>はビールが<u>大好</u>きです。　　　　(My husband likes beer very much.)

13. スモッグが<u>少</u>なくなるように<u>工夫</u>しなければなりません。(We must devise a way to reduce smog.)

14. <u>午後</u> <u>買物</u>に<u>行</u>きます。　　　　(I'll go shopping in the afternoon.)

15. きょうは<u>牛肉</u>ですきやきを<u>作</u>りましょう。　　　　(Let's make sukiyaki with beef today.)

16. スイスは<u>中立国</u>です。　　　　(Switzerland is a neutral country.)

17. <u>内金</u>はいくらおきましょうか。　　　　(How much of a down payment should I make (leave)?)

18. たいてい<u>右手</u>でおはしを<u>持</u>ちます。　　　　(We usually hold chopsticks with our right hand.)

19. かれは<u>先月</u> <u>目</u>の<u>手術</u>をしました。　　　　(He had eye surgery last month.)

20. <u>毛布</u>はなんまいいりますか。　　　　(How many blankets do you need?)

ANALYZING AND READING EXERCISE FOR EXAMPLE KANJI

Analyze the following Kanji. Write the *furigana* below the underlined Kanji. (Some familiar Kanji are included in this exercise.)

1. 語 ＝ ［　　］ ＋ ［　　］ ＋ ［　　］
   あなたはフランス<u>語</u>を<u>話</u>しますか。　　　　(Do you speak French?)

2. 星 ＝ ［　　］ ＋ ［　　］
   <u>今晩</u>は<u>星</u>がきれいです。　　　　(The stars are beautiful tonight.)

3. 明 ＝ [　] ＋ [　]
このへやはとても<u>明</u>るいですね。

(This room is very bright, isn't it?)

4. 秋 ＝ [　] ＋ [　]
<u>秋</u>は<u>山</u>のもみじが<u>美</u>しいです。

(In autumn, the maple trees of the mountains are beautiful.)

5. 線 ＝ [　] ＋ [　] ＋ [　]
<u>線路</u>にそって<u>歩</u>きました。
　　　　　　　　ある

(I walked along the railroad tracks.)

6. 栄 ＝ [　] ＋ [　] ＋ [　]
<u>日本</u>の<u>経済</u>(economy)はずいぶん<u>栄</u>えてきました。
　　　　　ざい

(Japan's economy has become prosperous.)

7. 賛 ＝ [　] ＋ [　] ＋ [　]
あなたの<u>考</u>えに<u>賛成</u>します。

(I agree with your idea.)

8. 許 ＝ [　] ＋ [　]
ごぶさたお<u>許</u>しください。

(Please forgive me for not contacting you sooner.)

9. 件 ＝ [　] ＋ [　]

10. 解 ＝ [　] ＋ [　] ＋ [　]
その<u>事件</u>はすぐ<u>解決</u>しました。

(That matter was solved immediately.)

11. 仲 ＝ [　] ＋ [　]
<u>山田</u>さんと<u>田中</u>さんはとても<u>仲</u>がいいです。

(Yamada-san and Tanaka-san are very close.)

12.　納＝　[　　]　＋　[　　]
　　　<u>日本</u>では<u>税金</u>は<u>三月</u>　<u>十五日</u>までに<u>納</u>めます。　(In Japan we pay our taxes by March 15th.)

13.　挙＝　[　　]　＋　[　　]　＋　[　　]　＋　[　　]
　　　どこで<u>結婚式</u>(wedding)を<u>挙</u>げますか。　(Where will you hold your wedding?)
　　　けっこんしき

14.　尾＝　[　　]　＋　[　　]
　　　<u>尾長鳥</u>を<u>知</u>っていますか。　(Do you know of [a bird called] the long-tailed cock?)

Four Stroke Kanji (Numbers 16 through 30)

Kanji and Examples			Stroke Order and Practice
16. 　　　　**4** 方 (direction, side, square, person, method)	訪	たず・ねる／ホウ (visit)	カ　亠　方　方　*方*　*方*
	防	ふせ・ぐ／ボウ (defend)	
	放	はな・す／ホウ (release, pg. 17)	
かた		作り方 (つくりかた way of making)　　　あの方 (あのかた that person)　　　夕方 (ゆうがた evening, pg. 105)	
ホウ		方法 (ホウホウ method)　　　正方形 (セイホウケイ square)　　　八方 (ハッポウ all sides, all directions)	
17. 　　　　**4** 文 (letter, sentence)	紋*	モン (crest)	カ　亠　方　文　*文*　*文*
	蚊*	か (mosquito)	
ふみ		恋*文 (こいぶみ love letter)	
ブン／モン		文化 (ブンカ culture)　　　文学 (ブンガク literature)　　　文句 (モンク complaint)	
18. 　　　　**4** 父 (father, pg. 6)	交	まじ・わる／コウ (cross, exchange)	ノ　バ　分　父　*父*　*父*
	校	コウ (school, pg. 17)	
ちち		父の日 (ちちのひ Father's Day)	
フ		父母 (フボ father & mother)　　　父兄 (フケイ father and/or elder brother, guardians)	
19. 　　　　**4** 今 (now, present, pg. 30)	念	ネン (sense, thought)	ノ　ハ　今　今　*今*　*今*
	琴*	こと／キン (koto (Japanese harp))	
いま		今 (いま now)	
コン／(キン)		今月 (コンゲツ this month)　　　今日 (コンニチ／(きょう) today)　　　今年 (コンネン／(ことし) this year)	

● 正 (セイ) will appear on pg. 141.

Kanji and Examples		Stroke Order and Practice
20. 分 4 (dividing, portion, minute, percentage, pg.91)	粉 こな／こ (powder, flour, pg. 18)　貧 まず・しい (poor, pg. 33)	ノ　八　分　分　分　分
わ・ける/わ・かれる/わ・かる	分ける (わける divide)　　分け前 (わけまえ share)　　分かれ道 (わかれみち fork in the road)	
ブン／フン／ブ	半分 (ハンブン half)　　五分 (ゴフン five minutes, pg. 113)　　大分 (ダイブ／ダイブン considerably)	
21. 公 4 (public, pg. 3)	松 まつ (pine tree)　総 ソウ (whole)	ノ　八　公　公　公　公
おおやけ	公 (おおやけ public, pg.3)	
コウ	公園 (コウエン public park)　　公社 (コウシャ public corporation)　　公共 (コウキョウ public, common)	
22. 友 4 (friend, pg. 7)	抜* ぬ・く／バツ (pull out, extract)	一　ナ　方　友　友　友
とも	友だち (ともだち friend, companion)	
ユウ	友人 (ユウジン friend)　　友情 (ユウジョウ friendship)	
23. 反 4 (opposite, anti-, unit of land area or cloth measurement, pg. xvi)	坂 さか／ハン (slope, pg. 16)　板 いた／ハン (board)　飯 めし／ハン (meal, pg. 24)	一　厂　反　反　反　反
そ・る/そ・り/そ・らす	反る (そる warp, curve, bend)　　反り (そり a curve)	
ハン／（ホン）／（タン）	反対 (ハンタイ opposition, objection)　　反日 (ハンニチ anti-Japanese)　　一反 (イッタン roll of cloth, about 1/4 acre)	

Kanji and Examples		Stroke Order and Practice						
24. 戸 (4) (door)	所 ところ／ショ (place, pg. 27) 房* ふさ／ボウ (tassel, cluster, room)	⇀ 一	㋐ ㋑	㋑ ㋐	戸	戸	戸	
と	戸だな (とだな cupboard, closet)　雨戸 (あまど shutter)　　あみ戸 (あみど screen door)							
コ	戸外 (コガイ outdoor)　　戸主 (コシュ head of household)							

| **25.** 尺 (4) (Japanese unit of length (about 1 ft., 30 cm.)) | 訳 わけ／ヤク (meaning, reason, translation)
釈* シャク (interpret, pg. 72)
駅 えき (station, pg. 20) | ㋑ ㋐ | ㋑ コ | 尸 | 尺 | 尺 | 尺 | |
| シャク | 尺八 (シャクハチ Japanese bamboo flute)　　一尺 (イッシャク about 1 foot or 30 cm.) | | | | | | | |

26. 化 (4) (transform, deceive, disguise, pg. 51)	貨 カ (currency, pg. 33) 花 はな／カ (flower, pg. 30)	ノ	イ	イ	化	化	化	
ば·ける	お化け (おばけ monster)							
カ／ケ	化学 (カガク chemistry)　　文化 (ブンカ culture, pg. 122)　　化しょう (ケショウ make-up)							

27. 比 (4) (compare)	階 カイ (stairs, pg.22) 批 ヒ (criticize) 混 ま·じる／コン (mix)	⇀ 一	上	比	比	比	比	
くら·べる	比べる (くらべる compare)　　比べ物 (くらべもの comparison, to match)							
ヒ	比率 (ヒリツ ratio, percentage)　　比較* (ヒカク comparison)							

● 主 (シュ) will appear on pg. 142.

Kanji and Examples			Stroke Order and Practice							
28. 王 ⁴	玉	たま (gem, ball)	二・	下	王・	王・	王	王		
	聖	セイ (holy)								
	全	ゼン (whole, all)								
(king, pg. xii)										

オウ	王さま (オウさま king)　　　王子 (オウジ prince)　　　王女 (オウジョ princess)

29. 円 ⁴		⁊	冂	円	円	円	円			
(round, circle, yen, pg. 40)										

まる・い	円い (まるい round)
エン	円形 (エンケイ round shape, a circle)　　一円 (イチエン one yen)　　半円 (ハンエン half circle)

30. 止 ⁴	歩	ある・く (walk)	⁊	㇄	屮	止・	止	止			
	歴	レキ (successive, pg. 36)									
(stop)	歯	は (teeth)									

と・まる／と・める	行き止まり (ゆきどまり dead end)　　止める (とめる to stop)
シ	休止 (キュウシ a pause, suspension)　　中止 (チュウシ discontinue, cancel)

EXERCISES FOR FOUR STROKE KANJI (NUMBERS 16 THROUGH 30)

WRITING EXERCISE
Fill in each box to make a word.

1. 正 □ 形 (square)
   セイ ホウ ケイ

2. あの □ (that person)
   かた

3. 日本 □ 学 (Japanese literature)
   ニ ホン ブン ガク

4. □ 句 (complaint)
   モン ク

5. □ の 日 (Father's Day)
   ちち ひ

6. □ 月 (this month)
   コン ゲツ

7. 半 □ (half)
   ハン ブン

8. □ 時 □ □ (9:05)
   ク ジ ゴ フン

9. □ け 前 (share)
   わ まえ

10. □ 共 (public)
    コウ キョウ

11. □ だ ち (friend)
    とも

12. □ 情 (friendship)
    ユウ ジョウ

13. □ 日 (anti-Japanese)
    ハン ニチ

14. あ み □ (screen door)
    ど

15. □ 外 (outdoor)
    コ ガイ

16. □ 八 (Japanese bamboo flute)
    シャク ハチ

17. □ 学 (chemistry)
    カ ガク

18. □ し ょ う (make-up)
    ケ

19. □ 較* (comparison)
    ヒ カク

20. □ 子 (prince)
    オウ ジ

21. □ 形 (round shape)
    エン ケイ

22. □ い テ ー ブ ル (round table)
    まる

23. 休 □ (pause, suspension)
    キュウ シ

24. 行 き □ ま り (dead end)
    ゆ ど

READING EXERCISE

Read the following sentences, and write the correct *furigana* (pronunciation of Kanji written in Hiragana regardless of whether the reading of the Kanji is On or Kun) below the underlined Kanji.

1. てんぷらの<u>作</u>り<u>方</u>を<u>知</u>っていますか。 (Do you know how to make tempura?)

2. <u>日本</u> <u>文化</u>について<u>知</u>りたいです。 (I'd like to know about Japanese culture.)

3. <u>父母</u>は<u>今</u>いなかにすんでいます。 (My father and mother live in the country.)

4. <u>今年</u>は<u>雨</u>が<u>多</u>いです。 (This year we are having a lot of rain.)

5. このパイを<u>八</u>つに<u>分</u>けてください。 (Please divide this pie into eight pieces.)

6. <u>大分</u>あたたかくなりましたね。 (It has become fairly warm, hasn't it?)

7. <u>公園</u>で<u>子</u>どもたちがあそんでいます。 (Children are playing in the park.)

8. これは<u>友人</u>の<u>本</u>です。 (This is my friend's book.)

9. あなたの意見には<u>反対</u>です。
   いけん (I disagree with your opinion.)

10. この<u>家</u>には<u>戸</u>だながたくさんあってべんりです。 (This house is convenient since it has many closets.)

11. <u>子</u>どもはお<u>化</u>けの<u>話</u>が<u>好</u>きです。 (Children like ghost stories.)

12. 京都は東京に比べてしずかな町です。 (Compared to Tōkyō, Kyōto is a quiet city.)

13. 今、円がかなり強いです。 (The yen is pretty strong now.)

14. 雨がふれば、あしたのベース・ボールゲームは中止です。 (If it rains, tomorrow's baseball game will be cancelled.)

ANALYZING AND READING EXERCISE FOR EXAMPLE KANJI

Analyze the following Kanji. Write the *furigana* below the underlined Kanji. (Some familiar Kanji are included in this exercise.)

1. 訪 ＝ [　] ＋ [　]
   きのう友だちを訪ねました。 (Yesterday I visited a friend.)

2. 放 ＝ [　] ＋ [　]
   かごから鳥を放してやりました。 (I freed the bird from the cage.)

3. 紋 ＝ [　] ＋ [　]
   あなたの家の紋はどんな紋ですか。 (What does your family crest look like?)

4. 校 ＝ [　] ＋ [　] ＋ [　]
   学校はおもしろいですか。 (Is school interesting?)

5. 粉 ＝ [　] ＋ [　]
   パンは小麦粉でできています。 (Bread is made from wheat flour.)

6. 貧 ＝ [　] ＋ [　]
   かれは貧しい家でそだちました。 (He grew up in a poor household.)

7. 総＝［　　］＋［　　］＋［　　］
　　<u>今</u>、<u>総理</u><u>大臣</u>はだれですか。
　　　　　　だいじん
　　(Who is the Prime Minister now?)

8. 抜＝［　　］＋［　　］
　　きょう<u>歯</u>を<u>抜</u>いたのでなにも<u>食</u>べることが
　　できません。
　　(Today I had my tooth extracted so I cannot eat anything.)

9. 飯＝［　　］＋［　　］
　　<u>夕飯</u>はなん<u>時</u>ですか。
　　(What time is dinner?)

10. 所＝［　　］＋［　　］
　　わたしのすんでいる<u>所</u>は<u>海</u>の<u>近</u>くです。
　　(The place where I live is near the ocean.)

11. 訳＝［　　］＋［　　］
　　この<u>日本語</u>の<u>文章</u>(sentence)を<u>英語</u>(English)に
　　　　　　　　　しょう　　　　　えい
　　<u>訳</u>してください。
　　(Please translate this Japanese sentence into English.)

12. 駅＝［　　］＋［　　］
　　<u>駅</u>まで<u>十分</u>かかります。
　　(It takes 10 minutes to get to the station.)

13. 貨＝［　　］＋［　　］
　　<u>昔</u>に<u>比</u>べると<u>貨</u>へい<u>価値</u>がずいぶん
　　　　　　　　　　　　　　　か　ち
　　<u>下</u>がりました。
　　(Compared to the past, the value of money has gone down a lot.)

14. 階 ＝ ［　　］ ＋ ［　　］ ＋ ［　　］
    わたしのアパートは二階です。

(My apartment is on the second floor.)

15. 批 ＝ ［　　］ ＋ ［　　］
    かれの批評はいつもしんらつです。

(His criticism is always severe.)

16. 聖 ＝ ［　　］ ＋ ［　　］ ＋ ［　　］
    あなたは聖書を読みますか。

(Do you read the Bible?)

17. 歩 ＝ ［　　］ ＋ ［　　］
    毎日 歩いて学校へ行きます。
    　　　い

(I walk to school every day.)

18. 歴 ＝ ［　　］ ＋ ［　　］ ＋ ［　　］
    日本の歴史を勉強したいです。
    　　　　　　　　べんきょう

(I would like to study Japanese history.)

Four Stroke Kanji (Numbers 31 through 46)

Kanji and Examples			Stroke Order and Practice
31. 元 4 (origin, base, pg. 90)	完 カン (completion) 院 イン (building, institute)		二· ー二· 亍 元 元 元
もと	元手 (もとで capital)		
ゲン / ガン	元気 (ゲンキ good spirits, vigor)　元金 (ガンキン principal)　元日 (ガンジツ New Year's Day)		
32. 予 4 (beforehand, previous, pg. 52)	預 あず·ける (deposit) 野 の / ヤ (field) 序 ジョ (preface, sequence)		マ· マ 予· 予 予 予
ヨ	予約 (ヨヤク reservation)　予定 (ヨテイ plan)　予習• (ヨシュウ lesson preparation)		
33. 区 4 (ward, pg. 3)	欧* オウ (Europe) 駆* か·ける / ク (run, gallop)		二· フ 又· 区· 区 区
ク	区別 (クベツ differentiation)　二十三区 (ニジュウサンク 23 wards [which make up central Tōkyō])		
34. 氏 4 (clan, suffix to a family name as an honorific)	紙 かみ / シ (paper, pg. 19) 底 そこ / テイ (bottom) 低 ひく·い / テイ (low)		ノ ㇄· ㇷ· 氏 氏 氏
うじ	氏神 (うじがみ patron deity)		
シ	氏名 (シメイ full name)		

• 習 (シュウ) will appear on pg. 140.

Kanji and Examples		Stroke Order and Practice
35. 片 4 (one side)	版 ハン (printing, printing plate)	ノ ∤ 片 片 片 片
かた	片かな (かたかな Katakana)　片方 (かたホウ one side)　片道 (かたみち one way)	
ヘン	一片 (イッペン a piece)	
36. 心 4 (heart, mind, pg. 3)	思 おも・う (think, pg. 33) 必 かなら・ず／ヒツ (by all means) 愛 アイ (love, pg. xii)	㇉ 心 心 心 心 心
こころ	心当たり (こころあたり knowledge, idea)　心強い (こころづよい reassuring)　女心 (おんなごころ a woman's feelings)	
シン	心理学 (シンリガク psychology)　安心 (アンシン relief, peace of mind)　決心 (ケッシン determination)	
37. 犬 4 (dog)	状 ジョウ (state or condition, letter, pg. 56) 獣* ジュウ／けもの (beast) 献* ケン (offer, contribute)	一 ナ 大 犬 犬 犬
いぬ	子犬 (こいぬ little dog, puppy)　秋田犬 (あきたいぬ Akita breed (of dog))	
ケン	番犬 (バンケン watchdog)	
38. 不 4 (not, un-, non-)	否 ヒ (no, negation) 杯* さかずき／ハイ (wine cup)	一 ナ 不 不 不 不
フ／ブ	不安 (フアン uneasiness)　不足 (フソク shortage)　不用心 (ブヨウジン unsafe, not secured)	

Kanji and Examples	Stroke Order and Practice

39. 支 **4**

(branch, support, pay)

枝 えだ／シ (branch)
技 ギ (skill)

二 十 步 支 支 支

ささ・える	支え (ささえ support)
シ	支社 (シシャ branch office)　支持 (シジ support)　支出 (シシュツ expenditure)

40. 少 **4**

(a little, a few, pg. 3)

歩 ある・く (walk, pg. 125)
砂 すな (sand, pg. 18)
秒 ビョウ (second, pg. 23)

リ 少 小 少 少 少

すく・ない／すこ・し	少ない (すくない few)　少し (すこし a little)
ショウ	少女 (ショウジョ young girl)　少年 (ショウネン boy)　少数 (ショウスウ small number)

41. 欠 **4**

(lacking, missing, defect, pg. 2)

飲 の・む (drink, pg. 24)
次 つぎ (next, pg. 21)
姿 すがた (figure, pg. 100)

ノ 欠 欠 欠 欠 欠

か・ける／か・く	欠ける (かける be lacking)
ケツ	欠点 (ケッテン a fault, shortcoming)　出欠 (シュッケツ attendance (or absence))

42. 斗 ***4**

(unit of volume (about 4.8 gal., 18 l.), measuring ladle)

料 リョウ (materials, pg.18)
科 カ (division, subject)
斜* なな・め (slanting, diagonal)

丶 冫 三 斗 斗 斗

ト	一斗 (イット about 4.8 gallons or 18 liters)　北斗七星 (ホクトシチセイ The Big Dipper)

133

Kanji and Examples			Stroke Order and Practice								
43. 井 *4 ([water] well, pg. 5)	囲	かこ・む (enclose, pg. 41)	二	二	丰	井	井	井			
	耕	たがや・す (to plow, pg. 23)									
い	井戸 (いど water well)										
セイ／ショウ	油井 (ユセイ oil well)			天井 (テンジョウ ceiling)							

44. 斤 ‡*4 (originally ax; unit of weight (about 1.3 lbs., 600 g.))	近	ちか・い／キン (near, pg. 38)	`	厂	斤	斤	斤	斤			
	折	お・る (fold, pg.27)									
キン	一斤 (イッキン about 1.3 pounds or 600 grams)										

45. 升 *4 (1/10 of a TO (see pg. 133.), square wooden measuring box)	昇*	のぼ・る (rise)	`	二	手	升	升	升			
ます	升 (ます wooden measuring box)										
ショウ	一升 (イッショウ about 0.48 gallons or 1.8 liters)										

46. 介 *4 (be in between, mediate, concern oneself with)	界	カイ (world, limit)	ノ	ヘ	介	介	介	介			
カイ	介入 (カイニュウ intervention) 介抱* (カイホウ nursing care) 紹介* (ショウカイ introduction)										

‡ 斤 appeared as *ono·zukuri* on pg. 27.
● 抱（ホウ）will appear on pg. 158.
● 紹（ショウ）will appear on pg. 166.

EXERCISES FOR FOUR STROKE KANJI (NUMBERS 31 THROUGH 46)

WRITING EXERCISE

Fill in each box to make a word.

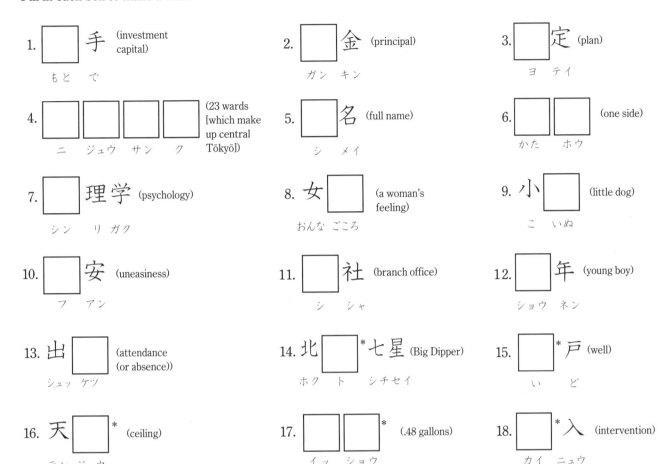

1. ☐ 手 (investment capital)
   もと で

2. ☐ 金 (principal)
   ガン キン

3. ☐ 定 (plan)
   ヨ テイ

4. ☐☐☐☐ (23 wards [which make up central Tōkyō])
   ニ ジュウ サン ク

5. ☐ 名 (full name)
   シ メイ

6. ☐☐ (one side)
   かた ホウ

7. ☐ 理学 (psychology)
   シン リ ガク

8. 女 ☐ (a woman's feeling)
   おんな ごころ

9. 小 ☐ (little dog)
   こ いぬ

10. ☐ 安 (uneasiness)
    フ アン

11. ☐ 社 (branch office)
    シ シャ

12. ☐ 年 (young boy)
    ショウ ネン

13. 出 ☐ (attendance (or absence))
    シュッ ケツ

14. 北 ☐ *七星 (Big Dipper)
    ホク ト シチセイ

15. ☐ *戸 (well)
    い ど

16. 天 ☐ * (ceiling)
    テン ジョウ

17. ☐☐ * (.48 gallons)
    イッ ショウ

18. ☐ *入 (intervention)
    カイ ニュウ

READING EXERCISE

Read the following sentences, and write the correct *furigana* (pronunciation of Kanji written in Hiragana regardless of whether the reading of the Kanji is On or Kun) below the underlined Kanji.

1. 元日には女の人はよく着物を着ます。 (On New Year's Day women usually wear kimonos.)

2. もうホテルの予約はしましたか。 (Have you made a hotel reservation yet?)

3. ウメとサクラの花の区別がつきますか。 (Can you tell the difference between plum and cherry blossoms?)

4. <u>日本</u>まで<u>片道</u>いくらですか。

(How much is a one way fare to Japan?)

5. あなたといっしょなら<u>心強</u>いです。

(If you accompany me, I will feel more at ease.)

6. みんな<u>元気</u>ですから<u>安心</u>してください。

(Everyone is doing well, so please don't worry.)

7. <u>秋田犬</u>はいい<u>番犬</u>です。

(An Akita is a good watchdog.)

8. <u>今年</u>は<u>雨</u>が<u>少</u>なくて<u>水</u>が<u>不足</u>しています。

(Because we had little rain, there is a shortage of water this year.)

9. だれがあの<u>一家</u>を<u>支</u>えていますか。
   いっか

(Who is supporting that household?)

10. あなたは<u>共和党</u>と<u>民主党</u>とどちらを<u>支持</u>しますか。
    きょうわとう　みんしゅとう

(Which party do you support, the Republicans or the Democrats?)

11. きょうは<u>少</u>し<u>寒</u>いですね。

(Today it's a little cold, isn't it?)

12. <u>少数</u>の<u>人</u>の<u>意見</u>もよく<u>聞</u>かなければなりません。
    いけん

(We must listen to minority opinions.)

13. この<u>茶</u>わんは<u>少</u>し<u>欠</u>けていますね。

(This rice bowl is slightly chipped, isn't it?)

14. かの<u>女</u>の<u>欠点</u>は<u>気</u>の<u>短</u>いことです。
    じょ

(Her weak point is a short temper.)

15. <u>昔</u>は<u>升</u>*で<u>お米</u>をはかりました。

(In the olden days, they measured rice with a *masu* [traditional wooden measuring box].)

16. わたしは<u>十年</u>も<u>母</u>の<u>介抱</u>をしました。 (I nursed my mother for ten [whole] years.)

ANALYZING AND READING EXERCISE FOR EXAMPLE KANJI

Analyze the following Kanji. Write the *furigana* below the underlined Kanji. (Some familiar Kanji are included in this exercise.)

1. 院 = [　] + [　] + [　]
   かれは<u>大学院</u>の<u>学</u>生です。
   　　　　　　　　　　せい
   (He is a student in graduate school.)

2. 預 = [　] + [　]
   <u>銀行</u>にいくらお<u>金</u>を<u>預</u>けましたか。
   ぎんこう
   (How much money did you deposit in the bank?)

3. 欧* = [　] + [　]
   いつか<u>欧州</u>を<u>旅行</u>したいです。
   　　　　　　　　りょこう
   (I would like to travel to Europe some day.)

4. 紙 = [　] + [　]
   この<u>紙</u>に<u>住所</u><u>氏名</u>を<u>書</u>いてください。
   　　　　じゅうしょ
   (Please write your name and address on this piece of paper.)

5. 版 = [　] + [　]
   <u>近</u>いうちに<u>本</u>を<u>出版</u>することになりました。
   ((It has been decided that) I will publish a book in the near future.)

6. 思 = [　] + [　]
   これはいい<u>本</u>だと<u>思</u>います。
   (I think this is a good book.)

7. 愛 = [　] + [　] + [　] + [　]
   わたしはかの<u>女</u>を<u>愛</u>しています。
   　　　　　　じょ
   (I love her.)

8. 状 ＝ ［　］ ＋ ［　］

    かれの<u>病状</u>はその後どうですか。
          ご

(How has he (the condition of his illness) been (after that)?)

9. 否 ＝ ［　］ ＋ ［　］

    かれの<u>考</u>えはいつも<u>否定</u>的です。
              てき

(He (His thinking) is always negative.)

10. 枝 ＝ ［　］ ＋ ［　］

    あの<u>松</u>の<u>木</u>の<u>枝</u>を<u>少</u>し<u>切</u>りましょう。

(Let's cut the branch of that pine tree a little.)

11. 技 ＝ ［　］ ＋ ［　］

    コンピューターの<u>技術</u>は

    どんどん<u>進</u>んでいます。

(Computer technology is improving rapidly.)

12. 砂 ＝ ［　］ ＋ ［　］

    <u>砂浜</u>•で<u>子</u>どもがあそんでいます。
      はま

(The children are playing on the sandy beach.)

13. 飲 ＝ ［　］ ＋ ［　］

    <u>毎日</u> <u>水</u>をたくさん<u>飲</u>みます。

(I drink a lot of water every day.)

14. 次 ＝ ［　］ ＋ ［　］

    <u>次</u>の<u>電車</u>はなん<u>時</u>ですか。

(What time is the next train?)

15. 科 ＝ ［　］ ＋ ［　］

    かれは<u>内科</u>の<u>医者</u>です。
       いしゃ

(He is a doctor of internal medicine.)

•浜（はま）will appear on pg. 198.

16. 囲 = [   ] + [   ]
　　　<u>京都</u>は<u>山</u>に<u>囲</u>まれた<u>町</u>です。

(Kyōto is a city surrounded by mountains.)

17. 近 = [   ] + [   ]
　　　うちの<u>近</u>くにいいすし<u>屋</u>があります。

(There is a good sushi bar near my house.)

18. 界 = [   ] + [   ]
　　　<u>世界</u>で<u>一番高</u>い<u>山</u>はどこですか。

(Where is the world's tallest mountain?)

Five Stroke Kanji (Numbers 1 through 14)

Kanji and Examples		Stroke Order and Practice
1. 白 5 (white)	泉 いずみ (fountain, pg. 114) 習 なら・う／シュウ (learn) 的 まと／テキ (target)	' ／ 亇 白 白 白 白
しろ・い／（しら）	白い（しろい white）	白黒（しろくろ black & white）　　白木（しらき plain unpainted wood）
ハク／ビャク	白米（ハクマイ polished rice）	明白（メイハク clear, obvious）　　白夜（ビャクヤ white night, midnight sun）
2. 目 5 (eye)	見 み・る (look, pg. 34) 眠* ねむ・る (sleep, pg. 18) 相 ソウ／ショウ (appearance, mutual)	｜ 冂 月 月 目 目 目
め／（ま）	目ぐすり（めぐすり eye drops）	目上（めうえ one's senior or superior）　　目のあたり（まのあたり before one's eyes）
モク／（ボク）	目的（モクテキ purpose）	注目（チュウモク attention）　　面目（メンボク face, honor）
3. 田 5 (rice field, pg. 5)	男 おとこ／ダン (man, pg. xv) 細 ほそ・い (slender, thin) 畑 はたけ／はた (field, farm, pg. 17)	｜ 冂 田 田 田 田 田
た	田畑（たはた farm）	田うえ（たうえ rice planting）
デン	水田（スイデン rice paddy）	油田（ユデン oil fields）
4. 由 5 (reason, signficance)	油 あぶら／ユ (oil) 宙 チュウ (space, sky) 笛 ふえ (flute)	｜ 冂 由 由 由 由 由
よし	…の由（…のよし I hear that…）	
ユ／ユウ／（ユイ）	由来（ユライ origin）	自由（ジユウ freedom）　　理由（リユウ reason, cause）

● 注（チュウ）will appear on pg. 142.
● 面（メン）will appear on pg. 228.

Kanji and Examples		Stroke Order and Practice
5. 申 5 (say, tell (humble form))	神 かみ／シン／ジン (God, pg. 22) 伸* の・ばす／シン (stretch, lengthen)	丨／ 冂 冂 日 申 申 申
もう・す	申し込み (もうしこみ proposal, application)	申しわけ (もうしわけ excuse)
シン	申告 (シンコク report)	答申 (トウシン submitting a written response to an inquiry)

6. 正 5 (correct, right, just)	証 ショウ (proof) 整 セイ (put in order) 政 セイ (politics)	一 丁 干 正 正 正 正
ただ・しい／まさ	正しい答え (ただしいこたえ right answer)	正に (まさに exactly)
セイ／ショウ	正門 (セイモン front gate)　公正 (コウセイ fair)　正月 (ショウガツ New Year's [holiday])	

7. 石 ‡5 (stone, pg. xii)	岩 いわ (rock, pg. 99) 碁* ゴ ([the game of] Go, pg. 70)	一 厂 石 石 石 石 石
いし	石だん (いしだん stone steps)　小石 (こいし pebble)	
セキ／シャク／ （コク）	石油 (セキユ petroleum)　磁石 (ジシャク magnet)　石高 (コクだか crop, stipend, yield)	

8. 立 5 (elect, stand up)	音 おと／オン (sound) 泣 な・く (cry) 堂 ドウ (hall, building)	丶 立 立 立 立 立 立
た・つ／た・てる	立つ (たつ stand up)　立場 (たちば stand point)　夕立 (ゆうだち evening [rain] shower)	
リツ／（リュウ）	立秋 (リッシュウ first day of autumn)　中立 (チュウリツ neutral, pg. 115)　建立 (コンリュウ construction of a Buddhist temple)	

‡石 appeared as *ishi·hen* on pg. 18.

Kanji and Examples		Stroke Order and Practice

9. 出 5
(go out, come out, put out, pg. 41)

堀* ほ・る／クツ (dig)
屈* クツ (bend, yield)
拙* セツ (unskillful, clumsy)

で・る／だ・す 思い出 (おもいで memories)　思い出す (おもいだす remember)

シュツ／（スイ） 外出 (ガイシュツ outing)　出発 (シュッパツ departure)　出納 (スイトウ accounts, revenue & expenditure)

10. 四 5
(four)

よ／よ・つ よっ・つ／よん 四時 (よ ジ four o'clock)　四日 (よっか fourth day, four days)　四分 (よんぷん four minutes)

シ 四方 (シホウ [all] four directions)　四季 (シキ four seasons)　四月 (シガツ April)

11. 生 5
(birth, life, living, be born, pupil, raw, grow)

星 ほし (star, pg. 113)
性 セイ (gender, pg.21)
産 う・む／サン (produce)

い・きる／い・ける う・まれる／き／なま は・える／お・う 長生き (ながいき long life)　生まれつき (うまれつき by nature)　生水 (なまみず unboiled water)

セイ／ショウ 生物学 (セイブツガク biology)　学生 (ガクセイ student)　一生 (イッショウ one's whole life, lifetime)

12. 主 5
(master, main, principal)

住 す・む／ジュウ (dwell)
柱 はしら／チュウ (pillar)
注 そそ・ぐ／チュウ (pour)

ぬし／おも 家主 (やぬし landlord)　持ち主 (もちぬし owner)　主に (おもに mainly)

シュ／（ス） 主食 (シュショク staple food)　主語 (シュゴ subject of a sentence)　主婦 (シュフ housewife)

• 食（ショク）will appear on pg. 197.

Kanji and Examples			Stroke Order and Practice							

| 13. 矢 ‡5 (arrow) | 医 イ (physician, pg. 6) 疑 うたが・う (doubt, pg. 65) 疾* シツ (illness, swift) | ノ | ﾆ | 仁 | 午 | 矢 | 矢 | 矢 | | |

| や | 弓矢 (ゆみや bow & arrow, pg. 105)　　矢印 (やじるし the arrow "→" symbol) |
| シ | 一矢をむくいる (イッシをむくいる shoot back, retaliate) |

| 14. 失 5 (lose, miss) | 鉄 テツ (iron, pg.20) 迭* テツ (alternate) | ノ | ﾆ | ﾆ | 失 | 失 | 失 | 失 | | |

| うしな・う | 失う (うしなう lose) |
| シツ | 失言 (シツゲン slip of the tongue)　　失礼 (シツレイ impolite)　　失敗 (シッパイ failure) |

‡ 矢 appeared as *ya·hen* on pg. 18.

EXERCISES FOR FIVE STROKE KANJI (NUMBERS 1 THROUGH 14)

WRITING EXERCISE
Fill in each box to make a word.

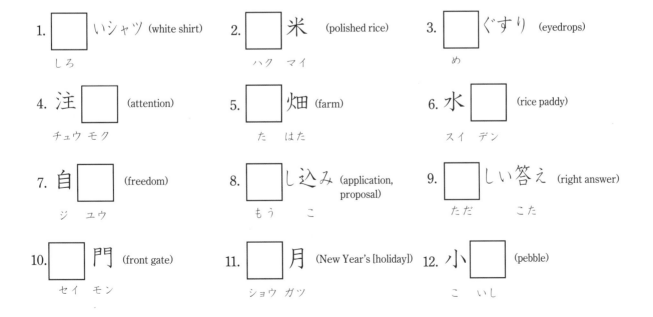

1. ☐ いシャツ (white shirt)　　しろ

2. ☐ 米 (polished rice)　　ハク マイ

3. ☐ ぐすり (eyedrops)　　め

4. 注 ☐ (attention)　　チュウ モク

5. ☐ 畑 (farm)　　た はた

6. 水 ☐ (rice paddy)　　スイ デン

7. 自 ☐ (freedom)　　ジ ユウ

8. ☐ し込み (application, proposal)　　もう こ

9. ☐ しい答え (right answer)　　ただ こた

10. ☐ 門 (front gate)　　セイ モン

11. ☐ 月 (New Year's [holiday])　　ショウ ガツ

12. 小 ☐ (pebble)　　こ いし

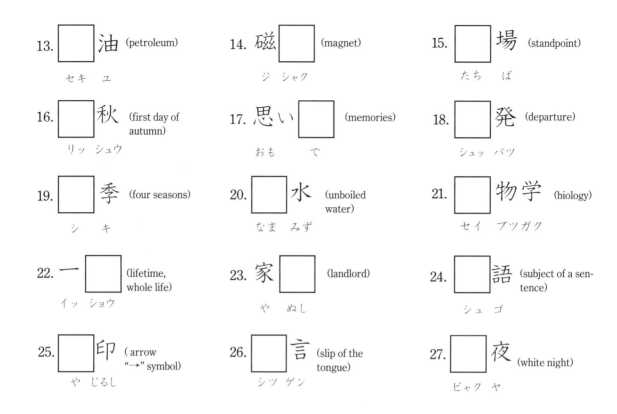

13. □油 (petroleum)
セキ ユ

14. 磁□ (magnet)
ジ シャク

15. □場 (standpoint)
たち ば

16. □秋 (first day of autumn)
リッ シュウ

17. 思い□ (memories)
おも で

18. □発 (departure)
シュッ パツ

19. □季 (four seasons)
シ キ

20. □水 (unboiled water)
なま みず

21. □物学 (biology)
セイ ブツガク

22. 一□ (lifetime, whole life)
イッ ショウ

23. 家□ (landlord)
や ぬし

24. □語 (subject of a sentence)
シュ ゴ

25. □印 (arrow "→" symbol)
や じるし

26. □言 (slip of the tongue)
シツ ゲン

27. □夜 (white night)
ビャク ヤ

READING EXERCISE

Read the following sentences, and write the correct *furigana* (pronunciation of Kanji written in Hiragana regardless of whether the reading of the Kanji is On or Kun) below the underlined Kanji.

1. このフィルムは<u>白黒</u>ですね。
   (This film is black and white, isn't it?)

2. かれがこのまちがいをした<u>事</u>は<u>明白</u>です。
   (It is obvious that he made this mistake.)

3. <u>日本語</u>を<u>習</u>う<u>目的</u>はなんですか。
   (What is your purpose for learning Japanese?)

4. カリフォルニアには<u>油田</u>がたくさんありますか。
   (Are there many oil fields in California?)

5. きのう<u>仕事</u>を<u>休</u>んだ<u>理由</u>はなんですか。
   (Why (What is the reason) you were absent from work yesterday?)

6. たいへんおそくなって<u>申</u>しわけございません。 (I am terribly sorry for being so late.)

7. <u>税金</u>の<u>申告</u>はもうすみましたか。 (Did you file (finish reporting) your income tax yet?)

8. <u>正</u>にそのとおりですね。 (You are absolutely right.)

9. <u>公正</u>な<u>取</u>り<u>引</u>きをしなければなりません。 (We must deal fairly [with everyone].)

10. <u>近</u>ごろよく<u>昔</u>のことを思い<u>出</u>します。
　　　ちか (These days I often reminisce about the past (events).)

11. <u>今晩</u>ちょっと<u>外出</u>します。 (I will be going out for a while tonight.)

12. <u>四月</u> <u>四日</u>はわたしのたん<u>生日</u>です。
　　　　　　　　　　　じょうび (April 4th is my birthday.)

13. <u>今</u>、<u>四時</u> <u>四分</u>です。 (It is now 4:04.)

14. いつまでも<u>長生</u>きしてください。 (May you live a long life.)

15. かれは<u>生</u>まれつき<u>体</u>がよわいです。 (He has been physically weak since birth.)

16. このさいふの<u>持ち主</u>はだれですか。 (Who is the owner of this wallet?)

17. <u>日本</u>では<u>米</u>が<u>主食</u>です。 (In Japan, rice is the staple food.)

18. 戦そうで<u>家</u>や<u>財産</u>を<u>失</u>った<u>人</u>がたくさんいます。
    <u>せん</u>
    (There are many (people) who lost houses and property due to the war.)

19. そろそろ<u>失礼</u>します。
    (Excuse me (my rudeness), [but I'd better be leaving] soon.)

20. <u>失敗</u>は<u>成功</u>のもとといいます。
    (It is said that failure is the basis of success.)

ANALYZING AND READING EXERCISE FOR EXAMPLE KANJI

Analyze the following Kanji. Write the *furigana* below the underlined Kanji. (Some familiar Kanji are included in this exercise.)

1. 習 = [　] + [　]
   かの女は<u>四</u>つの<u>時</u>からピアノを<u>習</u>っています。
   <u>じょ</u>
   (She has been learning the piano since she was four years old.)

2. 相 = [　] + [　]
   あなたの<u>手相</u>を<u>見</u>てあげましょうか。
   (Shall I read your palm for you?)

3. 細 = [　] + [　]
   あなたの<u>指</u>は<u>細</u>いですね。
   (Your fingers are slender, aren't they?)

4. 油 = [　] + [　]
   おいしいてんぷらにはいい<u>油</u>が<u>要</u>ります。
   (Delicious tempura requires good oil.)

5. 宙 = [　] + [　]
   <u>宇宙</u> <u>科学</u>の<u>研究</u>は<u>大切</u>です。
   (Space science research is important.)

6. 神 = [　] + [　]
   あなたは<u>神</u>を<u>信</u>じますか。
   (Do you believe in God?)

7. 証 ＝ ［　　］＋［　　］
　　　かれは<u>証券</u> <u>会社</u>に<u>勤</u>めています。

(He is working at a securities company.)

8. 整 ＝ ［　　］＋［　　］＋［　　］
　　　もう<u>少</u>し<u>机</u>の<u>上</u>を<u>整理</u>してください。

(Please organize the top of [your] desk a little better.)

9. 政 ＝ ［　　］＋［　　］
　　　かれは<u>政界</u>の大物です。
　　　　　　　　おおもの

(He is an important figure in the political world.)

10. 泣 ＝ ［　　］＋［　　］
　　　<u>子</u>どもが<u>大</u>きな<u>声</u>で<u>泣</u>いています。

(The child is crying in a loud voice.)

11. 童 ＝ ［　　］＋［　　］
　　　<u>日本</u>の<u>童話</u>をおしえてください。

(Please tell me some Japanese children's tales.)

12. 性 ＝ ［　　］＋［　　］
　　　かれの<u>性格</u>はみなに<u>好</u>かれます。

(He (his personality) is liked by everyone.)

13. 産 ＝ ［　　］＋［　　］＋［　　］
　　　カリフォルニアはオレンジの<u>産地</u>として
　　　<u>有名</u>です。

(California is famous as an orange producing area.)

14. 住 ＝ ［　　］＋［　　］
　　　あなたは<u>今</u>どこに<u>住</u>んでいますか。

(Where are you living now?)

15. 注 ＝ ［　　］＋［　　］
　　　<u>車</u>に<u>注意</u>してください。

(Please watch out for cars.)

16.　疑 ＝ ［　　］ ＋ ［　　］ ＋ ［　　］ ＋ ［　　］

　　　　証こがないのに人を疑ってはいけません。　(Without evidence [we] shouldn't suspect someone.)

17.　鉄 ＝ ［　　］ ＋ ［　　］

　　　　このすきやきなべは鉄でできています。　(This sukiyaki pan is made of iron.)

Five Stroke Kanji (Numbers 15 through 27)

Kanji and Examples			Stroke Order and Practice
15. 5 母 (mother, pg. 7)	(see 毋, variation of 母 on pg. 60)		ム　母　母　母　母　母　母
はは	母 (はは　mother, pg. 7)		母の日 (ははのひ　Mother's Day)
ボ	父母 (フボ　father & mother, pg. 122)		母音 (ボオン／ボイン　vowel)　　母校 (ボコウ　Alma Mater)
16. 5 半 (half, pg. 6)	判　ハン (seal, judgment) 伴*　ハン (accompany)		半　半　半
なか・ば	月の半ば (つきのなかば　middle of the month)		
ハン	半分 (ハンブン　half, pg. 123)	半日 (ハンニチ　a half day)	半月 (ハンつき　a half-month)
17. 5 平 (plain, flat, even)	評　ヒョウ (criticism) 坪*　つぼ (35.58 square feet)		平　平　平
たい・ら／ひら	平らな道 (たいらなみち　flat road)		平家 (ひらや　one story house)
ヘイ／ビョウ	平和 (ヘイワ　peace)	公平 (コウヘイ　fair)	平等 (ビョウドウ　equality)
18. 5 古 (old, pg. 91)	居　い・る (to be, pg. 36) 苦　くる・しい／ク (suffering, worries) 湖　みずうみ／コ (lake)		古　古　古
ふる・い	古本 (ふるホン　used book)	古顔 (ふるがお　old-timer)	中古 (チュウぶる　second hand)
コ	古代 (コダイ　ancient times)	古都 (コト　ancient city, capital)	中古車 (チュウコシャ　used car)

Kanji and Examples	Stroke Order and Practice

19. 兄 (5)
(elder brother, pg.3)

祝 いわ・う (celebrate)
党 トウ (party, faction)

| あに | 兄 (あに elder brother) | 兄よめ(あによめ elder brother's wife) |
| ケイ/(キョウ) | 父兄 (フケイ guardians, pg. 122) | 兄弟 (キョウダイ brothers, siblings) |

20. 史 (5)
(history, record)

使 つか・う / シ (use, employ)
吏* リ (public servant)

| シ | 史上 (シジョウ in history) 歴史 (レキシ history) 日本史 (ニホンシ Japanese history) |

21. 央 (5)
(middle)

映 うつ・る / エイ (reflect)
英 エイ (England, superb, talented)

| オウ | 中央 (チュウオウ center) |

22. 皮 (5)
(skin, leather)

波 なみ／ハ (wave)
破 やぶ・れる／ハ (rip, break)
彼* かれ／(かの)／ヒ (he)

| かわ | 毛皮 (けがわ fur, pg. 116) |
| ヒ | 皮膚* (ヒフ skin) 皮肉 (ヒニク sarcasm, irony) |

150

Kanji and Examples		Stroke Order and Practice

23. 世 (5) — (world, era, public, pg. 7)

葉 は／ヨウ (leaves)

二　十　廿　世　世　世　世

よ	世の中 (よのなか world)
セイ／セ	二世 (ニセイ second generation)　世界 (セカイ world)　世間 (セケン society)

24. 去 (5) — (leave, pass away, elapse)

法 ホウ (law)

脚* あし (leg, pg. 26)

二　十　土　去　去　去　去

さ・る	去る五月 (さるゴガツ last May)
キョ／コ	去年 (キョネン last year)　過去 (カコ the past)

25. 皿 (‡5) — (dish, plate, platter)

盟 メイ (ally, pg. 33)

監* カン (supervise, pg. 82)

盆* ボン (tray)

丨　冂　冊　皿　皿　皿　皿

さら	小皿 (こざら small dish)　灰皿 (はいざら ashtray)

26. 以 (5) — (with, from, than)

似 に・る (resemble)

丨　以　以　以　以　以　以

イ	以外 (イガイ other than, except)　以上 (イジョウ more than)　以下 (イカ less than)

‡ 皿 appeared as *sara·ashi* on pg. 33.

Kanji and Examples			Stroke Order and Practice							

| 27.   5
 必 | 秘 ヒ (secret)

 密 ミ・ツ (intimate, secret, dense) | `ソ` | 心 | 心 | 必 | 必 | 必 | 必 | | |

(certain, sure, necessity, pg. 132)

かなら・ず	必ず (かならず by all means, pg. 132)		
ヒ ツ	必然 (ヒツゼン inevitable)	必要 (ヒツヨウ necessary)	必読 (ヒツドク a must read)

EXERCISES FOR FIVE STROKE KANJI (NUMBERS 15 THROUGH 27)

WRITING EXERCISE
Fill in each box to make a word.

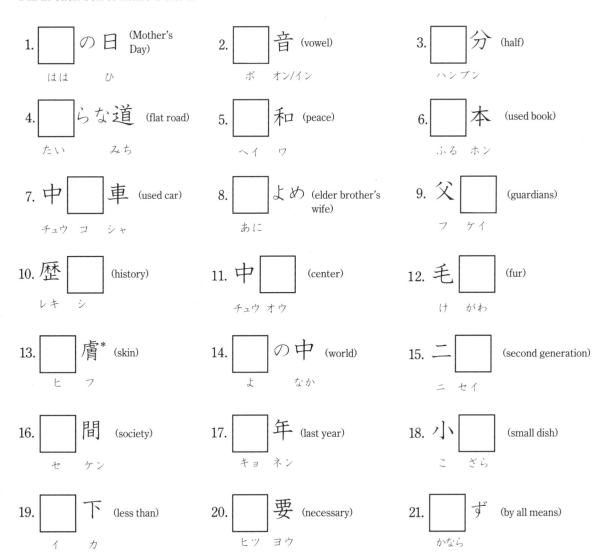

1. ☐ の日 (Mother's Day)
   はは ひ

2. ☐ 音 (vowel)
   ボ オン/イン

3. ☐ 分 (half)
   ハンブン

4. ☐ らな道 (flat road)
   たい みち

5. ☐ 和 (peace)
   ヘイ ワ

6. ☐ 本 (used book)
   ふる ホン

7. 中 ☐ 車 (used car)
   チュウ コ シャ

8. ☐ よめ (elder brother's wife)
   あに

9. 父 ☐ (guardians)
   フ ケイ

10. 歴 ☐ (history)
   レキ シ

11. 中 ☐ (center)
   チュウ オウ

12. 毛 ☐ (fur)
   け がわ

13. ☐ 膚* (skin)
   ヒ フ

14. ☐ の中 (world)
   よ なか

15. 二 ☐ (second generation)
   ニ セイ

16. ☐ 間 (society)
   セ ケン

17. ☐ 年 (last year)
   キョ ネン

18. 小 ☐ (small dish)
   こ ざら

19. ☐ 下 (less than)
   イ カ

20. ☐ 要 (necessary)
   ヒツ ヨウ

21. ☐ ず (by all means)
   かなら

READING EXERCISE

Read the following sentences, and write the correct *furigana* (pronunciation of Kanji written in Hiragana regardless of whether the reading of the Kanji is On or Kun) below the underlined Kanji.

1. <u>父母</u>は<u>旅行</u>が<u>好</u>きです。
りょこう
(My father and mother like to travel.)

2. <u>今月</u>の<u>半</u>ばに<u>東京</u>へ<u>行</u>きます。
(I am going to Tōkyō in the middle of this month.)

3. きょうは<u>半日</u> <u>仕事</u>を<u>休</u>みました。
(Today I took a half-day off from work.)

4. わたしの<u>家</u>は<u>平家</u>です。
(My home is a one story house.)

5. <u>父</u>の<u>残</u>したお<u>金</u>を<u>兄弟</u>で<u>公平</u>に<u>分</u>けました。
(We siblings evenly divided the money our father left us among ourselves.)

6. <u>男女</u>は<u>平等</u>に<u>扱</u>われなければなりません。
(Men and women should be treated equally.)

7. <u>中古</u>の<u>自転車</u>を<u>買</u>いました。
じてんしゃ
(I bought a used bicycle.)

8. <u>古代</u>ローマの<u>文化</u>を<u>研究</u>しています。
(I am researching the culture of ancient Rome.)

9. <u>先月</u>のハリケーンは<u>史上</u> <u>最大</u>(maximum)のものでした。
さいだい
(Last month's hurricane was the strongest in history.)

10. <u>彼</u>はいつも<u>皮肉</u>を<u>言</u>います。
(He always says sarcastic things.)

11. <u>今</u> <u>世界</u>の<u>人口</u>はどのぐらいですか。
(What is the current world population?)

12. それはもう<u>過去</u>のことです。 (It's already a thing of the past.)

13. すみませんが、ちょっと<u>灰皿</u>をとって
くださいませんか。 (Excuse me, but could you please pass me the ashtray?)

14. きょうは<u>九十度</u><u>以上</u>あります。 (Today it is over 90 degrees.)

15. わたしは<u>肉</u><u>以外</u>はなんでも<u>食</u>べます。
　　　　　　　　　　　　　た (I'll eat anything except meat.)

16. これは<u>学生</u>にとって<u>必読</u>の<u>本</u>です。 (This book is a "must read" for students.)

ANALYZING AND READING EXERCISE FOR EXAMPLE KANJI

Analyze the following Kanji. Write the *furigana* below the underlined Kanji. (Some familiar Kanji are included in this exercise.)

1. 判＝［　］＋［　］
　　<u>女性</u>の<u>判事</u>はまだ<u>少</u>ないです。 (There are still only a few women judges.)

2. 評＝［　］＋［　］
　　あの<u>映画</u>はとても<u>評判</u>がいいです。 (People have a high opinion of that movie. (That movie's reputation is very good.))

3. 居＝［　］＋［　］
　　うちにはとても<u>広</u>い<u>居間</u>があります。 (Our home has a very spacious living room.)

4. 湖＝［　］＋［　］＋［　］
　　<u>富士山</u>のそばに<u>大</u>きな<u>湖</u>があります。 (There is a big lake by Mt. Fuji.)

5. 祝 = [　] + [　]

今晩子どものたん生日のお祝いをします。　(Tonight we are celebrating
　　　　じょうび　　　　　　　　　　　　　　my child's birthday.)

6. 党 = [　] + [　] + [　]

あなたはどの政党を支持しますか。　(Which political party do you
　　　　　　　　　　　　　　　　　　support?)

7. 使 = [　] + [　] + [　]

わたしはよくこの字引を使います。　(I use this dictionary a lot.)

8. 映 = [　] + [　]

きのう友だちと映画を見に行きました。　(Yesterday I went to see a movie
　　　　　　　　　　　　　　　　　　　with my friend.)

9. 英 = [　] + [　]

彼女は英語も日本語も上手です。　(She is fluent (skilled) in both
　　　　　　　　　じょうず　　　　　English and Japanese.)

10. 波 = [　] + [　]

きょうはサンタモニカで波のりをしました。　(Today I went surfing (surfed) at
　　　　　　　　　　　　　　　　　　　　Santa Monica.)

11. 破 = [　] + [　]

若い人はなぜ破れたジーンズをはくのでしょう。(I wonder why young people wear
　　　　　　　　　　　　　　　　　　　　torn jeans.)

12. 葉 = [　] + [　] + [　]

にわに木の葉がたくさんおちています。　(Many leaves have fallen in the
　　　　　　　　　　　　　　　　　　yard.)

13. 法 = [　] + [　]

彼は大学の法科に入りました。　(He entered the university's law
　　　　　　　　　　　　　　　school (department).)

14. 盟＝［　］＋［　］
    <u>今</u>、<u>世界</u>のほとんどの<u>国</u>が国連(United Nations)
    こくれん
    に<u>加盟</u>しています。

(Most countries of the world have
now joined the United Nations.)

15. 似＝［　］＋［　］
    あなたはお<u>母</u>さんによく<u>似</u>ていますね。
    かあ

(You resemble your mother
very much, don't you?)

16. 秘＝［　］＋［　］

17. 密＝［　］＋［　］＋［　］
    これはわたしたちだけの<u>間</u>の<u>秘密</u>です。

(This is a secret just between the
two of us.)

Five Stroke Kanji (Numbers 28 through 41)

Kanji and Examples		Stroke Order and Practice
28. 広 5 (wide, spacious, pg. 36)	拡 カク (expand, extend) 鉱 コウ (ore, mine)	⺜ ⺬ 广 広 広 広 広
ひろ・い∕ひろ・まる∕ ひろ・がる	広い (ひろい wide, broad)　　広場 (ひろば open space, plaza)　　広島 (ひろしま Hiroshima)	
コウ	広告 (コウコク advertisement)　広大 (コウダイ vast)	
29. 司 5 (manage, govern)	詞 シ (words) 飼* かう∕シ (raise, breed) 伺* うかが・う∕シ (ask, visit)	⺆ ⺋ ⺆ 司 司 司 司
シ	司会 (シカイ presiding)　　司法 (シホウ administration of justice)　　上司 (ジョウシ one's superiors)	
30. 可 5 (possible, can, acceptable, approval)	何 なに∕(なん)∕カ (what) 河 かわ∕カ (river, pg. xvi) 歌 うた∕カ (song, pg. 25)	一 ⺮ 可 ⺄ 可 可 可
カ	可否 (カヒ right & wrong, pros & cons)　　不可 (フカ improper, not right, not good)　　許可 (キョカ permission)	
31. 句 5 (phrase, pg. 41)	敬 ケイ (respect) 警 ケイ (warn) 驚* おどろ・く∕キョウ (to be surprised)	⺈ ⺈ 勺 句 句 句 句
ク	俳句 (ハイク haiku (17 syllable Japanese poem))　　字句 (ジク words & phrases)　　文句 (モンク complaint, pg. 122)	

Kanji and Examples		Stroke Order and Practice
32. **包** **5** (wrap)	抱* だ・く／ホウ (hug) 砲* ホウ (gun) 飽* あ・きる／ホウ (get tried)	ク ク 勹 匀 包 包 包
つつ・む	包み紙 (つつみがみ wrapping paper)　　小包 (こづつみ a parcel, postal package)	
ホウ	包囲 (ホウイ surround, encirclement)　　包装 (ホウソウ packing, wrapping)　　包丁 (ホウチョウ kitchen knife)	

33. **示** **5** (indicate, show, pg. 90)	祭 まつ・り (festival, pg. 61) 票 ヒョウ (vote, pg. 69) 禁 キン (prohibition)	二 二 示 示 示 示 示
しめ・す	示す (しめす to show)	
ジ／（シ）	指示 (シジ indication, instruction)　　公示 (コウジ public announcement)	

34. **永** **5** (long (time))	泳 およ・ぐ／エイ (swim, pg. 21) 詠* エイ (chant)	ヺ 刃 刃 永 永 永 永
なが・い	日永 (ひなが long (spring) day)	
エイ	永久 (エイキュウ forever, pg. 106)　　永遠 (エイエン eternity)　　永住 (エイジュウ permanent residence)	

36. **穴** **‡5** (hole, cave, pg. 91)	究 キュウ (study thoroughly, pg. 29) 空 そら／クウ (sky, pg. 2) 窓 まど (window, pg. 29)	ヽ ヾ 宀 宀 穴 穴 穴
あな	穴ぐら (あなぐら cellar)　　穴子 (あなご sea eel)　　大穴 (おおあな great loss, jackpot)	
ケツ	穴居時代 (ケッキョジダイ the [prehistoric] cave period)	

‡ 穴 appeared as *ana・kammuri* on pg. 29.

Kanji and Examples		Stroke Order and Practice
36. 冊 **5** (counter for books & magazines)		丿 冂 冊 冊 冊 冊 冊
サツ／（サク）	五冊 (ゴサツ five books)	短冊 (タンザク strip of paper for tanka or haiku)
37. 用 **5** (errand, use)	通 とお·る／ツウ (pass) 備 そな·える (provide) 痛 いた·い／ツウ (painful, pg. 36)	丿 刀 月 月 用 用 用
もち·いる	用いる (もちいる to use)	
ヨウ	用件 (ヨウケン things to be done, business)	社用 (シャヨウ company business) 利用 (リヨウ utilize)
38. 民 **5** (the people, the populace)	眠* ねむ·る／ミン (sleep, pg. 18)	� ﾖ 尸 尺 民 民 民
たみ	民 (たみ the people)	
ミン	国民 (コクミン the people, citizens)	民族 (ミンゾク a race, a people) 民主的 (ミンシュテキ democratic)
39. 台 **5** (a stand, counter for vehicles or machines, pg. 52)	始 はじ·める／シ (begin) 治 おさ·める／ジ (govern)	厶 厶 台 台 台 台 台
ダイ／タイ	台所 (ダイどころ kitchen) 一台 (イチダイ one vehicle or machine) 舞台 (ブタイ stage)	

Kanji and Examples			Stroke Order and Practice								
40. 北 5 (north, pg. 3)	背	せ／せい (one's back, height)	⸝	⺊	⺌	⺅	北	北	北		
きた	北風 (きたかぜ north wind)		北国 (きたぐに northern province)								
ホク	北西 (ホクセイ northwest)		北部 (ホクブ northern part)			東北 (トウホク northeast, the Tōhoku district)					
41. 市 5 (market, city, pg. 55)	姉 肺	あね (older sister, pg. 16) ハイ (lungs)	⺀	亠	广	市	市	市	市		
いち	市場 (いちば market place)										
シ	市場 (シジョウ market)		市長 (シチョウ mayor)								

EXERCISES FOR FIVE STROKE KANJI (NUMBERS 28 THROUGH 41)

WRITING EXERCISE

Fill in each box to make a word.

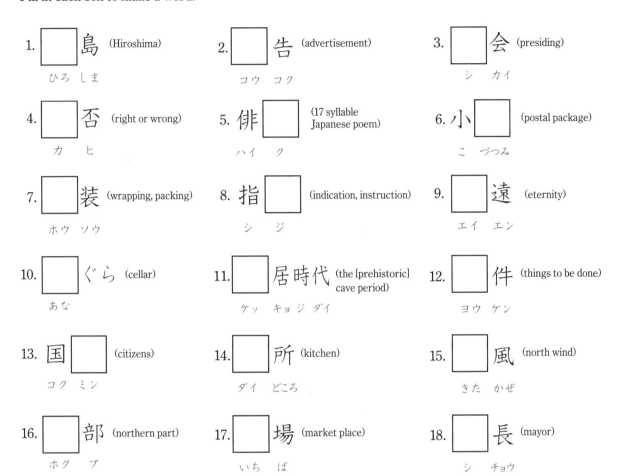

1. ☐島 (Hiroshima)
ひろ　しま

2. ☐告 (advertisement)
コウ　コク

3. ☐会 (presiding)
シ　カイ

4. ☐否 (right or wrong)
カ　ヒ

5. 俳☐ (17 syllable Japanese poem)
ハイ　ク

6. 小☐ (postal package)
こ　づつみ

7. ☐装 (wrapping, packing)
ホウ　ソウ

8. 指☐ (indication, instruction)
シ　ジ

9. ☐遠 (eternity)
エイ　エン

10. ☐ぐら (cellar)
あな

11. ☐居時代 (the [prehistoric] cave period)
ケッ　キョジ　ダイ

12. ☐件 (things to be done)
ヨウ　ケン

13. 国☐ (citizens)
コク　ミン

14. ☐所 (kitchen)
ダイ　どころ

15. ☐風 (north wind)
きた　かぜ

16. ☐部 (northern part)
ホク　ブ

17. ☐場 (market place)
いち　ば

18. ☐長 (mayor)
シ　チョウ

READING EXERCISE

Read the following sentences, and write the correct *furigana* (pronunciation of Kanji written in Hiragana regardless of whether the reading of the Kanji is On or Kun) below the underlined Kanji.

1. 駅前の広場に人がたくさんいます。 (There are many people in the square in front of the [train] station.)

2. 広大な宇宙の研究がさかんになってきました。 (Deep (Vast) space research is starting to flourish.)

3. わたしの上司はとてもしんせつです。 (My boss is very kind.)

4. <u>父</u>の<u>許可</u>をもらってアメリカの<u>大学</u>に<u>入</u>りました。 (I got my father's permission and entered college in America.)

5. あのデパートの<u>包</u>み<u>紙</u>はきれいですね。 (That department store's wrapping paper is very pretty, isn't it?)

6. この<u>包丁</u>はよく<u>切</u>れます。 (This kitchen knife cuts well.)

7. <u>子</u>どもにはいつもよいお<u>手本</u>を<u>示</u>してください。 (Always set a good example for the children, please.)
　　　　　　　て　ほん

8. とうとうロス・アンジェルスに<u>永住</u>することになりました。 (Finally, it has been settled that I will reside in Los Angeles permanently.)

9. ホース・レースで<u>大穴</u>を<u>当</u>てました。 (I made a killing at the horse races.)

10. <u>本</u>を<u>五冊</u> <u>買</u>いました。 (I bought five books.)

11. <u>短冊</u>に<u>俳句</u>を<u>書</u>いてください。 (Please write a haiku on this strip of paper.)

12. <u>社用</u>で<u>東京</u>へ<u>行</u>きました。 (I went to Tōkyō on company business.)

13. <u>自由</u>と<u>平等</u>が<u>民主主義</u>の<u>精神</u>です。 (Freedom and equality are the spirit of democracy.)

14. <u>新</u>しい<u>車</u>を<u>一台</u> <u>買</u>いました。 (I bought a new car.)

15. <u>北国</u>の<u>春</u>はおそいですね。 (Spring comes late in the northern province, doesn't it?)

16. きょうは<u>北西</u>の<u>風</u>が<u>強</u>いです。 (Today the northwest wind is strong.)

17. これはまだ<u>市場</u>に<u>出</u>ていない<u>新</u>しい<u>製品</u>です。 (This is a new product which hasn't
    せいひん   come on the market yet.)

ANALYZING AND READING EXERCISE FOR EXAMPLE KANJI

Analyze the following Kanji. Write the *furigana* below the underlined Kanji. (Some familiar Kanji are included in this exercise.)

1. 拡 = [　] + [　]
   あの<u>会社</u>はだんだん<u>事業</u>(business)を<u>拡大</u>しています。(That company is gradually
   　　　　　　　　　　じ ぎょう　　　　　　　　　　　　　　expanding its business.)

2. 鉱 = [　] + [　]
   <u>父</u>は<u>鉱山技師</u>でした。 (My father was a mining engineer.)
   　　　　　　ぎ し

3. 詞 = [　] + [　]
   あの<u>歌</u>の<u>歌詞</u>をおぼえていますか。 (Do you remember the words to
   　　　　　　　　　　　　　　　　　　　　 that song?)

4. 何 = [　] + [　]
   <u>今晩何</u>をしますか。 (What are you doing tonight?)

5. 敬 = [　] + [　] + [　]
   <u>日本人</u>は<u>目上</u>の<u>人</u>に<u>敬語</u>をつかいます。 (The Japanese use *keigo* (honorific
   　　　　　め うえ　　　　　　　　　　　　　　　 expressions) with their superiors.)

6. 警 = [　] + [　] + [　] + [　]
   <u>警官</u>の<u>仕事</u>はたいへんです。 (A policeman's job is hard [work].)

7. 抱 = [　] + [　]
   お<u>母</u>さんが<u>赤</u>ちゃんを<u>抱</u>いています。 (A mother is holding her infant.)
   　　かあ

163

8.　禁 ＝ ［　　］ ＋ ［　　］
　　　学校ではたばこは禁止されています。　　　　　　(Smoking is forbidden at school.)

9.　泳 ＝ ［　　］ ＋ ［　　］
　　　夏は毎日プールで泳ぎます。　　　　　　(I swim in the pool every day during the summer.)

10.　窓 ＝ ［　　］ ＋ ［　　］ ＋ ［　　］
　　　あついから窓を開けてくださいませんか。　　　　　　(Since it's hot, won't you please open the window?)

11.　通 ＝ ［　　］ ＋ ［　　］ ＋ ［　　］
　　　毎日 花屋の前を通って学校へ行きます。　　　　　　(Every day I pass the florist on my way (going) to school.)

12.　痛 ＝ ［　　］ ＋ ［　　］ ＋ ［　　］
　　　昨晩おそくねたので少し頭が痛いです。　　　　　　(I have a slight headache because I went to bed late last night.)

13.　眠* ＝ ［　　］ ＋ ［　　］
　　　子どもがよく眠っています。　　　　　　(The child is sleeping soundly.)

14.　始 ＝ ［　　］ ＋ ［　　］
　　　いつから日本語の勉強を始めましたか。　　　　　　(When did you begin your studies of Japanese?)

15.　背 ＝ ［　　］ ＋ ［　　］
　　　あなたは背が高いですね。　　　　　　(You are tall, aren't you?)

16.　姉 ＝ ［　　］ ＋ ［　　］
　　　姉は小学校の校長です。　　　　　　(My older sister is an elementary school principal.)

Five Stroke Kanji (Numbers 42 through 54)

Kanji and Examples		Stroke Order and Practice
42. **5** 代 (generation, on behalf of, fee, pg. 3)	貸 か・す／タイ (lend, loan, pg. 33) 袋* ふくろ／タイ (bag)	ノ　亻　仁　代　代　代　代
よ／か・わる／しろ	神代 (かみよ the age of gods (in Japanese mythology))	私の代わりに (わたくしのかわりに on my behalf)　身の代金 (みのしろキン ransom)
ダイ／タイ	現代 (ゲンダイ modern times)	車代 (くるまダイ transportation fee, fare)　交代 (コウタイ taking turns)
43. **5** 加 (add, increase, join in, pg. 92)	賀 ガ (congratulate) 架* カ (to span, to bridge)	ア　カ　カ　加　加　加　加
く わ・える／く わ・わる	加える (くわえる add, pg. 92)	加わる (くわわる join)
カ	加州 (カシュウ state of California)	加入 (カニュウ joining, entry)　増加 (ゾウカ increase)
44. **5** 未 (not yet, un-, still)	味 あじ／ミ (taste, pg. 16) 妹 いもうと (younger sister, pg. 16)	二　二　キ　オ　未　未　未
ミ	未来 (ミライ future)	未知 (ミチ unknown)　未定 (ミテイ undecided)
45. **5** 末 (end)	抹 マツ (erase)	二　二　キ　オ　末　末　末
すえ	末っ子 (すえっこ youngest child)	五月の末 (ゴガツのすえ end of May)
マツ／バツ	月末 (ゲツマツ end of the month)	末弟 (バッテイ youngest brother)

Kanji and Examples		Stroke Order and Practice
46. 5 令 (order, command, honorable)	冷 つめ・たい／レイ (cold, pg. 21) 領 リョウ (territory, dominion) 鈴* すず (bell)	⼃ ⼈ ⼈ 令 令 令 令
レイ	命令 (メイレイ command) 法令 (ホウレイ laws)	
47. 5 冬 (winter, pg. 2)	終 お・わる (end, finish)	⼃ ⼑ 冬 冬 冬 冬 冬
ふゆ	冬休み (ふゆやすみ winter vacation) 冬服 (ふゆふく winter clothes)	
トウ	冬眠* (トウミン hibernation) 初冬 (ショトウ beginning of winter)	
48. 5 付 (attach, affix, stick)	府 フ (urban prefecture, government office) 符* フ (sign, mark) 附* フ (attached, affiliation)	⼃ ⼈ 仁 付 付 付 付
つ・く／つ・ける	付き合い (つきあい association) 手付け (てつけ deposit, down payment) 日付け (ひづけ [calendar] date)	
フ	交付金 (コウフキン grant-in-aid, subsidize)	
49. *5 召 (summon, honorific form of take, eat, wear)	招 まね・く／ショウ (invite) 紹* ショウ (introduce, help) 照 て・る／ショウ (shine)	⼅ ⼑ 刀 召 召 召 召
め・す	召し上がる (めしあがる eat (polite form))	
ショウ	召集 (ショウシュウ a call, convocation)	

Kanji and Examples		Stroke Order and Practice

50. *5

占

(occupy, divination)

店 みせ／テン (store, pg. 36)

点 テン (dot, pg. 2)

し・める／うらな・う	買い占める (かいしめる buy up)　　　星占い (ほしうらない astrology, horoscope)
セン	占領 (センリョウ occupation, capture)　　　独占 (ドクセン monopolize)

51. *5

丙

(third in a series)

病 やまい／ビョウ (illness, pg. 36)

柄* え／がら／ヘイ (handle, pattern)

ヘイ	甲乙丙 (コウ・オツ・ヘイ 1st, 2nd, 3rd in a series; equivalent to ABC)

52. *5

且

(also, furthermore)

組 くみ／ソ (group, pg. 19)

祖 ソ (ancestor)

租* ソ (tribute, tax)

か・つ	且つ (かつ furthermore)

53. *5

甘

(sweet, indulgent)

紺* コン (navy blue)

某* ボウ (a certain one)

あま・い	甘み (あまみ sweetness)　　　甘える (あまえる be indulged)
カン	甘言 (カンゲン sweet talk, cajolery)

Kanji and Examples		Stroke Order and Practice
54. ‡*5 矛 (halberd)	柔* ジュウ (soft, tender) 務 つと・め/ム (duty, pg. 18)	⇁⇁ マ ⇁⇁ 予 矛 矛 矛
ほこ	矛先 (ほこさき point of a spear)	
ム	矛盾▲* (ムジュン contradiction)	

‡ 矛 appeared as *hoko·hen* on pg. 18.
▲ 盾 (たて/ジュン) shield

EXERCISES FOR FIVE STROKE KANJI (NUMBERS 42 THROUGH 54)

WRITING EXERCISE
Fill in each box to make a word.

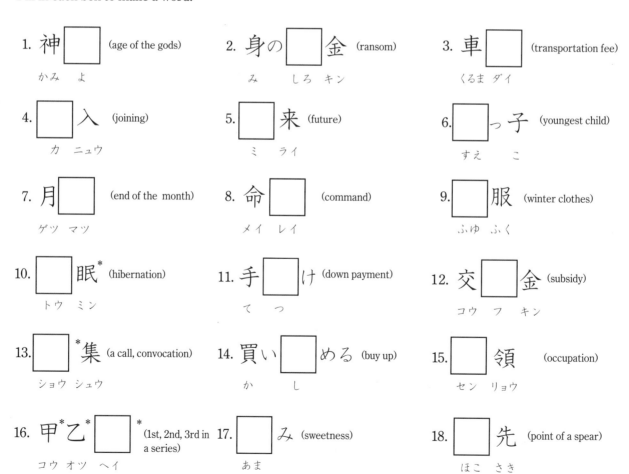

1. 神☐ (age of the gods)　かみ よ

2. 身の☐金 (ransom)　み しろ キン

3. 車☐ (transportation fee)　くるま ダイ

4. ☐入 (joining)　カ ニュウ

5. ☐来 (future)　ミ ライ

6. ☐っ子 (youngest child)　すえ こ

7. 月☐ (end of the month)　ゲツ マツ

8. 命☐ (command)　メイ レイ

9. ☐服 (winter clothes)　ふゆ ふく

10. ☐眠* (hibernation)　トウ ミン

11. 手☐け (down payment)　て つ

12. 交☐金 (subsidy)　コウ フ キン

13. ☐*集 (a call, convocation)　ショウ シュウ

14. 買い☐める (buy up)　か し

15. ☐領 (occupation)　セン リョウ

16. 甲*乙*☐* (1st, 2nd, 3rd in a series)　コウ オツ ヘイ

17. ☐み (sweetness)　あま

18. ☐先 (point of a spear)　ほこ さき

READING EXERCISE

Read the following sentences, and write the correct *furigana* (pronunciation of Kanji written in Hiragana regardless of whether the reading of the Kanji is On or Kun) below the underlined Kanji.

1. きょうはわたしの<u>代</u>わりに<u>会議</u>に<u>出</u>てください。
   かいぎ

   (Please attend the meeting today in my place.)

2. <u>妹</u>と<u>交代</u>で<u>皿洗</u>いをします。
   あら

   (My younger sister and I take turns washing the dishes.)

3. <u>一</u>に<u>二</u>を<u>加</u>えると<u>三</u>になります。

   (Adding two to one makes (becomes) three.)

4. <u>世界</u>の<u>人口</u>は<u>毎年 増加</u>しています。

   (The world's population is increasing every year.)

5. あしたの<u>予定</u>はまだ<u>未定</u>です。

   (Tomorrow's plans are still undecided.)

6. <u>五月</u>の<u>末</u>に<u>日本</u>へ<u>行</u>きます。

   (I am going to Japan at the end of May.)

7. <u>冬休</u>みにはスキーに<u>行</u>きます。

   (I will go skiing during winter vacation.)

8. わたしは<u>近</u>ごろ<u>林</u>さんとお<u>付</u>き<u>合</u>いしています。

   (Lately I have been spending time (associating) with Hayashi-san.)

9. <u>何</u>もございませんが、どうぞ<u>召</u>し<u>上</u>がってください。

   (I'm afraid there isn't much, but please enjoy (eat) the meal.)

10. あなたは<u>星占</u>いを<u>信</u>じますか。
    しん

    (Do you believe in astrology?)

11. <u>彼</u>は<u>独占欲</u>が<u>強</u>いです。

    (His desire to control (monopolize) is strong.)

12. 彼はよくはたらき、且つよく勉強します。 (He works hard; furthermore, he studies hard.)

13. 彼のいうことはときどき矛盾しています。 (The things he says are sometimes contradictory.)

ANALYZING AND READING EXERCISE FOR EXAMPLE KANJI

Analyze the following Kanji. Write the *furigana* below the underlined Kanji. (Some familiar Kanji are included in this exercise.)

1. 貸＝［　］＋［　］
   友だちに字引を貸してあげました。
   じびき
   (I lent the dictionary to my friend.)

2. 賀＝［　］＋［　］
   もう年賀状を書きましたか。
   (Have you written your New Year's cards yet?)

3. 味＝［　］＋［　］
   このスープはとてもいい味です。
   (This soup tastes (has a) very good (flavor).)

4. 妹＝［　］＋［　］
   妹は今十五です。
   (My younger sister is now 15.)

5. 冷＝［　］＋［　］
   あなたの手は冷たいですね。
   (Your hands are cold, aren't they?)

6. 領＝［　］＋［　］
   1945年に日本はアメリカに占領されました。
   (In 1945, Japan was occupied by America.)

7. 終＝［　］＋［　］
   仕事はもう終わりましたか。
   (Have you finished your work already?)

8. 府 ＝ [　] ＋ [　]
   東京は日本の首府です。　　　　　　　　　　(Tōkyō is Japan's capital.)

9. 符* ＝ [　] ＋ [　]
   東京までの切符はもう買いましたか。　　　　(Have you already bought your
   　　　　　　　　　　　　　　　　　　　　　ticket to Tōkyō?)

10. 招 ＝ [　] ＋ [　]
    きょうはお招きありがとうございました。　(Thank you for inviting me today.)

11. 紹 ＝ [　] ＋ [　]
    友だちを紹介します。　　　　　　　　　　(I will introduce my friend
    　　　　　　　　　　　　　　　　　　　　[to you].)

12. 店 ＝ [　] ＋ [　]
    この店のケーキはおいしいです。　　　　　(The cake at this store is delicious.)

13. 病 ＝ [　] ＋ [　]
    病気はもうなおりましたか。　　　　　　　(Have you recovered from your
    　　　　　　　　　　　　　　　　　　　　illness yet?)

14. 組 ＝ [　] ＋ [　]
    あなたは労働組合に加入していますか。　(Do you belong to the labor union?)
    　　　　ろうどう

15. 祖 ＝ [　] ＋ [　]
    わたしの祖先はさむらいでした。　　　　　(My ancestors were samurai.)

16. 紺* ＝ [　] ＋ [　]
    日本の男の人はよく紺のスーツを着ます。　(Japanese men often wear
    　　　　　　　　　　　　　　　　　　　　navy blue suits.)

17. 柔* = [　] + [　]
　　彼は柔道がとくいです。

(He is very skilled at jūdō.)

18. 務 = [　] + [　] + [　]
　　今度の会議で彼は議長を務めることになりました。
　　こんど　　　　　　　　　　　　ぎちょう

(It has been decided that he will be the Chairman of the upcoming meeting.)

Six Stroke Kanji (Numbers 1 through 13)

Kanji and Examples			Stroke Order and Practice

1. ‡6 糸 (thread)

紫* むらさき／シ (purple)

素 ソ／ス (element, base, uncovered, simple)

| いと | 生糸 (きいと raw silk) | 毛糸 (けいと woolen yarn, pg. 116) |
| シ | 銀糸 (ギンシ silver thread) | |

2. ‡6 耳 (ear)

聖 セイ (holy, pg. 125)

聞 き・く／ブン (hear, pg. 40)

| みみ | 耳に入る (みみにはいる reach one's ears) | 早耳 (はやみみ sharp ears, esp. for gossip) |
| ジ | 耳鼻科 (ジビカ otorhinology (ear & nose specialty)) | |

3. 6 虫 (insect)

蚕 かいこ (silk worm, pg. 114)

独 ドク (alone, pg. 22)

風 かぜ (wind, pg. 3)

| むし | 虫歯 (むしば decayed tooth) | 虫めがね (むしめがね magnifying glass) |
| チュウ | 益虫 (エキチュウ beneficial insect) | 幼虫(ヨウチュウ larva) |

4. 6 羽 (feather, wing)

翌 ヨク (next, following)

習 なら・う／シュウ (learn)

翼* つばさ／ヨク (wing)

| は／はね | 羽織 (はおり Japanese half-coat) | 一羽 (イチわ one bird) | 羽ぶとん (はねぶとん down quilt) |
| ウ | 羽毛 (ウモウ feathers, down) | | |

‡ 糸 appeared as *ito·hen* on pg. 19.
‡ 耳 appeared as *mimi·hen* on pg. 19.

Kanji and Examples		Stroke Order and Practice
5. ‡6 竹 (bamboo)	筆 ふで (writing brush, pg. 69) 節 ふし (joint, pg. 26) 答 こた・える (answer, pg. 29)	ノ ⺊ 竹 ⺮ ⺮ 竹 竹 竹
たけ	竹の子 (たけのこ bamboo shoot)	竹やぶ (たけやぶ bamboo grove)
チク	竹馬の友 (チクバのとも childhood playmate)	竹林 (チクリン bamboo grove)
6. ‡6 米 (rice, America, meter (about 39 in.))	迷 まよ・う (stray) 歯 は／シ (teeth) 継 つ・ぐ (succeed, inherit)	⺊ ⺌ 半 米 米 米 米
こめ	米屋 (こめや rice store)	もち米 (もちごめ sweet rice)
ベイ／マイ	米国 (ベイコク U.S.A.)	米価 (ベイカ price of rice) 白米 (ハクマイ polished rice, pg. 140)
7. 6 色 (color, pg. 3)	絶 た・える (become extinct, discontinue)	⺈ ⺈ 刍 刍 色 色 色 色
いろ	色紙 (いろがみ colored paper)	水色 (みずいろ light blue, pg. 114) 茶色 (チャいろ light brown)
ショク／シキ	特色 (トクショク characteristic) 原色 (ゲンショク primary color) 色彩 (シキサイ color)	
8. 6 羊 (sheep, pg. 51)	洋 ヨウ (ocean, pg. x) 群 む・れ (flock) 鮮* セン (fresh)	⺌ ⺍ 半 半 羊 羊 羊
ひつじ	子羊 (こひつじ lamb)	
ヨウ	羊毛 (ヨウモウ wool, pg. 116)	

‡ 竹 appeared as *take·kammuri* on pg. 29.
‡ 米 appeared as *kome·hen* on pg. 18.

Kanji and Examples	Stroke Order and Practice

9. 6 肉 （meat, flesh, pg. xii）

腐* くさ・る／フ (rot)

肉 ｜ 冂 内 肉 肉 肉 肉 肉

| ニク | 牛肉（ギュウニク beef, pg. 115）　鳥肉（とりニク poultry）　肉屋（ニクや butcher） |

10. 6 血 （blood）

衆 シュウ (the people, the masses)

血 ノ 亻 占 冊 帅 血 血 血

| ち | 鼻血（はなぢ nose bleed） |
| ケツ | 血色（ケッショク color in one's cheeks）　出血（シュッケツ bleeding） |

11. 6 舌 （tongue, pg. 97）

活 カツ (vigor)
乱 ラン (disorder, pg. 50)
話 はな・す／ワ (speak, pg. 19)

舌 ノ 二 千 千 舌 舌 舌 舌

| した | 舌（した tongue, pg. 97） |
| ゼツ | 弁舌（ベンゼツ a speech, eloquence）　毒舌（ドクゼツ malicious tongue, blistering remarks） |

12. 6 寺 （temple, pg. 107）

待 ま・つ (wait, pg. 21)
等 ひと・しい (equal, pg. 29)
詩 シ (verse, poetry)

寺 二 十 土 圭 寺 寺 寺 寺

| てら | 山寺（やまでら mountain temple）　あま寺（あまでら convent） |
| ジ | 寺院（ジイン [Buddhist] temple） |

Kanji and Examples			Stroke Order and Practice							
13. ‡6 衣 (clothes)	裁	サイ (cut, pass judgment, pg. 71)	⺌	亠	产	产	衣	衣	衣	衣
	製	セイ (manufacture)								
	装	ショウ／ソウ (dress, pg. 56)								
ころも		衣がえ（ころもがえ seasonal change in clothes）								
イ		衣服（イフク clothes）　　衣食（イショク food & clothing）　　白衣（ハクイ white [lab] coat or uniform）								

‡ 衣 appeared as *koromo·hen* on pg. 23.

EXERCISES FOR SIX STROKE KANJI (NUMBERS 1 THROUGH 13)

WRITING EXERCISE

Fill in each box to make a word.

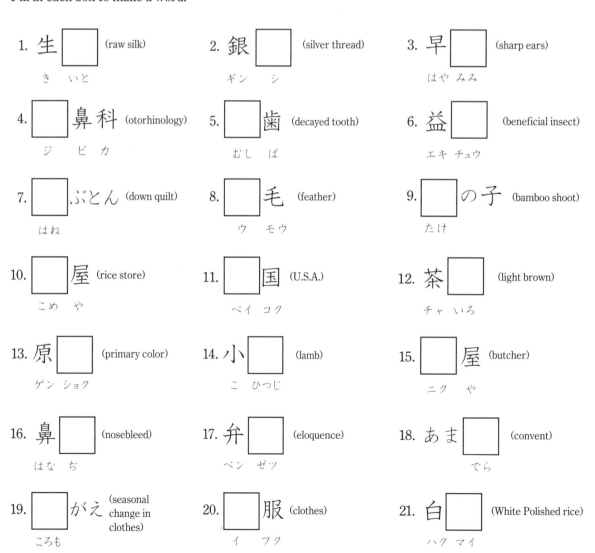

1. 生 ☐ (raw silk)
き いと

2. 銀 ☐ (silver thread)
ギン シ

3. 早 ☐ (sharp ears)
はや みみ

4. ☐ 鼻科 (otorhinology)
ジ ビ カ

5. ☐ 歯 (decayed tooth)
むし ば

6. ☐ 益 (beneficial insect)
エキ チュウ

7. ☐ ぶとん (down quilt)
はね

8. ☐ 毛 (feather)
ウ モウ

9. ☐ の子 (bamboo shoot)
たけ

10. ☐ 屋 (rice store)
こめ や

11. ☐ 国 (U.S.A.)
ベイ コク

12. 茶 ☐ (light brown)
チャ いろ

13. 原 ☐ (primary color)
ゲン ショク

14. 小 ☐ (lamb)
こ ひつじ

15. ☐ 屋 (butcher)
ニク や

16. 鼻 ☐ (nosebleed)
はな ち

17. 弁 ☐ (eloquence)
ベン ゼツ

18. あま ☐ (convent)
でら

19. ☐ がえ (seasonal change in clothes)
ころも

20. ☐ 服 (clothes)
イ フク

21. 白 ☐ (White Polished rice)
ハク マイ

READING EXERCISE

Read the following sentences, and write the correct *furigana* (pronunciation of Kanji written in Hiragana regardless of whether the reading of the Kanji is On or Kun) below the underlined Kanji.

1. この<u>毛糸</u>でセーターをあむつもりです。   (I am planning to knit a sweater with this yarn.)

2. へんなうわさが<u>耳</u>に<u>入</u>ってきました。   (An unpleasant rumor reached my ears.)

3. <u>虫</u>めがねがなければこの<u>字</u>は<u>読</u>めません。   (I cannot read this character without a magnifying glass.)

4. わたしは<u>小鳥</u>を<u>一羽</u>かっています。   (I own one bird.)

5. <u>彼</u>とわたしは<u>竹馬</u>の<u>友</u>です。   (He and I have been friends since we were childhood playmates.)

6. <u>日本</u>では<u>米価</u>をきめるのは<u>大</u>きな政治問題です。   (Setting the price of rice is a big political issue in Japan.)
   せいじもんだい

7. この<u>映画</u>の<u>特色</u>は音楽のすばらしさです。   (The most striking feature of this movie is its beautiful music.)

8. <u>牛肉</u>と<u>鳥肉</u>とどっちが<u>好</u>きですか。   (Which do you like [better], beef or chicken?)

9. あなたは<u>近</u>ごろ<u>血色</u>がいいですね。   (Your complexion is good these days, isn't it?)

10. <u>彼</u>はときどき<u>毒舌</u>をはきます。   (He sometimes makes blistering remarks.)

11. <u>京都</u>には<u>寺院</u>がたくさんあります。   (There are many temples in Kyōto.)

12. <u>衣食住</u>は人間の<u>生活</u>にとって<u>大切</u>なものです。
　　　　　　　　にんげん

(Clothing, food, and shelter are important things for human life.)

ANALYZING AND READING EXERCISE FOR EXAMPLE KANJI

Analyze the following Kanji. Write the *furigana* below the underlined Kanji. (Some familiar Kanji are included in this exercise.)

1. 素 ＝ [　　] ＋ [　　]

　　"Oxygen" は<u>日本語</u>で<u>酸素</u>といいます。

(Oxygen is called "sanso" in Japanese.)

2. 紫* ＝ [　　] ＋ [　　] ＋ [　　]

　　この<u>紫</u>の<u>洋服</u>はとてもきれいです。

(This purple dress is very beautiful.)

3. 聞 ＝ [　　] ＋ [　　]

　　<u>彼</u>の<u>話</u>を<u>聞</u>きましたか。

(Did you hear his story?)

4. 独 ＝ [　　] ＋ [　　]

　　<u>七月</u><u>四日</u>は<u>米国</u>の<u>独立</u><u>記念日</u>です。
　　　　　　　　　　　　　　　　きねんび

(The 4th of July is America's Independence Day.)

5. 翌 ＝ [　　] ＋ [　　]

　　<u>雨</u>がふった<u>翌日</u>はあまりスモッグがありません。

(There isn't much smog the day after it rains.)

6. 答 ＝ [　　] ＋ [　　]

　　わたしの<u>質問</u>(question)にはっきり<u>答</u>えてください。
　　　　　しつもん

(Please answer my question clearly.)

7. 迷 ＝ [　　] ＋ [　　]

　　<u>友</u>だちを<u>訪</u>ねた<u>時</u>、<u>道</u>に<u>迷</u>ってしまいました。

(I got completely lost when I went to visit my friend.)

8. 継 ＝ [　　] ＋ [　　] ＋ [　　]

　　<u>彼</u>は<u>大学</u>を<u>出</u>るとすぐ<u>父</u>の<u>店</u>を<u>継</u>ぎました。

(As soon as he finished college he took over his father's store.)

9.　絶 = [　　] + [　　]
　　　彼と連絡(contact)が絶えてしまいました。　　　(I completely lost contact with him.)
　　　　　れんらく

10.　洋 = [　　] + [　　]
　　　飛行機(airplane)は今太平洋の上を飛んでいます。(The airplane is flying over
　　　ひこうき　　　　　　　　　　　　　と　　　　　the Pacific Ocean now.)

11.　鮮 = [　　] + [　　]
　　　この魚は新鮮ですね。　　　　　　　　　　(This fish is fresh, isn't it?)

12.　腐 = [　　] + [　　] + [　　]
　　　豆腐が好きですか。　　　　　　　　　　　(Do you like tōfu?)
　　　とう

13.　衆 = [　　] + [　　] + [　　] + [　　]
　　　このへんに公衆電話がありますか。　　　　(Is there a public telephone around
　　　　　　　　　　　　　　　　　　　　　　　here?)

14.　活 = [　　] + [　　]
　　　東京では生活費はどのぐらいかかりますか。(Approximately how much is the
　　　　　　　　　　　　　　　　　　　　　　　cost of living in Tōkyō?)

15.　待 = [　　] + [　　]
　　　たいへんお待たせいたしました。　　　　　(I'm sorry to have kept you waiting.)

16.　詩 = [　　] + [　　]
　　　彼は有名な(famous)詩人です。　　　　　　(He is a famous poet.)
　　　　　ゆうめい

17.　製 = [　　] + [　　] + [　　]
　　　これは新しい製品です。　　　　　　　　　(This is a new product.)

Six Stroke Kanji (Numbers 14 through 26)

Kanji and Examples	Stroke Order and Practice

14. 百 6 (hundred)

	Stroke order: 一 丆 丆 而 百 百 百 百

宿 やど／シュク (lodging, inn)

ヒャク	百万 (ヒャクマン one million) 二百人 (ニヒャクニン 200 people) 三百円 (サンビャクエン ¥300)

15. 兆 6 (sign, indication, trillion)

	Stroke order: ノ リ リ 兆 兆 兆 兆 兆

桃* もも／トウ (peach)
逃* に・げる／トウ (flee)
跳* と・ぶ／チョウ (jump, pg. 23)

きざ・す	兆し (きざし sign, indication)
チョウ	前兆 (ゼンチョウ sign, omen) 一兆円 (イッチョウエン one trillion yen)

16. 光 6 (light, ray, sunlight, pg. 34)

	Stroke order: ｜ ⺌ ⺌ 丷 半 光 光 光

ひかり／ひか・る	光 (ひかり light, ray, sunlight, pg. 34) いな光り (いなびかり lightning) 光る (ひかる to shine, twinkle)
コウ	光線 (コウセン ray of light) 日光 (ニッコウ sunshine)

17. 先 6 (previous, in advance, point, pg. 34)

	Stroke order: ⺊ 𠂉 牛 生 歩 先 先 先

洗 あら・う／セン (wash)
銑* セン (pig iron)

さき	先ばらい (さきばらい advance payment) ペン先 (ペンさき tip of a pen) 先に (さきに previously, ahead)
セン	先生 (センセイ teacher) 先月 (センゲツ last month) 先日 (センジツ the other day, pg. 113)

Kanji and Examples		Stroke Order and Practice
18. **2** 毎 (every, pg. 50)	梅 うめ (plum, pg. 60) 海 うみ／カイ (sea, pg. xii) 悔*カイ (regret)	⼃　⼇．　⼌．　勽．　毎　毎．　毎　毎
	マイ	毎日(マイニチ every day) 毎朝 (マイあさ every morning) 毎晩 (マイばん every night [evening])

19. **6** 年 (year, pg. 50)		⼃　⼇．　乍　仨　仨．　年　年　年
	とし	年上（としうえ older, senior) 今年（ことし this year, pg. 122） 毎年（マイとし every year）
	ネン	年末（ネンマツ year end) 年令（ネンレイ age) 一年（イチネン one year）

20. **6** 合 (together, combine, match, gō = 0.18 liters or 0.381 pt.)	答 こた・える (answer, pg. 29) 拾 ひろ・う (pick up) 給 キュウ (supply)	⼃　⼂　今　合　合　合　合　合
	あ・う／あ・わす	合かぎ（あいかぎ duplicate key) 知り合い（しりあい acquaintance) 見合い（みあい arranged marriage interview)
	ゴウ／ガッ／（カッ）	合計 (ゴウケイ total) 合衆国 (ガッシュウコク United States) 合戦 (カッセン a battle)

21. **6** 各 (each)	客 キャク (guest, pg. 55) 格 カク (status, standard) 落 お・ちる／ラク (fall)	⼃　勿　冬　冬　各　各　各　各
	おのおの	各（おのおの each one)
	カク	各自（カクジ each individual) 各国 (カッコク each country) 各地 (カクチ each place)

Kanji and Examples		Stroke Order and Practice
22. 自 6 (oneself)	息 いき (breath) 鼻 はな (nose)	′ ⁄ 丷 ⁄ 宀 → 白 → 自 ↓ 自 | 自 | 自
みずか・ら	自ら (みずから oneself)	
ジ／シ	自分 (ジブン self)　　　　自由 (ジユウ freedom, pg. 140)　　　　自然 (シゼン nature)	

23. 同 6 (same, pg. 3)	銅 ドウ (copper, pg. 20) 胴* ドウ (torso)	′ ⁊ → 冂 ⁄ 冋 → 同 → 同 → 同 | 同 | 同
おな・じ	同じ (おなじ same, pg. 3)　　　　同じ年 (おなじとし same year)	
ドウ	同一 (ドウイツ identical, pg. 90)　　　同窓 (ドウソウ alumni)　　　共同 (キョウドウ cooperation, partnership)	

24. 曲 6 (to curve, to bend, melody)	豊 ゆた・か (rich, abundant) 農 ノウ (agriculture, pg. 72)	′ ⁊ → 冂 ⁄ 団 ⁄ 曲 → 曲 | 曲 | 曲
ま・がる／ま・げる	曲がり角 (まがりかど corner)　　　　曲げる (ま・げる to bend, to curve)	
キョク	曲線 (キョクセン curved line)　　　曲目 (キョクモク title of a piece of music)　　　作曲 (サッキョク musical composition)	

25. 西 ‡6 (west)		′ ⁻ ⁄ 一 ⁄ 两 ⁄ 西 ⁄ 西 → 西 | 西 | 西
にし	西日 (にしび afternoon sun)　　　西日本 (にしニホン western Japan)　　　西むき (にしむき facing west)	
セイ／サイ	西洋 (セイヨウ the West)　　　西北 (セイホク northwest)　　　東西 (トウザイ east & west, the East & the West)	

‡ 西 A variation of this Kanji appeared on pg. 69 as 西.

Kanji and Examples	Stroke Order and Practice
26. 2 両 (both)	一 丆 丙 両 両 両 両 両
リョウ	両方 (リョウホウ both sides)　両手 (リョウて both hands)　両親 (リョウシン parents)

EXERCISES FOR SIX STROKE KANJI (NUMBERS 14 THROUGH 26)

WRITING EXERCISE
Fill in each box to make a word.

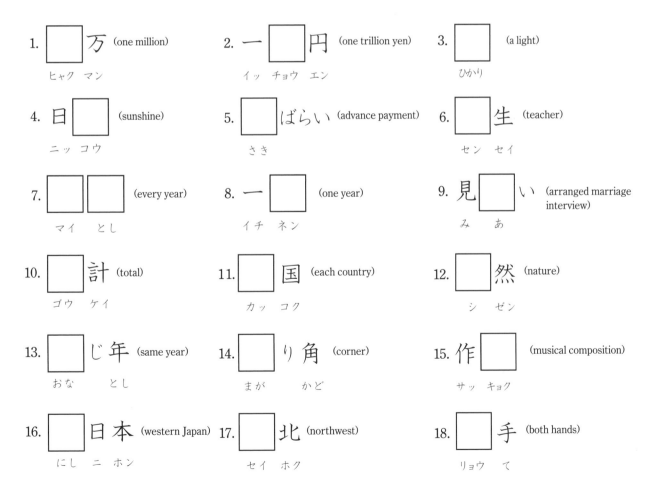

1. ☐ 万 (one million)
ヒャク　マン

2. 一 ☐ 円 (one trillion yen)
イッ　チョウ　エン

3. ☐ (a light)
ひかり

4. 日 ☐ (sunshine)
ニッ　コウ

5. ☐ ばらい (advance payment)
さき

6. ☐ 生 (teacher)
セン　セイ

7. ☐ ☐ (every year)
マイ　とし

8. 一 ☐ (one year)
イチ　ネン

9. 見 ☐ い (arranged marriage interview)
み　あ

10. ☐ 計 (total)
ゴウ　ケイ

11. ☐ 国 (each country)
カッ　コク

12. ☐ 然 (nature)
シ　ゼン

13. ☐ じ 年 (same year)
おな　とし

14. ☐ り 角 (corner)
まが　かど

15. 作 ☐ (musical composition)
サッ　キョク

16. ☐ 日本 (western Japan)
にし　ニ　ホン

17. ☐ 北 (northwest)
セイ　ホク

18. ☐ 手 (both hands)
リョウ　て

READING EXERCISE

Read the following sentences, and write the correct *furigana* (pronunciation of Kanji written in Hiragana regardless of whether the reading of the Kanji is On or Kun) below the underlined Kanji.

1. この<u>本</u>は<u>三百円</u>でした。 (This book cost ¥ 300.)

2. <u>木</u>の<u>芽</u>が<u>出</u>て<u>春</u>の<u>兆</u>しが<u>見</u>えてきました。 (Buds on the trees have come out marking [the arrival of] spring.)

3. UFOは<u>地震</u>*の<u>前兆</u>かもしれないといいます。
   じしん (They say that UFOs may be a sign of earthquakes.)

4. <u>夜空</u>に<u>星</u>が<u>光</u>っています。
   よぞら (Stars are twinkling in the night sky.)

5. <u>夏</u>は<u>太陽</u>の<u>光線</u>が<u>強</u>いからサングラスをかけます。
   こうせん (In summer, I wear sunglasses because the sunlight is strong.)

6. お<u>先</u>に<u>失礼</u>します。 (Please excuse me (going before you.))

7. <u>彼</u>は<u>毎晩</u>ビールを<u>飲</u>みます。 (He drinks beer every night.)

8. <u>年末</u>にハワイへ<u>行</u>くつもりです。 (I'm planning to go to Hawaii at the end of this year.)

9. <u>田中</u>さんは<u>昔</u>からの<u>知</u>り<u>合</u>いです。 (Tanaka-san is an old acquaintance [of mine].)

10. わたしはアメリカ<u>合衆国</u>の<u>国民</u>です。 (I am a citizen of the United States.)

11. <u>各地</u>でさくらの<u>花</u>がさきはじめました。 (Cherry blossoms began to bloom everywhere.)

12. <u>母</u>はいつも「<u>自分</u>のことは<u>自分</u>でしなさい。」と<u>言</u>います。　(Mother always says, "Take care of your own business by yourself.")

13. <u>彼</u>とわたしは<u>同窓生</u>です。　(He and I are alumni of the same school.)

14. <u>今晩</u>のコンサートの<u>曲目</u>は<u>何</u>ですか。　(What is the program for tonight's concert?)

15. <u>夏</u>、このへやは<u>西日</u>がさして<u>暑</u>いです。
　　　　　　　　　　　　　あつ
(The afternoon (west) sun shines in this room making it very warm in summer.)

16. あなたは<u>西洋</u><u>料理</u>が<u>好</u>きですか。　(Do you like Western food?)

17. シルクロードを<u>通</u>じて<u>東西</u><u>文化</u>の<u>交流</u>が
　　　　　　　　　　　　　　　　　こうりゅう
(Through the Silk Road, cultural exchange between East and West flourished.)

　　さかんになりました。

18. <u>両方</u>の<u>意見</u>を<u>聞</u>かないと<u>決</u>めることができません。
　　　　　い けん
(Unless we listen to both sides' opinions, we cannot reach a conclusion.)

ANALYZING AND READING EXERCISE FOR EXAMPLE KANJI

Analyze the following Kanji. Write the *furigana* below the underlined Kanji. (Some familiar Kanji are included in this exercise.)

1. 宿＝［　　］＋［　　］＋［　　］
　　　<u>毎日</u><u>宿題</u>がたくさんあります。
　　　　　　　　だい
(I have a lot of homework every day.)

2. 逃＝［　　］＋［　　］
　　　<u>犬</u>がほえるとどろぼうは<u>逃</u>げていきました。
(When the dog barked, the burglar ran away.)

3. 洗＝［　　］＋［　　］
　　　<u>車</u>を<u>洗</u>ったら<u>雨</u>がふりました。
(It rained after I washed my car.)

4. 梅 = [   ] + [   ]

梅の花がさいて春はもうすぐです。

(The plum blossoms are blooming, so spring is near.)

5. 拾 = [   ] + [   ]

きょう道でお金を拾いました。

(Today I found some money on the street.)

6. 給 = [   ] + [   ]

毎月、月末に給料をもらいます。

(I receive my salary at the end of every month.)

7. 格 = [   ] + [   ]

男女の賃金にはまだ格差があります。
　　　ちんぎん

(There is still a difference between men's and women's salaries.)

8. 息 = [   ] + [   ]

坂を登ると息が苦しいです。

(When I walk uphill I get short of breath (breathing is painful).)

9. 鼻 = [   ] + [   ] + [   ]

犬はよく鼻がききます。

(Dogs have a keen sense of smell.)

10. 銅 = [   ] + [   ]

オリンピックで彼女は銅メダルをもらいました。

(She received a bronze medal at the Olympics.)

11. 豊 = [   ] + [   ]

カリフォルニアは一年中くだものが豊かです。
　　　　　　　　　じゅう

(California is rich in fruits all year round.)

12. 農 = [   ] + [   ]

農家の人はいつがひまですか。

(When do farmers have free time?)

Six Stroke Kanji (Numbers 27 through 38)

Kanji and Examples		Stroke Order and Practice
27. **6** 州 (state, province, sandbank, pg. 2)	酬* シュウ (repay, reward)	⺀ 丿丨 丿𝗅 州 州 州 州 州
す	三角州 (サンカクす delta)	
シュウ	本州 (ホンシュウ Honshū (main island of Japan)) 欧*州 (オウシュウ Europe) 九州 (キュウシュウ Kyūshū island)	
28. **6** 共 (both, all, as well as, pg. 60)	異 イ (difference, uncommon) 供 キョウ (offer) 選 えら・ぶ／セン (choose)	二 十 艹 共 共 共 共 共
とも	共かせぎ (ともかせぎ [husband & wife] both working)	
キョウ	共学 (キョウガク coeducation) 共通 (キョウツウ common) 公共 (コウキョウ public, pg. 123)	
29. **6** 行 (go, conduct, line, row)	街 まち／ガイ (street, pg. 40) 術 ジュツ (tactics, pg. 40) 衛 エイ (defense, pg. 40)	丿 彳 彳 行 行 行 行 行
い・く／ゆ・く／ おこな・う	行く先 (いくさき／ゆくさき destination)	
コウ／ギョウ／(アン)	旅行 (リョコウ travel) 一行 (イチギョウ one line) 行火 (アンカ foot warmer)	
30. **6** 成 (become, consist of, do, form, pg. 65)	誠 まこと／セイ (truth, faithful-ness) 城 しろ／ジョウ (castle) 盛 さか・ん／セイ (thrive, pg. 33)	一 厂 厈 成 成 成 成 成
な・る／な・す	成り立つ (なりたつ consist of) 成り行き (なりゆき course [of events])	
セイ／(ジョウ)	成人 (セイジン adult) 成長 (セイチョウ growth) 成功 (セイコウ success)	

Kanji and Examples			Stroke Order and Practice

31. 式 **6**

(ceremony, formula, style, pg. 41)

試 ため・す／シ (try, attempt)

二 三 亍 式 式 式 式 式

シキ	形式 (ケイシキ formality)　　入学式 (ニュウガクシキ ceremony for entering school)　　洋式 (ヨウシキ Western style)

32. 交 **6**

(cross, intersect, exchange, pg. 122)

校 コウ (school, pg. 17)

効 コウ (be effective)

較* カク (compare)

亠 广 交 六 交 交 交 交

まじ・わる／か・わす	交わり (まじわり association, friendship)
コウ	交通 (コウツウ traffic)　　交流 (コウリュウ alternating current, exchange)　　外交 (ガイコウ diplomacy)

33. 因 **6**

(cause, factor, pg. 98)

恩 オン (debt of gratitude)

姻* イン (marriage, matrimony)

刂 冂 冃 因 因 因 因 因

よ・る	…に因る (…による due to, caused by)
イン	因果 (インガ cause & effect)　　原因 (ゲンイン cause)

34. 至 **6**

(utmost, attain, lead to)

室 シツ (room)

屋 や (shop, pg. 36)

倒 たお・れる (fall, collapse)

二 互 互 至 至 至 至 至

いた・る	至る所 (いたるところ everywhere)　　今に至るまで (いまにいたるまで until now)
シ	至急 (シキュウ urgent)　　至上 (シジョウ supreme, highest)　　必至 (ヒッシ inevitable)

Kanji and Examples			Stroke Order and Practice

35. ‡*6

舟

(boat)

船 ふね／セン (boat, pg. 19)

航 コウ (voyage, pg. 19)

Stroke order: ⸜ ノ ⼌ 月 月 舟 舟 舟

| ふね／(ふな) | わたし舟 (わたしぶね ferry)　舟歌 (ふなうた boatman's song) |
| シュウ | 舟行 (シュウコウ navigation, sailing) |

36. *6

吉

(good luck)

結 むす・ぶ／ケツ (bind, connect)

詰* つ・める／キツ (pack)

Stroke order: 一 十 士 吉 吉 吉 吉 吉

| キチ／キツ | 吉日 (キチジツ lucky day)　大吉 (ダイキチ splendid luck)　吉報 (キッポウ good news) |

37. *6

朱

(vermilion, red)

株 かぶ／シュ (stocks, shares, a stump)

殊* こと・に／シュ (especially)

珠* シュ (gem, jewel)

Stroke order: ⸜ 仁 仁 牛 牛 朱 朱 朱

| シュ | 朱色 (シュいろ vermilion)　朱肉 (シュニク red ink pad) |

38. *6

充

(fill, allocate)

統 トウ (govern, control)

銃* ジュウ (gun)

Stroke order: ⼍ 亠 充 云 亢 充 充 充

| あ・てる | 充てる (あてる allocate) |
| ジュウ | 充分 (ジュウブン enough, full)　充電 (ジュウデン charging [a battery]) |

‡ 舟 appeared as *fune·hen* on pg. 19.

EXERCISES FOR SIX STROKE KANJI (NUMBERS 27 THROUGH 38)

WRITING EXERCISE

Fill in each box to make a word.

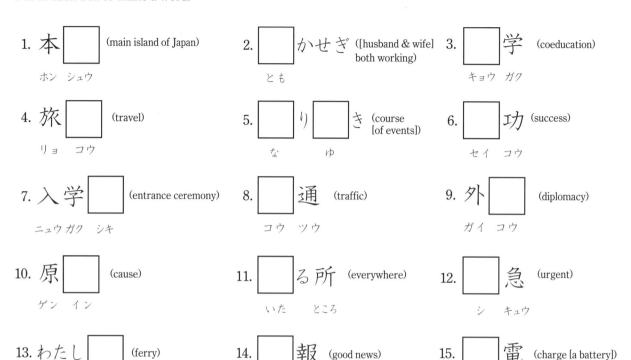

1. 本☐ (main island of Japan)
   ホン シュウ

2. ☐かせぎ ([husband & wife] both working)
   とも

3. ☐学 (coeducation)
   キョウ ガク

4. 旅☐ (travel)
   リョ コウ

5. ☐り☐き (course [of events])
   な ゆ

6. ☐功 (success)
   セイ コウ

7. 入学☐ (entrance ceremony)
   ニュウ ガク シキ

8. ☐通 (traffic)
   コウ ツウ

9. 外☐ (diplomacy)
   ガイ コウ

10. 原☐ (cause)
    ゲン イン

11. ☐る所 (everywhere)
    いた ところ

12. ☐急 (urgent)
    シ キュウ

13. わたし☐ (ferry)
    ぶね

14. ☐報 (good news)
    キッ ポウ

15. ☐電 (charge [a battery])
    ジュウ デン

READING EXERCISE

Read the following sentences, and write the correct *furigana* (pronunciation of Kanji written in Hiragana regardless of whether the reading of the Kanji is On or Kun) below the underlined Kanji.

1. 九州は本州の西南にあります。　(Kyūshū is southwest of Honshū.)
   せいなん

2. 近ごろの若い人の話題は何ですか。　(Currently, what are the [common] topics of conversation among young people?)
   わだい

3. 彼はだれにも行く先を言わないで家を出ました。　(He left home without telling anybody where he was going.)

4. 一行おきに書いてください。　(Please write on every other line.)

5. <u>子</u>どもの<u>成長</u>は<u>早</u>いですね。

(Children grow fast, don't they?
(Children's growth is fast, isn't it?))

6. <u>日本</u>は<u>四</u>つの<u>島</u>とおきなわから<u>成り立</u>っています。

(Japan consists of four islands and Okinawa.)

7. <u>日本人</u>はわりあいに<u>形式</u>を<u>重</u>んじます。
おも

(The Japanese place considerable importance upon formality.)

8. あなたのうちのおふろは<u>洋式</u>ですか、<u>和式</u>ですか。

(Is your bath Western style or Japanese style?)

9. <u>良</u>い<u>友</u>だちと<u>交</u>わるのはいいことです。
よ

(It is nice to associate with good friends.)

10. <u>世界</u><u>各国</u>と<u>文化</u><u>交流</u>をすすめていきたいです。

(We would like to promote cultural exchange with various countries of the world.)

11. <u>彼</u>の<u>病気</u>はストレスに<u>因</u>るものです。

(His illness is a result of stress.)

12. これは社長の<u>至上</u><u>命令</u>です。
しゃちょう

(This is the company president's absolute (highest authority) order.)

13. きょう<u>神社</u>で<u>大吉</u>のおみくじをひきました。

(Today at the shrine I drew a (written oracle with a) very lucky fortune.)

14. <u>日本</u>ではサインの<u>代</u>わりに<u>朱肉</u>をつけた<u>判</u>をつかいます。

(In Japan we use a seal with red ink in place of a signature.)

15. このお<u>金</u>は<u>本代</u>に<u>充</u>てるつもりです。

(I am budgeting this money for the purchase of books.)

16. 「もう<u>少</u>しいかがですか。」「いいえ、もう<u>充分</u>いただきました。」

("Would you like to have some more?" "No, thank you; I've had plenty.")

ANALYZING AND READING EXERCISE FOR EXAMPLE KANJI

Analyze the following Kanji. Write the *furigana* below the underlined Kanji. (Some familiar Kanji are included in this exercise.)

1. 酬 ＝ ［　　］ ＋ ［　　］
   コンサルタントへの報酬はいくらはらいますか。　(How much (compensation) are you paying the consultant?)

2. 異 ＝ ［　　］ ＋ ［　　］
   この夏の暑さは異常ですね。　(This summer's heat is unusual.)
   　　あつ

3. 供 ＝ ［　　］ ＋ ［　　］
   車の需要に対して供給が追いつきません。　(The supply of cars hasn't caught up with the demand.)
   　　じゅよう　たい

4. 選 ＝ ［　　］ ＋ ［　　］ ＋ ［　　］ ＋ ［　　］
   どのネクタイを選びますか。　(Which tie are you going to choose?)

5. 街 ＝ ［　　］ ＋ ［　　］
   ニューヨークの五番街を歩いたことがありますか。　(Have you ever walked [along] 5th Avenue in New York?)

6. 誠 ＝ ［　　］ ＋ ［　　］
   彼は人にたのまれたことは誠意をもってします。　(Whatever he is asked to do [by other people] he does conscientiously.)

7. 城 ＝ ［　　］ ＋ ［　　］
   日本にはあちらこちらにきれいなお城が　(Throughout Japan there are many beautiful castles.)
   たくさんあります。

8. 盛 ＝ ［　　］ ＋ ［　　］
   日本では今サッカーがとても盛んです。　(In Japan, soccer is very popular now.)

9.　試＝［　］＋［　］
　　　こんどの<u>試験</u>はいつですか。 　　　　　　　　(When is the next test?)

10.　較＝［　］＋［　］
　　　わたしは<u>比較</u><u>文学</u>を<u>研究</u>しています。 　　(I am doing research in comparative literature.)

11.　恩＝［　］＋［　］
　　　<u>父母</u>の<u>恩</u>は<u>山</u>より<u>高</u>く<u>海</u>よりもふかいです。 (My debt to my parents is higher than the mountains and deeper than the ocean.)

12.　室＝［　］＋［　］
　　　<u>教室</u>に<u>学生</u>が<u>二十人</u>ほどいます。 　　(There are about twenty students in the classroom.)

13.　屋＝［　］＋［　］
　　　パン<u>屋</u>のとなりに<u>本屋</u>があります。 　　(Next to the bakery there is a bookstore.)

14.　船＝［　］＋［　］
　　　<u>船</u>で<u>世界</u><u>旅行</u>をしたいです。 　　　(I want to take a trip around the world by boat.)

15.　航＝［　］＋［　］＋［　］
　　　<u>彼</u>は<u>航空</u><u>会社</u>に<u>勤</u>めています。 　　(He is working for an airline company.)

16.　結＝［　］＋［　］
　　　くつのひもを<u>結</u>ばないところびますよ。 　　(If you don't tie your shoelace you'll trip.)

17.　株＝［　］＋［　］
　　　<u>今</u>、<u>銀行株</u>を<u>買</u>ったらいいかもしれません。 (It may be a good idea to purchase bank stocks right now.)

18. 統＝ ［　］ ＋ ［　］
　　　ハンドバッグと靴は<u>同</u>じ<u>色</u>で
　　　　　　　　　くっ
　　　<u>統一</u>した<u>方</u>がいいです。

(It's better to match (unify) the
color of your shoes and handbag.)

Seven Stroke Kanji (Numbers 1 through 14)

Kanji and Examples			Stroke Order and Practice

1. 見 **7**

(see, visible, show, pg. 34)

親	おや／シン (parent)
覚	おぼ・える (remember, memorize)
規	キ (regulation, pg. 115)

Stroke order: 刂 冂 门 月 目 貝 見 見 見

み・る／み・える／み・せる：見本 (みホン sample)　見方 (みかた way of looking at, viewpoint)　花見 (はなみ flower viewing)

ケン：見物 (ケンブツ sightseeing)　意見 (イケン opinion)　発見 (ハッケン discover)

2. 貝 ‡**7**

(shellfish)

負	ま・ける (lose)
員	イン (member)
賞	ショウ (prize, pg. 55)

Stroke order: 刂 冂 门 月 目 貝 貝 貝 貝

かい：貝柱 (かいばしら scallop)　貝がら (かいがら shell)　赤貝 (あかがい ark shell)

3. 足 ‡**7**

(leg, foot, counter for pairs of footwear, enough, add, pg. 3)

促*	うなが・す／ソク (urge)

Stroke order: 口 早 早 早 足 足 足

あし／た・りる／た・る／た・す：足あと (あしあと footprint)　足りる (たりる enough)　足し算 (たしザン addition)

ソク：遠足 (エンソク excursion)　一足 (イッソク pair of shoes, socks)

4. 走 ‡**7**

(run)

徒	ト (stroll, fellow, purposeless)
起	お・きる (get up, pg. 38)

Stroke order: 一 十 土 キ キ 走 走 走 走

はし・る：走る (はしる run)　走り高跳び (はしりたかとび running high jump)

ソウ：競走 (キョウソウ race)

‡ 貝　appeared as *kai·hen* on pg. 19 and *kai·ashi* on pg. 33.
‡ 足　appeared as *ashi·hen* on pg. 23.
‡ 走　appeared as *sō·nyo* on pg. 38.

Kanji and Examples		Stroke Order and Practice
5. ‡7 車 (vehicle, car, wheel, pg. 6)	連 つ・れる／レン (accompaniment, link) 軍 グン (the military, pg. 29) 庫 コ (storehouse)	一 厂 厉 盲 百 亘 車 車 車
くるま	車いす（くるまいす wheelchair）　車代（くるまダイ fare for transportation, pg. 165）	
シャ	電車（デンシャ electric train）　車内（シャナイ inside (the car)）　新車（シンシャ new car）	
6. 7 里 (village, old unit of distance)	野 の／ヤ (field, pg. 131) 量 リョウ (quantity, volume) 理 リ (reason, pg. 17)	丿 口 臼 日 甲 里 里 里 里
さと	里心（さとごころ homesickness）　里帰り（さとがえり bride's first visit back to her old home）	
リ	一里（イチリ 2.44miles, 3.927km.）　郷里（キョウリ hometown）	
7. ‡7 言 (say, word)	信 しん・じる (trust) 警 ケイ (warn, pg. 157)	` 亠 宀 言 言 言 言 言 言
い・う／こと	言い方（いいかた manner in which something is said）　言葉（ことば word）	
ゲン／ゴン	言語（ゲンゴ language, speech）　方言（ホウゲン dialect）　伝言（デンゴン message）	
8. 7 豆 (bean)	頭 あたま／トウ (head, pg. 27) 短 みじか・い／タン (short, pg. 18) 登 のぼ・る／トウ (climb, pg. 30)	亠 一 厂 亘 豆 豆 豆 豆 豆
まめ	豆もち（まめもち rice cake with black soybeans）　黒豆（くろまめ black soybean）	
トウ／（ズ）	豆腐*（トウフ tōfu, beancurd）　大豆（ダイズ soybean）	

‡ 車 appeared as *kuruma·hen* on pg. 19.

‡ 言 appeared as *gomben* on pg. 19.

Kanji and Examples			Stroke Order and Practice

9. 谷 **7** (valley)

容 ヨウ (appearance, content)
欲 ヨク (desire, pg. 25)
浴 あ・びる／ヨク (bathe)

Stroke order: 丷 丷 〵 〴 谷 谷 谷 谷 谷

たに — 谷川 (たにがわ mountain stream)　谷間 (たにま valley, ravine)

コク — けい谷 (けいコク valley, gorge)

10. 角 **7** (angle, corner, animal horn)

解 と・く／カイ (solve, pg. 115)
触* ふ・れる (touch, feel)

Stroke order: 丿 𠂉 勹 ⺈ 角 角 角 角 角

かど／つの — 四つ角 (よつかど cross roads)　しかの角 (しかのつの antler)

カク — 角度 (カクド angle)　三角 (サンカク triangle)　方角 (ホウガク direction)

9. 身 **2** (body)

射 い・る／シャ (shoot, pg. 25)
謝 シャ (thank)

Stroke order: 丿 𠂉 冂 𠃌 身 身 身 身 身

み — 身内 (みうち relatives)　身分証明 (みブンショウメイ identification)　中身 (なかみ contents)

シン — 身長 (シンチョウ height)　独身 (ドクシン unmarried)　自身 (ジシン oneself)

12. 良 **7** (good)

食 た・べる (eat)
浪* ロウ (wander, waves)
娘* むすめ (daughter)

Stroke order: 丶 ㇇ ヨ ヨ 良 良 良 良 良

よ・い — 良い友だち (よいともだち good friend)

リョウ — 良心 (リョウシン conscience)　改良 (カイリョウ improvement, reform)

Kanji and Examples			Stroke Order and Practice								
13. **臣** 7	緊 キン (tense, tight) 覧 ラン (look, pg. 82)		二	厂	厂	戸	臣	臣	臣	臣	臣
(subject, vassal)											
シン / ジン	近臣 (キンシン trusted vassal)　大臣 (ダイジン cabinet member, minister of state)										

Kanji and Examples			Stroke Order and Practice								
14. **兵** 7	浜 はま／ヒン (beach, seashore)		'	宀	戸	丘	兵	兵	兵	兵	兵
(soldier)											
ヘイ／(ヒョウ)	兵隊 (ヘイタイ military serviceman)　歩兵 (ホヘイ infantryman)　兵糧 (ヒョウリョウ rations, provisions)										

EXERCISES FOR SEVEN STROKE KANJI (NUMBERS 1 THROUGH 14)

WRITING EXERCISE
Fill in each box to make a word.

1. 花☐ (flower viewing)
はな み

2. ☐物 (sight seeing)
ケン ブツ

3. ☐柱 (scallop)
かい ばしら

4. ☐あと (footprint)
あし

5. 遠☐ (excursion)
エン ソク

6. ☐り高跳び (running high jump)
はし たかと

7. 競☐ (race)
キョウ ソウ

8. ☐いす (wheel chair)
くるま

9. 電☐ (electric train)
デン シャ

10. ☐帰り (bride's first visit back to her old home)
さと がえ

11. 一☐ (2.44mi., 3.927km)
イチ リ

12. ☐い方 (manner in which something is said)
い

13. ☐葉 (word)
こと ば

14. 方☐ (dialect)
ホウ ゲン

15. 黒☐ (black soybean)
くろ まめ

16. 大☐ (soy bean)
ダイ ズ

17. ☐川 (mountain stream)
たに がわ

18. ☐度 (angle)
カク ド

19. しかの☐ (antler)
つの

20. ☐分証明 (identification)
み ブンショウメイ

21. ☐長 (height)
シン チョウ

22. ☐心 (conscience)
リョウ シン

23. 大☐ (governmental minister)
ダイ ジン

24. ☐隊 (military serviceman)
ヘイ タイ

READING EXERCISE

Read the following sentences, and write the correct *furigana* (pronunciation of Kanji written in Hiragana regardless of whether the reading of the Kanji is On or Kun) below the underlined Kanji.

1. その<u>見本</u>を<u>見</u>せてください。 (Please show me that sample.)

2. コロンブスがアメリカ<u>大陸</u>を<u>発見</u>したと<u>言</u>われています。 (It is said that Colombus discovered the American continent.)

3. わたしは<u>赤貝</u>のさしみが<u>大好</u>きです。 (I like ark-shell sashimi very much.)

4. <u>本</u>を<u>買</u>うお<u>金</u>が<u>足</u>りません。 (I don't have enough money to buy the book.)

5. きょう靴を<u>一足</u> <u>買</u>いました。
　　　くつ (I bought a pair of shoes today.)

6. 「<u>今度</u><u>買</u>った<u>新車</u>は<u>何</u>ですか。」「ニッサンです。」 ("What kind of new car did you buy this time?" "It's a Nissan.")

7. <u>家</u>を<u>出</u>てから<u>長</u>いので<u>里心</u>がついてきました。 (It has been a long time since I left home, and I am starting to feel homesick.)

8. あなたの<u>郷里</u>はどちらですか。 (What is the name of (where is) your home town?)

9. あの<u>方</u>は<u>言語学</u>を<u>勉強</u>しています。 (He/she (that person) is studying linguistics.)

10. <u>何</u>か<u>伝言</u>がございますか。 (Is there any message?)

11. <u>彼女</u>は<u>谷間</u>の<u>白</u>ゆりのような<u>人</u>です。
　　　　　　　しら (She is like [as modest and refined as] a white lily blooming in the valley (ravine).)

12. その<u>四</u>つ<u>角</u>を<u>左</u>へ<u>曲</u>がるとすぐきっさ<u>店</u>が<u>見</u>えます。 (Right after turning left at that intersection you will see the coffee shop.)

13. この<u>箱</u>の<u>中身</u>は<u>何</u>ですか。
   はこ
   (What are the contents of this box?)

14. わたしはまだ<u>独身</u>です。 (I am still single.)

15. <u>車</u>は<u>毎年</u><u>改良</u>されています。 (Cars are being improved every year.)

16. <u>山田</u>さんとわたしは<u>良</u>い<u>友</u>だちです。 (Yamada-san and I are good friends.)

ANALYZING AND READING EXERCISE FOR EXAMPLE KANJI

Analyze the following Kanji. Write the *furigana* below the underlined Kanji. (Some familiar Kanji are included in this exercise.)

1. 親 ＝ ［　］ ＋ ［　］ ＋ ［　］
   あの<u>子</u>は<u>父親</u>にとてもよく<u>似</u>ています。 (That child resembles its father very much.)

2. 覚 ＝ ［　］ ＋ ［　］ ＋ ［　］
   あしたまでに<u>漢字</u>を<u>二十</u>
   <u>覚</u>えなければなりません。 (I have to memorize 20 Kanji by tomorrow.)

3. 負 ＝ ［　］ ＋ ［　］
   サッカーの<u>試合</u>で<u>彼</u>のティームが
   しあい
   <u>負</u>けました。 (His team lost in the soccer match.)

4. 賞 ＝ ［　］ ＋ ［　］ ＋ ［　］ ＋ ［　］
   スピーチ・コンテストに<u>出</u>て<u>賞品</u>をもらいました。 (I entered the speech contest and won a prize.)

5. 促*＝［　］＋［　］
   <u>彼女</u>に<u>貸</u>したお<u>金</u>のさい<u>促</u>をしました。 (I demanded that she pay me back the money I lent her.)

6. 徒＝［　］＋［　］
   <u>今</u> <u>日本語</u>のクラスに<u>生徒</u>が<u>何人</u>いますか。 (Currently how many students are there in your Japanese class?)

7. 連＝［　］＋［　］
   <u>子</u>どもを<u>連</u>れて<u>公園</u>へ<u>行</u>きました。 (I took the children and went to the park.)

8. 軍＝［　］＋［　］
   <u>彼</u>は<u>空軍</u>のパイロットです。 (He is a pilot in the Air Force.)

9. 野＝［　］＋［　］
   <u>野原</u>で<u>子</u>どもたちとあそびました。 (I played with the children in the field.)

10. 理＝［　］＋［　］
    <u>彼女</u>は<u>料理</u>がじょうずです。 (She is good at cooking.)

11. 信＝［　］＋［　］
    わたしの<u>言</u>うことを<u>信</u>じてください。 (Please believe what I say.)

12. 頭＝［　］＋［　］
    <u>彼</u>はとても<u>頭</u>がいいです。 (He is very intelligent.)

13. 短＝［　］＋［　］
    <u>短</u>いスカートはまだはやっていますか。 (Are short skirts still in style?)

14. 容 ＝ ［　　］ ＋ ［　　］
　　　この本の内容はたいしたことはありません。　(There isn't much to the content of this book.)

15. 謝 ＝ ［　　］ ＋ ［　　］ ＋ ［　　］
　　　お世話になった人に感謝しましょう。　(We should (Let's) show gratitude to people to whom we are indebted.)

16. 娘 ＝ ［　　］ ＋ ［　　］
　　　わたしの娘は今大学生です。　(My daughter is currently a college student.)

17. 覧 ＝ ［　　］ ＋ ［　　］ ＋ ［　　］
　　　これをご覧ください。　(Please take a look at this.)

18. 浜 ＝ ［　　］ ＋ ［　　］
　　　砂浜で子どもたちがあそんでいます。　(The children are playing on the beach (sandy shore).)

Seven Stroke Kanji (Numbers 15 through 26)

Kanji and Examples		Stroke Order and Practice
15. 求 **7** (seek, request, demand, pg. 64)	球 たま／キュウ (ball, bulb, sphere, pg. 17) 救 すく・う／キュウ (rescue)	一　寸　寸　求　求　求　求　求
もと・める	求める（もとめる　seek, request, demand, pg. 64）	
キュウ	求人（キュウジン　Help Wanted）　　要求（ヨウキュウ　demand）　　追求（ツイキュウ　pursuit）	
16. 束 **7** (bunch, ream)	速 はや・い／ソク (speedy) 整 セイ (put in order, pg. 141) 頼* たよ・る (rely on)	一　一　戸　戸　束　束　束　束　束
たば	一束（ひとたば　a bundle, a bunch）　　花束（はなたば　bouquet）　　札束（さつたば　roll of notes）	
ソク	約束（ヤクソク　promise）　　結束（ケッソク　unity）	
17. 来 **7** (come)		一　一　平　平　平　来　来　来　来
く・る／き・ます／こ・ない	来る（くる　come）　　来ます（きます　come）　　来ない（こない　not come）	
ライ	来週（ライシュウ　next week）　　来月（ライゲツ　next month）　　来年（ライネン　next year）	
18. 余 **7** (remainder, surplus, not very)	途* ト (way, route) 除 のぞ・く (exclude) 斜* なな・め (diagonal, pg. 133)	ノ　ハ　合　今　余　余　余　余　余
あま・る／あま・す	余り（あまり　remainder, too much, not very）	
ヨ	余分（ヨブン　excess）　　余地（ヨチ　room, margin）　　余計（ヨケイ　surplus, extra）	

Kanji and Examples		Stroke Order and Practice
19. 赤 7 (red, pg. 99)	赦* シャ (pardon) 嚇* カク (threaten)	二　亠　赤　赤　赤　赤　赤　赤　赤
あか / あか・い	赤字 (あかじ deficit, in the red)　赤んぼう (あかんぼう baby)　赤い花 (あかいはな red flower)	
セキ / (シャク)	赤道 (セキドウ equator)　赤十字 (セキジュウジ Red Cross)　赤銅 (シャクドウ gold-copper alloy)	
20. 我 7 (oneself, pg. 27)	義 ギ (righteousness) 議 ギ (deliberation, debate) 餓* ガ (hunger)	ノ　二　千　手　我　我　我　我　我
われ / わ	我我 (われわれ we)　我が国 (わがくに our country)	
ガ	我まん (ガまん patience)　自我 (ジガ self, ego)	
21. 君 7 (suffix for younger person, you, ruler, pg. 57)	郡 グン (county, pg. 26) 群 むれ / グン (flock, pg. 174)	ヲ　ヲ　ヲ　尹　尹　君　君　君　君
きみ	君が代 (きみがよ "Kimi ga Yo", Japan's national anthem)	
クン	君主国 (クンシュコク monarchy)　中村君 (なかむらクン (Mr./Ms.) Nakamura)	
22. 告 7 (announce, inform)	造 つく・る / ゾウ (make, build) 酷* コク (cruel, severe)	ノ　广　牛　生　告　告　告　告　告
つ・げる	告げ口 (つげぐち tell on, tattle)	
コク	告白 (コクハク confession)　広告 (コウコク advertisement, pg. 157)　申告 (シンコク report, pg. 141)	

Kanji and Examples	Stroke Order and Practice

23. 7 系 (lineage, system)

係 かかり／ケイ (in charge, duty)
孫 まご (grandchildren, pg. 16)

Stroke order: `ゝ` `乄` `幺` `幺` `乒` `系` `系` 系 系

ケイ	アジア系 (アジアケイ Asian descent)　　日系 (ニッケイ Japanese descent)　　体系 (タイケイ system)

24. 7 図 (diagram, plan, pg. 41)

Stroke order: `丨` `冂` `冈` `冈` `図` `図` 図 図 図

はか・る	図る (はかる to plan, to scheme)
ズ／ト	地図 (チズ map)　　図書館 (トショカン library)

25. 7 麦 (barley, wheat, pg. 55)

Stroke order: `二` `十` `キ` `圭` `声` `麦` `麦` 麦 麦

むぎ	麦茶 (むぎチャ barley tea)　　小麦 (こむぎ wheat, pg. 98)
バク	麦芽 (バクガ malt, wheat germ)

26. 7 卵 (egg)

Stroke order: `ゝ` `乍` `仁` `卩` `卵` `卵` `卵` 卵 卵

たまご	卵焼き (たまごやき omelette)　生卵 (なまたまご raw egg)
ラン	卵白 (ランパク egg white)　卵黄 (ランオウ yolk)

EXERCISES FOR SEVEN STROKE KANJI (NUMBERS 15 THROUGH 26)

WRITING EXERCISE
Fill in each box to make a word.

1. 要 ☐ (demand)
ヨウ キュウ

2. 花 ☐ (bouquet)
はな たば

3. 約 ☐ (promise)
ヤク ソク

4. ☐ る (come)
く

5. ☐ 週 (next week)
ライ シュウ

6. ☐ 分 (excess)
ヨ ブン

7. ☐ 字 (deficit, in the red)
あか ジ

8. ☐ 道 (equator)
セキ ドウ

9. ☐ が 国 (our country)
わ くに

10. 自 ☐ (self)
ジ ガ

11. ☐ が 代 (Japan's national anthem)
きみ よ

12. ☐ 主 国 (monarchy)
クン シュ コク

13. ☐ げ口 (tell on)
つ ぐち

14. 広 ☐ (advertisement)
コウ コク

15. 日 ☐ (Japanese descent)
ニッ ケイ

16. 地 ☐ (map)
チ ズ

17. 小 ☐ (wheat)
こ むぎ

18. 生 ☐ (raw egg)
なま たまご

READING EXERCISE
Read the following sentences, and write the correct *furigana* (pronunciation of Kanji written in Hiragana regardless of whether the reading of the Kanji is On or Kun) below the underlined Kanji.

1. 人人 はみんな 世界 の 平和 を 求 めています。 (Everyone wants world peace.)
ひとびと

2. 求人 広告 が 新聞 にたくさん 出 ています。 (Many Help Wanted ads are listed in the newspaper.)

3. ほうれんそうを 一束 買 いました。 (I bought one bunch of spinach.)

207

4. 「<u>山田</u>さんはいつロス・アンジェルスへ<u>来</u>ますか。」
「<u>今年</u>は<u>来</u>ないそうです。」

("When is Yamada-san coming to Los Angeles?" "I hear that he is not coming this year.")

5. <u>余</u>り<u>食</u>べ<u>過</u>ぎておなかが<u>痛</u>くなりました。

(I overate and got a stomachache.)

6. <u>一人</u>でできますから<u>余計</u>な<u>心配</u>をしないでください。
   しんぱい

(I can do it by myself, so don't worry (too much.))

7. <u>赤</u>いセーターを<u>買</u>いました。

(I bought a red sweater.)

8. <u>彼</u>は<u>赤十字</u><u>病院</u>に<u>入院</u>しました。

(He was admitted to the Red Cross Hospital.)

9. <u>歯</u>が<u>痛</u>くて<u>我</u>まんできませんでした。

(My tooth was so painful that I couldn't bear it.)

10. <u>中村</u><u>君</u>はわたしの<u>友</u>だちです。

(Nakamura is my friend.)

11. <u>彼女</u>にわたしの<u>気持</u>ちを<u>告白</u>するつもりです。

(I intend to reveal (confess) my feelings to her.)

12. ロス・アンジェルスではアジア<u>系</u>の<u>人口</u>が
    ずいぶんふえています。

(The Asian population has been increasing greatly in Los Angeles.)

13. <u>毎日</u><u>図書館</u>で<u>勉強</u>します。

(I study at the library every day.)

14. <u>卵黄</u>にはコレストロールが<u>多</u>いといいます。

(They say there is a lot of cholesterol in egg yolks.)

ANALYZING AND READING EXERCISE FOR EXAMPLE KANJI

Analyze the following Kanji. Write the *furigana* below the underlined Kanji. (Some familiar Kanji are included in this exercise.)

1. 球 = [   ] + [   ]
   日本では野球がとてもさかんです。　　　　(Baseball is very popular in Japan.)

2. 速 = [   ] + [   ]
   新幹線はとても速いです。　　　　(The bullet train is very fast.)

3. 途* = [   ] + [   ]
   うちへ帰る途中本屋によりました。　　　　(I stopped at the bookstore on my way home.)

4. 除 = [   ] + [   ]
   日曜日を除いて彼はほとんど家にいません。　　(Excepting Sundays, he is almost never at home.)

5. 赦* = [   ] + [   ]
   彼は恩赦*をうけて罪になりませんでした。　　(He was pardoned and was not punished.)

6. 議 = [   ] + [   ] + [   ]
   彼は議論が好きです。　　　　(He enjoys arguing.)

7. 郡 = [   ] + [   ]
   "County"は日本語で郡といいます。　　(A county is called a "gun" in Japanese.)

8. 造 = [   ] + [   ]
   彼は造船会社に勤めています。　　(He works at a shipbuilding company.)

9. 係＝ ［　］ ＋ ［　］

小川さんは会社の受付係です。
　おがわ　　　　　　　　うけつけ

(Ogawa-san is a receptionist for the
　company.)

10. 孫＝ ［　］ ＋ ［　］

わたしには孫が五人あります。

(I have five grandchildren.)

Eight Stroke Kanji (Numbers 1 through 10)

Kanji and Examples		Stroke Order and Practice
1. 青 8 (blue, green, pg. 60)	晴 は・れる／セイ (clear up, pg. 17) 清 きよ・い／セイ／ショウ (pure, clear, pg. xvi) 静 しず・か／セイ／ジョウ (quiet, silent)	二・ 十 丰・ 圭・ 青 青 青 青 青 青
あお／あお・い	青色 (あおいろ blue color) 青空 (あおぞら blue sky) 青物 (あおもの green vegetable)	
セイ／ショウ	青年 (セイネン a youth, young people) 青春 (セイシュン one's youth, spring of life) 緑青 (ロクショウ green copper rust)	
2. 金 ‡8 (gold, metal, money, Friday)	銀 ギン (silver, pg. 20) 鉄 テツ (iron, pg. 20) 銅 ドウ (copper, pg. 20)	ソ ハ ハ 今 全 金 金 金 金
かね／(かな)	金持ち (かねもち rich person) お金 (おかね money) 金物 (かなもの hardware)	
キン／コン	金曜日 (キンヨウび Friday) 現金 (ゲンキン cash) 金色 (コンジキ golden color)	
3. 雨 ‡8 (rain)	漏* も・る (leak)	二・ 广・ 厅 雨 雨 雨 雨 雨 雨
あめ／あま	雨上り (あめあがり after the rain) 大雨 (おおあめ heavy rain) 雨戸 (あまど window shutter, pg. 124)	
ウ	雨天 (ウテン rainy weather) 雨期 (ウキ rainy season) 風雨 (フウウ wind & rain, rain storm)	
4. 東 8 (east)	練 レン (knead, train) 凍 こお・る／トウ (frozen, pg. 21)	一・ 厂 厅 百 車 東 東 東
ひがし	東風 (ひがしかぜ east wind) 東口 (ひがしぐち east exit or entrance)	
トウ	東京 (トウキョウ Tōkyō) 東洋 (トウヨウ the Orient) 中東 (チュウトウ the Middle East)	

‡ 金 appeared as *kane·hen* on pg. 20.

‡ 雨 appeared as *ame·kammuri* on pg. 29.

Kanji and Examples			Stroke Order and Practice

5. 京 8 (capital, pg. 30)

景 ケイ (scenery, view)

就 シュウ (take a position, get a job)

涼* すず・しい (cool)

Stroke order: 亠 → 亠 → 宀 → 京 → 京 → 京 → 京 → 京

キョウ/(ケイ)	京都 (キョウト Kyōto) 上京 (ジョウキョウ going to Tōkyō) 京浜* (ケイヒン Tōkyō & Yokohama)

6. 長 8 (long, eldest, chief, pg. 2)

張 チョウ (stretch)

帳 チョウ (notebook, pg. 22)

Stroke order: ⌐ → ⌐ → 﨑 → 長 → 長 → 長 → 長

なが・い	長生き (ながいき longevity, pg. 142) 長さ (ながさ length) 長年 (ながネン many years)
チョウ	長男 (チョウナン eldest son) 成長 (セイチョウ growth) 社長 (シャチョウ company president)

7. 表 8 (surface, appear, chart, pg. 60)

俵* たわら/ヒョウ (straw bag)

Stroke order: 一 → 十 → 圭 → 圭 → 声 → 表 → 表 → 表

おもて/あらわ・す	表 (おもて surface, front, pg. 60) 表す (あらわす to express)
ヒョウ	表紙 (ヒョウシ cover) 表現 (ヒョウゲン expression) 時間表 (ジカンヒョウ timetable)

8. 門 ‡8 (gate)

閉 と・じる (to close, shut)

関 せき/カン (barrier, check point, pg. 71)

問 と・う/モン (ask, inquire)

Stroke order: ｜ → ｢ → 門 → 門 → 門 → 門 → 門 → 門

かど	門口 (かどぐち gate, door) 門出 (かどで on one's departure)
モン	▲専門 (センモン school major, specialty) 校門 (コウモン school gate) 表門 (おもてモン front gate)

‡ 門 appeared as *mon·gamae* on pg. 40.

▲ 専 (セン) exclusive

Kanji and Examples		Stroke Order and Practice
9. 8 並 (average, be in a row or line, arrange, as well)	普* フ (widely, generally) 譜* フ (sheet of music, genealogy)	゛ ゛ ゛ ゛ 氺 並 並 並 並 並
なみ/なら・ぶ/ なら・びに	人並 (ひとなみ ordinary, average) 並ぶ (ならぶ line up) 並べる (ならべる put things side by side)	
ヘイ	並行 (ヘイコウ parallel)	
10. 8 幸 (happiness, good fortune)	報 ホウ (report, pg. 61) 執* と・る (take, execute)	一 十 土 士 寺 幸 幸 幸 幸 幸
さいわ・い/ しあわ・せ/(さち)	幸い (さいわい fortunate) 幸せ (しあわせ happiness) 山の幸 (やまのさち mountain delicacy)	
コウ	幸福 (コウフク happiness) 不幸 (フコウ unhappiness)	

EXERCISES FOR EIGHT STROKE KANJI (NUMBERS 1 THROUGH 10)

WRITING EXERCISE
Fill in each box to make a word.

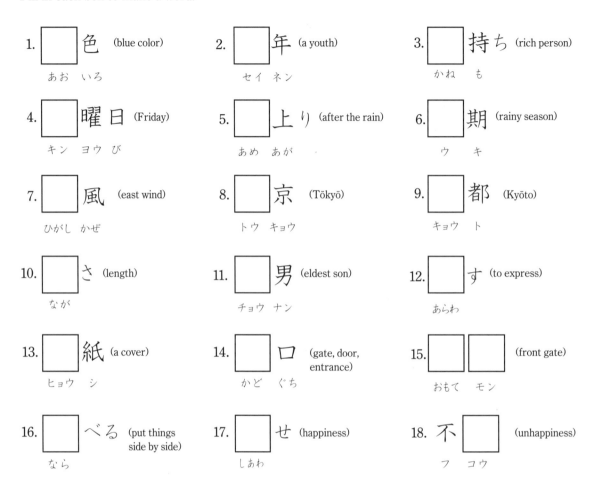

1. ☐ 色 (blue color)
   あお　いろ

2. ☐ 年 (a youth)
   セイ　ネン

3. ☐ 持ち (rich person)
   かね　も

4. ☐ 曜日 (Friday)
   キン　ヨウ　び

5. ☐ 上り (after the rain)
   あめ　あが

6. ☐ 期 (rainy season)
   ウ　キ

7. ☐ 風 (east wind)
   ひがし　かぜ

8. ☐ 京 (Tōkyō)
   トウ　キョウ

9. ☐ 都 (Kyōto)
   キョウ　ト

10. ☐ さ (length)
    なが

11. ☐ 男 (eldest son)
    チョウ　ナン

12. ☐ す (to express)
    あらわ

13. ☐ 紙 (a cover)
    ヒョウ　シ

14. ☐ 口 (gate, door, entrance)
    かど　ぐち

15. ☐ ☐ (front gate)
    おもて　モン

16. ☐ べる (put things side by side)
    なら

17. ☐ せ (happiness)
    しあわ

18. 不 ☐ (unhappiness)
    フ　コウ

READING EXERCISE

Read the following sentences, and write the correct *furigana* (pronunciation of Kanji written in Hiragana regardless of whether the reading of the Kanji is On or Kun) below the underlined Kanji.

1. 青空に白い雲がうかんでいます。 (White clouds are floating in a blue sky.)

2. 青春は二度とかえってきません。 (Youth never returns (again).)

3. 今いくらお金をもっていますか。 (How much money do you have right now?)

4. いつも現金はあまり持たない方がいいです。 　(It is always better not to carry too much cash.)

5. きのうは大雨のため仕事を休みました。 　(Yesterday, because of heavy rain, I was absent from work.)

6. 雨天の時は試合は中止です。 　(In the event of rain, the game will be canceled.)

7. 駅の東口で待っています。 　(I will be waiting at the east exit of the station.)

8. 今、中東の平和が大きな問題です。
　もんだい
　(At present, peace in the Middle East is a big issue.)

9. 今度いつ上京しますか。 　(When is your next trip to Tōkyō?)

10. 社長は今外出中です。 　(The president of the company is out now.)

11. 自分の気持ちをすなおに表現する方がいいです。 　(It's better to express one's feelings frankly.)

12. あなたの門出をお祝いしましょう。 　(We wish you good luck in your new life (on your departure).)

13. 彼の専門は何ですか。 　(What is his area of specialty?)

14. やっと人並みの生活ができるようになりました。 　(Finally, I have managed to make a decent (average) living.)

15. 幸い、きょうのピクニックはいいお天気でした。 　(Fortunately, the weather was fine at today's picnic.)

16. わたしたちは<u>健康</u>で<u>幸福</u>な<u>生活</u>をおくっています。　(We are living a healthy and happy life.)

ANALYZING AND READING EXERCISE FOR EXAMPLE KANJI

Analyze the following Kanji. Write the *furigana* below the underlined Kanji. (Some familiar Kanji are included in this exercise.)

1. 晴＝［　　］＋［　　］
   きょうは<u>空</u>がよく<u>晴</u>れています。　(The sky is very clear today.)

2. 清＝［　　］＋［　　］
   この<u>谷川</u>の<u>水</u>は<u>清</u>くすんでいます。　(The water in this mountain stream is clear.)

3. 静＝［　　］＋［　　］＋［　　］＋［　　　］
   <u>静</u>かな<u>海</u>を<u>見</u>ていると<u>心</u>が<u>休</u>まります。　(When I look at the quiet ocean, my mind is at peace (rests).)

4. 銀＝［　　］＋［　　］
   お<u>友</u>だちに<u>銀</u>のネックレスをいただきました。　(I received a silver necklace from my friend.)

5. 漏*＝［　　］＋［　　］＋［　　　］
   このバケツは<u>水</u>が<u>漏</u>っています。　(Water is leaking from this bucket.)

6. 練＝［　　］＋［　　］
   <u>毎日</u>ピアノの<u>練習</u>をします。　(I practice the piano every day.)

7. 凍*＝［　　］＋［　　］
   <u>冷凍</u><u>食品</u>はあまり<u>好</u>きではありません。　(I don't care much for frozen foods.)
   しょくひん

8. 景＝［　　］＋［　　］
   <u>窓</u>から<u>美</u>しい<u>山</u>の<u>風景</u>を<u>見</u>るのが<u>好</u>きです。(I like to look at the beautiful mountain scenery from the window.)

9. 涼* = [　　] + [　　]
   今年の夏はわりあいに涼しいです。　　(This (year's) summer has been fairly cool.)

10. 張 = [　　] + [　　]
   彼はいつも自分の意見を強く主張します。　(He always asserts his opinions strongly.)

11. 帳 = [　　] + [　　]
   わたしはいつもポケットに手帳をもっています。(I always carry a memo book in my pocket.)

12. 閉 = [　　] + [　　]
   本を閉じてください。　　(Please close your book.)

13. 関 = [　　] + [　　]
   あなたはこの事件とどんな関係がありますか。(How are you involved in (what kind of connection do you have to) this incident?)

14. 問 = [　　] + [　　]
   きょうの試験の問題はとてもむずかしかったです。(The problems on today's test were very difficult.)

15. 譜* = [　　] + [　　] + [　　]
   このピアノの曲は楽譜がなくても　　(I can play this piano piece without the sheet music.)
   ひくことができます。

16. 報 = [　　] + [　　]
   そのことについての情報はまだ入っていません。(No information has come in on that matter yet.)

Eight Stroke Kanji (Numbers 11 through 20)

Kanji and Examples			Stroke Order and Practice

11. 者 (8)

(person, pg. 30)

暑	あつ・い／ショ (hot)	
都	みやこ／ト (capital, pg. 26)	
諸	ショ (various)	

Stroke order: 一　ナ　土　耂　耂　者　者　者　*者*
Practice: *者*

もの	若者 (わかもの young people)　　独り者 (ひとりもの unmarried person)
シャ	医者 (イシャ physician)　　作者 (サクシャ author)　　学者 (ガクシャ scholar)

12. 昔 (8)

(long ago, pg. 60)

借	か・りる／シャク (borrow)	
惜*	お・しい／セキ (regret)	
籍*	セキ (legal residence)	

Stroke order: 一　十　艹　共　昔　昔　昔　昔　*昔*
Practice: *昔*

むかし	昔話 (むかしばなし old tale, legend)　　昔なじみ (むかしなじみ old friend)
セキ／（シャク）	昔日 (セキジツ olden days)　　今昔 (コンジャク past & present)

13. 果 (8)

(fruit, result, accomplish, end)

課	カ (section, lesson)	
菓*	カ (cake, fruit)	

Stroke order: 丨　口　日　日　旦　果　果　果　*果*
Practice: *果*

は・たす／は・てる／は・たして／は・て	約束を果たす (ヤクソクをはたす keep one's promise)　　果たして (はたして as was expected)　　果てしない (はてしない endless)
カ	果実 (カジツ fruit)　　結果 (ケッカ result)

14. 非 (8)

(non-, un-, wrong)

悲	かな・しい／ヒ (sorrow)	
罪	つみ (sin, pg. 31)	
俳	ハイ (witty, actor)	

Stroke order: 丿　ヲ　ヺ　ヲ　非　非　非　非　*非*
Practice: *非*

ヒ	非行 (ヒコウ misconduct)　　非常に (ヒジョウに extraordinarily)　　非科学的 (ヒカガクテキ unscientific)

Kanji and Examples			Stroke Order and Practice

15. 8 直
(straight, immediate, direct, correct)

植	う・える／ショク (plant)
置	お・く／チ (to place, pg. 31)
値*	ね／チ (price, cost)

一 十 +ナ 疒 直 直 直 **直** 直

直

| ただ・ちに／なお・す／なお・る | 直ちに (ただちに immediately)　　直す (なおす correct, fix, mend) |
| チョク／ジキ | 直前 (チョクゼン just before)　　直通 (チョクツウ direct communication)　　正直 (ショウジキ upright, honest) |

16. 8 周
(circuit, circumference)

週	シュウ (week)
調	しら・べる／チョウ (investigate)
彫*	ほ・る／チョウ (carve)

丿 冂 冂 用 用 周 周 周 周

周

| まわ・り | 家の周り (いえのまわり around the outside of the house) |
| シュウ | 一周 (イッシュウ once around)　周囲 (シュウイ surroundings)　円周 (エンシュウ circumference) |

17. 8 固
(hard, solid, firm)

| 個 | コ (individual, counter for objects) |
| 箇* | カ (counter for some abstract objects) |

丨 冂 冂 用 用 周 固 固 固

固

| かた・い／かた・める／かた・まる | 固い (かたい hard, solid)　　固める (かためる harden, strengthen)　　固まる (かたまる to gel, become hard/firm) |
| コ | 固定 (コテイ fixed, fastened)　強固 (キョウコ firm, solid, strong) |

18. 8 官
(government official)

| 館 | カン (hall, pg. 24) |
| 管 | くだ／カン (pipe, tube) |

丷 宀 宀 宀 宁 官 官

官

| | |
| カン | 官吏* (カンリ government official)　高官 (コウカン high official)　警官 (ケイカン policeman) |

Kanji and Examples		Stroke Order and Practice								
19. 8 垂 (hang down, drip)	郵 ユウ (mail) 睡* スイ (sleep)	ノ	二	三	亖	垂	垂	垂	垂	垂
た・れる	垂れる (たれる drip, hang down)									
スイ	垂直 (スイチョク vertical, perpendicular)									
20. *8 免 (exemption, permission)	勉 ベン (endeavor, pg. 92) 晩 バン (evening, pg. xii)	ノ	久	今	叴	叴	免	免	免	免
まぬか・れる	免れる (まぬかれる be exempted, escape)									
メン	免許 (メンキョ license) 免除 (メンジョ exemption) 免税品 (メンゼイヒン duty free goods)									

EXERCISES FOR EIGHT STROKE KANJI (NUMBERS 11 THROUGH 20)

WRITING EXERCISE
Fill in each box to make a word.

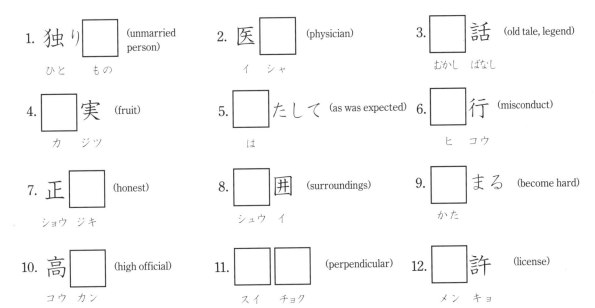

1. 独り □ (unmarried person)
   ひと　もの

2. 医 □ (physician)
   イ　シャ

3. □ 話 (old tale, legend)
   むかし　ばなし

4. □ 実 (fruit)
   カ　ジツ

5. □ たして (as was expected)
   は

6. □ 行 (misconduct)
   ヒ　コウ

7. 正 □ (honest)
   ショウ　ジキ

8. □ 囲 (surroundings)
   シュウ　イ

9. □ まる (become hard)
   かた

10. 高 □ (high official)
    コウ　カン

11. □ □ (perpendicular)
    スイ　チョク

12. □ 許 (license)
    メン　キョ

READING EXERCISE
Read the following sentences, and write the correct *furigana* (pronunciation of Kanji written in Hiragana regardless of whether the reading of the Kanji is On or Kun) below the underlined Kanji.

1. 東京の原宿は若者の町です。
   はらじゅく
   (Harajuku, in Tōkyō, is a town for young people.)

2. この小説の作者はだれですか。
   (Who is the author of this novel?)

3. 彼女はわたしの昔なじみです。
   (She is an old friend from when I was a child.)

4. 彼には昔日のおもかげがありません。
   (He no longer bears any trace of his former self (from the old days).)

5. 若者のゆめは果てしなく広がります。
   (The dreams [aspirations] of young people grow endlessly.)

6. テストの<u>結果</u>はどうでしたか。

(What were the results of your test?)

7. あの<u>映画</u>は<u>非常</u>におもしろいです。

(That movie is extremely nteresting.)

8. けがをしたので<u>直</u>ちに<u>病院</u>へ<u>行</u>きました。

(I had an injury, so I immediately went to the hospital.)

9. まちがった<u>字</u>は<u>直</u>してください。

(Please correct the incorrect characters.)

10. わたしの<u>事務所</u>には<u>直通</u> <u>電話</u>があります。
    じむしょ

(There is a direct telephone line in my office.)

11. <u>家</u>の<u>周</u>りをさんぽしました。

(I took a walk around my house.)

12. <u>彼女</u>は<u>世界</u> <u>一周</u>の<u>旅</u>に<u>出</u>かけました。

(She set out on a trip around the world.)

13. <u>彼</u>は意思の<u>強固</u>な<u>人</u>です。
    いし

(He is a strong-willed person.)

14. <u>水道</u>のじゃ<u>ロ</u>(faucet)から<u>水</u>がぽたぽた<u>垂</u>れています。
    ぐち

(Water is dripping from the faucet.)

15. <u>車</u>がしょうとつしましたが、けがは<u>免</u>れました。

(My car was hit, but I escaped injury.)

16. <u>日本</u>からの<u>旅行者</u>はたいてい<u>免税品店</u>へ<u>行</u>きます。

(Tourists from Japan usually go to the duty free shop.)

ANALYZING AND READING EXERCISE FOR EXAMPLE KANJI

Analyze the following Kanji. Write the *furigana* below the underlined Kanji. (Some familiar Kanji are included in this exercise.)

1. 暑 ＝ ［　］＋［　］
   きょうはとても暑いですね。 (It's very hot today, isn't it?)

2. 都 ＝ ［　］＋［　］
   京都は古い都です。 (Kyōtō is an old capital.)

3. 借 ＝ ［　］＋［　］
   これは友だちに借りた本です。 (This is a book I borrowed from my friend.)

4. 惜* ＝ ［　］＋［　］
   この服をすてるのはまだ惜しいです。 (It's a shame to throw away this dress yet.)

5. 籍* ＝ ［　］＋［　］＋［　］
   あなたの国籍はどこですか。 (What (where) is your nationality?)

6. 課 ＝ ［　］＋［　］
   今だい八課を習っています。 (We are now studying section eight.)

7. 菓* ＝ ［　］＋［　］
   このお菓子はおいしいですね。 (This sweet tastes good, doesn't it?)

8. 悲 ＝ ［　］＋［　］
   死んだ犬のことを考えるととても悲しいです。 (I become very sad whenever I think about my dog that died.)

9. 罪 ＝ ［　　］ ＋ ［　　］
　　おかした<u>罪</u>はつぐなわなければなりません。

(One must pay for the sins one has committed.)

10. 俳 ＝ ［　　］ ＋ ［　　］
　　<u>俳句</u>は<u>十七音</u>で<u>表</u>す<u>短</u>い<u>詩</u>です。
　　　　　　　おん

(A haiku is a short poem expressed in 17 syllables.)

11. 置 ＝ ［　　］ ＋ ［　　］
　　テレビはどこに<u>置</u>きましょうか。

(Where shall we put the television?)

12. 値 ＝ ［　　］ ＋ ［　　］
　　<u>買</u>い<u>値</u>はいくらでしたか。

(How much was the purchase price?)

13. 週 ＝ ［　　］ ＋ ［　　］
　　<u>先週</u>この<u>本</u>を<u>買</u>いました。

(I bought this book last week.)

14. 調 ＝ ［　　］ ＋ ［　　］
　　この<u>問題</u>はよく<u>調</u>べてください。

(Please investigate this matter thoroughly.)

15. 個 ＝ ［　　］ ＋ ［　　］
　　それは<u>彼女</u>の<u>個人</u>的な<u>問題</u>です。

(That is her personal problem.)

16. 館 ＝ ［　　］ ＋ ［　　］
　　<u>図書館</u>はうちの<u>近</u>くにあります。

(The library is near my house.)

17. 管 ＝ ［　　］ ＋ ［　　］
　　<u>水道管</u>をかえなければなりません。

(We have to change the water pipes.)

18. 郵 ＝ [   ] ＋ [   ]
    きょうの<u>郵便</u>はもう<u>来</u>ましたか。　　　　　　　(Has today's mail come yet?)

19. 勉 ＝ [   ] ＋ [   ]

20. 晩 ＝ [   ] ＋ [   ]
    わたしは<u>毎晩</u> <u>勉強</u>します。　　　　　　　(I study every night.)

Nine Stroke Kanji

Kanji and Examples			Stroke Order and Practice
1. 南 9 (south)	献* ケン (contribute, pg. 132)		一 十 十 冎 冎 南 南 南 南 南 南
みなみ	南アフリカ (みなみアフリカ South Africa)		南口 (みなみぐち south exit or entrance)
ナン／(ナ)	南北 (ナンボク north & south)		東南アジア (トウナンアジア Southeast Asia)
2. 風 9 (wind, style, pg. 3)			) 几 凧 凪 凧 凬 風 風 風 風 風
かぜ／(かざ)	雨風 (あめかぜ rain & wind)	大風 (おおかぜ strong wind)	風上 (かざかみ windward)
フウ／(フ)	風車 (フウシャ windmill)	台風 (タイフウ typhoon)	和風 (ワフウ Japanese style)
3. 音 9 (sound, pg. 141)	暗 くら・い (dark) 意 イ (intention, pg. 33) 鏡 かがみ (mirror, pg. 83)		亠 亠 产 立 产 产 音 音 音 音 音
おと／ね	足音 (あしおと sound of footsteps)	物音 (ものおと sound, noise)	音色 (ねいろ tone)
オン／イン	音読み (オンよみ On (Chinese) reading of a Kanji)	発音 (ハツオン pronunciation)	母音 (ボイン／ボオン vowel, pg. 149)
4. 食 ‡9 (food, eating)	養 やしな・う／ヨウ (raise, support, feed)		ノ ハ 个 今 今 仐 食 食 食 食 食
た・べる／く・う／ (く・らう)	食べ物 (たべもの food)	食い止める (くいとめる hold back)	
ショク／(ジキ)	夕食 (ゆうショク supper)	主食 (シュショク staple food, pg. 142)	和食 (ワショク Japanese food)

‡ 食 appeared as *shoku·hen* on pg. 24.

Kanji and Examples			Stroke Order and Practice								

5. **9**

品

(article, goods, refinement, pg. 105)

操 ソウ (operate)

臨 リン (look out over, attend)

Stroke order: ⺊ ⼝ 口 吕 品 品 品 品 品

Practice: 品 品

しな	品物 (しなもの goods, merchandise)	品切れ (しなぎれ out of stock)	手品 (てじな magic tricks, sleight of hand)
ヒン	品行 (ヒンコウ behavior)	上品 (ジョウヒン elegant, pg. 98)	作品 (サクヒン piece of work, production)

6. **9**

首

(neck, head, pg. 56)

道 みち／ドウ (way, road, pg. 38)

導 みちび・く／ドウ (guide, pg. 107)

Stroke order: ⺌ ⺍ 丷 䒑 产 首 首 首 首

Practice: 首 首

くび	首切り (くびきり firing, dismissal)	手首 (てくび wrist)	
シュ	首都 (シュト capital of a country)	首相 (シュショウ Prime Minister)	部首 (ブシュ Kanji radical)

7. **9**

重

(heavy, serious, pile)

動 うご・く／ドウ (move, pg. 25)

働 はたら・く／ドウ (work)

種 たね／シュ (seed)

Stroke order: ⼂ 亠 千 舌 盲 重 重 重

Practice: 重 重

おも・い／ かさ・ねる／(え)	重さ (おもさ weight, importance)	重ねる (かさねる pile one on top of another)	八重ざくら (やえざくら double petalled cherry blossom, pg. 91)
ジュウ／チョウ	重大 (ジュウダイ important)	体重 (タイジュウ body weight)	自重 (ジチョウ prudence, caution)

8. **9**

相

(mutual, appearance, government minister, pg. 140)

想 ソウ (thought, image)

箱 はこ (box)

Stroke order: 一 十 才 木 村 机 相 相 相

Practice: 相 相

あい	相手 (あいて the other party, partner)		
ソウ／ショウ	相当 (ソウトウ correspond to, considerable)	手相 (てソウ lines of the palm)	外相 (ガイショウ Minister of Foreign Affairs)

Kanji and Examples			Stroke Order and Practice								

9. 則 (9)

側 かわ／ソク (side)
測 はか・る／ソク (measure)

(rule, law)

刂	冂	刖	刖	目	目	貝	則	則
則	則							

ソク	原則（ゲンソク principle, fundamental rule）　　規則（キソク rules, regulations）

10. 革 (9)

靴* くつ (shoes)

(animal skin, reform)

一	廿	廿	廿	苎	苎	苫	苴	革
革	革							

かわ	革靴*（かわぐつ leather shoes）　革のかばん（かわのかばん leather bag, briefcase）
カク	革命（カクメイ revolution）　　革新（カクシン reform）　　　改革（カイカク reorganize）

11. 面 (9)

(face, mask, surface)

一	ァ	石	百	而	而	而	面
面	面						

おもて／おも／（つら）	面（おもて surface）　　　　面長（おもなが oval face）　　面白い（おもしろい interesting）
メン	面会（メンカイ an interview, visit）　　お面（おメン mask）　　　表面（ヒョウメン surface）

12. 単 (9)

戦 たたか・う／セン (fight, pg. 27)
弾* たま／ダン (bullet)
禅* ゼン (Zen Buddhism)

(single, simple, mere, pg. 57)

⌯	⌯⌯	⌯⌯	兴	肖	肖	畄	単
単	単						

タン	単語（タンゴ word, vocabulary）　　単に（タンに merely, simply）　　単独（タンドク independent, single-handed）

Kanji and Examples	Stroke Order and Practice

13. 軍 (9)

運 はこ・ぶ／ウン (carry, transport, luck)

揮 キ (scatter, command)

(the military, pg. 29)

Stroke order: ㇀ 冖 冖 冃 宕 冒 冒 冒 軍

軍 軍

| グン | 軍人 (グンジン soldier) | 空軍 (クウグン Air Force) | 海軍 (カイグン Navy) |

14. 飛 (9)

(to fly, pg. 3)

Stroke order: 飞 乜 飞 飞 飞 飛 飛 飛 飛

飛 飛

| と・ぶ | 飛ぶ (とぶ to fly, pg. 3) | 飛び込む (とびこむ jump in) |
| ヒ | 飛行 (ヒコウ flight) | 飛行場 (ヒコウジョウ airport) |

15. 乗 (9)

剰 ジョウ (surplus, besides)

(ride, get on, multiply)

Stroke order: ㇒ 二 三 乒 乒 垂 垂 乗 乗

乗 乗

| の・る | 乗り物 (のりもの vehicle) | 乗り場 (のりば place to board or get in [a vehicle]) |
| ジョウ | 乗客 (ジョウキャク passenger) | 乗車 (ジョウシャ board a bus or train) |

16. 是 (*9)

提 さ・げる／テイ (carry, submit)

題 ダイ (title, topic)

堤* つつみ／テイ (bank, levee)

(correct, policy)

Stroke order: ㇀ 甲 目 日 旦 昇 昰 昰 是

是 是

| ゼ | 是非 (ゼヒ right & wrong, by all means) | 是正 (ゼセイ correction) |

EXERCISES FOR NINE STROKE KANJI

WRITING EXERCISE

Fill in each box to make a word.

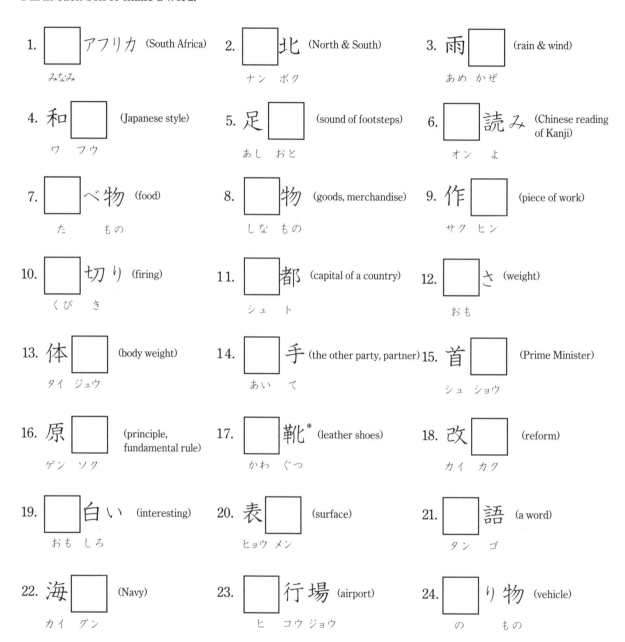

1. ☐ アフリカ (South Africa)
みなみ

2. ☐ 北 (North & South)
ナン ボク

3. 雨 ☐ (rain & wind)
あめ かぜ

4. 和 ☐ (Japanese style)
ワ フウ

5. 足 ☐ (sound of footsteps)
あし おと

6. ☐ 読み (Chinese reading of Kanji)
オン よ

7. ☐ べ物 (food)
た もの

8. ☐ 物 (goods, merchandise)
しな もの

9. 作 ☐ (piece of work)
サク ヒン

10. ☐ 切り (firing)
くび き

11. ☐ 都 (capital of a country)
シュ ト

12. ☐ さ (weight)
おも

13. 体 ☐ (body weight)
タイ ジュウ

14. ☐ 手 (the other party, partner)
あい て

15. 首 ☐ (Prime Minister)
シュ ショウ

16. 原 ☐ (principle, fundamental rule)
ゲン ソク

17. ☐ 靴* (leather shoes)
かわ ぐつ

18. 改 ☐ (reform)
カイ カク

19. ☐ 白い (interesting)
おも しろ

20. 表 ☐ (surface)
ヒョウ メン

21. ☐ 語 (a word)
タン ゴ

22. 海 ☐ (Navy)
カイ グン

23. ☐ 行場 (airport)
ヒ コウ ジョウ

24. ☐ り物 (vehicle)
の もの

READING EXERCISE

Read the following sentences, and write the correct *furigana* (pronunciation of Kanji written in Hiragana regardless of whether the reading of the Kanji is On or Kun) below the underlined Kanji.

1. 近いうちに東南アジアを旅行するつもりです。　(I am planning to tour Southeast Asia in the near future.)

2. 今、外は大風がふいています。 (Outside, a strong wind is blowing right now.)

3. 日本では九月が台風の季節です。 (In Japan, September is the typhoon season.)

4. 「何か物音がしませんでしたか。」「こわいですね。」 ("Didn't you hear a noise?" "I am scared; aren't you?")

5. 彼女のフルートの音色はすばらしいですね。 (The tone of her flute is spectacular, isn't it?)

6. あのアナウンサーの発音はとてもきれいです。 (That announcer's pronunciation is very clear.)

7. 夕飯は和食にしましょうか、洋食にしましょうか。 (Shall we have Japanese food or Western food for dinner?)

8. このＣＤは今品切れです。 (This CD is currently out of stock.)

9. 漢字を習うためには部首を知ることが大切です。 (In order to learn Kanji, it is important to know the radicals.)

10. 机の上に本が重ねてあります。 (The books are piled on top of the desk.)

11. 今年の重大なニュースは何でしたか。 (What were this year's important news events?)

12. この夏は相当暑くなりそうです。 (It looks like this summer will be quite hot.)

13. 彼は革新政党にぞくしています。 (He belongs to the reformist political party.)

14. <u>病院</u>の<u>面会</u><u>時間</u>は何時からですか。

(What time do the hospital's visiting hours begin?)

15. <u>彼</u>は<u>単独</u>でアルプスに<u>登</u>りました。

(He went climbing in the Alps by himself.)

16. あまり<u>暑</u>いのでプールに<u>飛</u>び<u>込</u>みました。

(It was so hot that I jumped into the swimming pool.)

17. あのステュワーデスはとても<u>乗客</u>にしんせつですね。

(That stewardess is very kind to passengers, isn't she?)

18. あした<u>是非</u>わたしのうちへあそびに<u>来</u>てください。

(By all means, please come and visit me at my home tomorrow.)

ANALYZING AND READING EXERCISE FOR EXAMPLE KANJI

Analyze the following Kanji. Write the *furigana* below the underlined Kanji. (Some familiar Kanji are included in this exercise.)

1. 献*＝[　]＋[　]
  <u>毎月</u>お<u>寺</u>に<u>献金</u>をします。

(I make a donation to the temple every month.)

2. 暗＝[　]＋[　]
  <u>夜</u>、この<u>道</u>は<u>暗</u>いですね。

(This road is very dark at night, isn't it?)

3. 意＝[　]＋[　]
  この<u>言葉</u>の<u>意味</u>を<u>知</u>っていますか。

(Do you know the meaning of this word?)

4. 養＝[　]＋[　]
  <u>今</u>、<u>三人</u>の子どもを<u>養</u>っています。

(I am supporting three children now.)

5.　操 ＝ [　] ＋ [　] ＋ [　]
　　彼は体操の先生です。　　　　　　　　　　(He is a physical education instructor.)

6.　導 ＝ [　] ＋ [　] ＋ [　]
　　彼は週末にサッカーの指導をします。　　　(He coaches soccer on the weekends.)
　　　　しゅうまつ　　　　　　　　し

7.　動 ＝ [　] ＋ [　]
　　ここを動かないで待っていてください。　　(Please wait without moving from this spot.)

8.　働 ＝ [　] ＋ [　] ＋ [　]
　　彼女は朝から晩までよく働きます。　　　　(She works hard from morning till night.)

9.　想 ＝ [　] ＋ [　]
　　これについてあなたの感想を聞かせてください。　(Let me hear your thoughts on this matter.)

10.　箱 ＝ [　] ＋ [　]
　　この箱の中に何がありますか。　　　　　　(What is inside this box?)

11.　側 ＝ [　] ＋ [　]
　　わたしの家はこの道の左側にあります。　　(My house is on the left hand side of this road.)

12.　戦 ＝ [　] ＋ [　]
　　わたしたちは戦争のない世界をのぞんでいます。　(We are hoping for a world without war.)

13. 運 ＝ [   ] ＋ [   ]

   あなたは<u>毎日</u><u>運動</u>しますか。　　　　　　　(Do you exercise everyday?)

   この<u>スーツ・ケース</u>を<u>運</u>んでください。　　(Please carry this suitcase.)

14. 揮 ＝ [   ] ＋ [   ]

   あの<u>オーケストラ</u>の<u>指揮者</u>はだれですか。　(Who is the conductor of that orchestra?)

15. 剰 ＝ [   ] ＋ [   ]

   <u>東京</u>は<u>人口</u><u>過剰</u>で<u>住</u>みにくいです。　(Since the population is so dense (excessive) in Tōkyō, it is difficult to live there.)

16. 題 ＝ [   ] ＋ [   ]

17. 提 ＝ [   ] ＋ [   ]

   <u>毎日</u><u>宿題</u>を<u>提出</u>しなければなりません。　(We must turn in homework everyday.)

Ten through Twelve Stroke Kanji
Ten Stroke Kanji

Kanji and Examples			Stroke Order and Practice

1. ‡10 馬 (horse)

驚* おどろ・く／キョウ (to be surprised, pg. 157)

騰* トウ (rise)

Stroke order: 丨 广 厂 厈 馬 馬 馬 馬 馬

うま／(ま)	馬小屋 (うまごや stable) 小馬 (こうま pony) 絵馬 (えま picture of a horse used as a religious offering)
バ	馬力 (バリキ horsepower) 馬券 (バケン horse race betting ticket) 名馬 (メイバ fine horse)

2. 10 骨 (bone)

滑* すべ・る (slide, glide, ski)

髄* ズイ (marrow)

Stroke order: 丨 冂 冎 骨 骨 骨 骨 骨

ほね	骨組 (ほねぐみ body frame, framework) 骨休め (ほねやすめ relaxation) 背骨 (せぼね backbone, spine)
コツ	骨格 (コッカク skeleton, body frame) 骨折 (コッセツ bone fracture) 鉄骨 (テッコツ steel frame)

3. 10 高 (high, pg. 30)

稿* コウ (manuscript)

Stroke order: 丶 亠 亠 市 产 户 高 高 高

たか・い	高値 (たかね highest price in a fluctuating market) 名高い (なだかい famous) 円高 (エンだか strong yen)
コウ	高校 (コウコウ high school) 高速道路 (コウソクドウロ expressway)

4. 10 原 (origin, field, plain, pg. 36)

源 みなもと／ゲン (fountainhead, source, origin)

願 ねが・う／ガン (wish, pg. 27)

Stroke order: 一 厂 厂 厂 厉 原 原 原 原

はら	草原 (くさはら (ソウゲン) grassy plain) 野原 (のはら field, plain)
ゲン	原子 (ゲンシ atom, pg. 100) 原因 (ゲンイン cause, pg. 188) 高原 (コウゲン plateau)

‡ 馬 appeared as *uma·hen* on pg. 20.

235

	Kanji and Examples		Stroke Order and Practice
5. **10** 員 (member, pg. 195)	損 ソン (loss) 韻* イン (rythme)		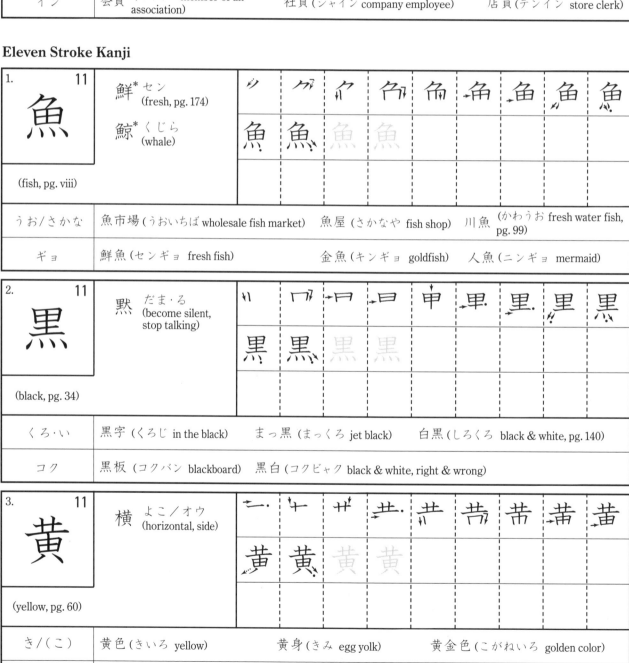
	イン	会員 （カイイン member of an association) 社員 （シャイン company employee) 店員 （テンイン store clerk)	

Eleven Stroke Kanji

	Kanji and Examples	
1. **11** 魚 (fish, pg. viii)	鮮* セン (fresh, pg. 174) 鯨* くじら (whale)	
	うお／さかな	魚市場 （うおいちば wholesale fish market) 魚屋 （さかなや fish shop) 川魚 （かわうお fresh water fish, pg. 99)
	ギョ	鮮魚 （センギョ fresh fish) 金魚 （キンギョ goldfish) 人魚 （ニンギョ mermaid)

	Kanji and Examples	
2. **11** 黒 (black, pg. 34)	黙 だま・る (become silent, stop talking)	
	くろ・い	黒字 （くろじ in the black) まっ黒 （まっくろ jet black) 白黒 （しろくろ black & white, pg. 140)
	コク	黒板 （コクバン blackboard) 黒白 （コクビャク black & white, right & wrong)

	Kanji and Examples	
3. **11** 黄 (yellow, pg. 60)	横 よこ／オウ (horizontal, side)	
	き／（こ）	黄色 （きいろ yellow) 黄身 （きみ egg yolk) 黄金色 （こがねいろ golden color)
	コウ／オウ	黄河 （コウガ the Yellow River) 黄金 （オウゴン gold)

Kanji and Examples		Stroke Order and Practice								
4. 11 責 (condemn, blame, burden, pg. 60)	積 つ・もる／セキ (accumulate) 績 セキ (achievement, spinning) 債* サイ (debt)	一	十	キ	主	青	青	青	青	責
		責	責	責	責					
せ・める	責める（せめる condemn, blame, pg. 60)									
セキ	責任（セキニン responsibility)　責務（セキム duty, obligation)　職責（ショクセキ work responsibility)									

Twelve Stroke Kanji

Kanji and Examples		Stroke Order and Practice								
1. 12 歯 (tooth)	齢* レイ (age)	丨	｜	⺊	止	止	歩	歩	歩	歩
		柴	歯	歯	歯	歯				
は	歯医者（はイシャ dentist)　虫歯（むしば decayed tooth, pg. 173)									
シ	歯石（シセキ [dental] tartar)　歯科（シカ dentistry)									
2. 12 象 (elephant, image)	像 ゾウ (image, statue)	⺈	⺈	⺈	龱	岛	岛	象	象	象
		象	象	象	象	象				
ショウ／ゾウ	象形文字（ショウケイモジ pictorial Kanji)　印象（インショウ impression)　象げ（ゾウげ ivory)									

EXERCISES FOR TEN THROUGH TWELVE STROKE KANJI

WRITING EXERCISE
Fill in each box to make a word.

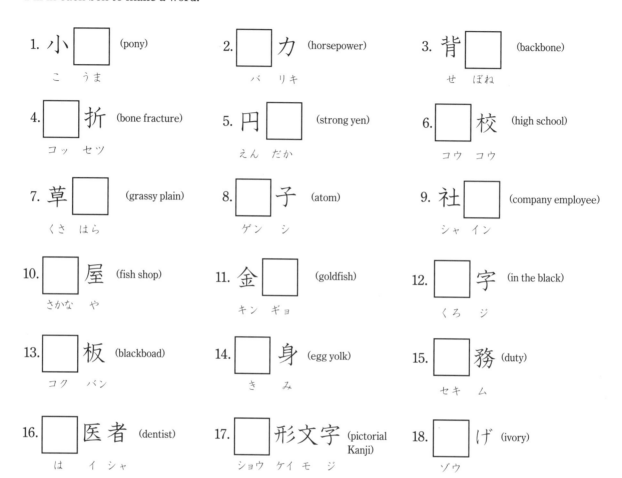

1. 小☐ (pony)
こ うま

2. ☐力 (horsepower)
バ リキ

3. 背☐ (backbone)
せ ぼね

4. ☐折 (bone fracture)
コッ セツ

5. 円☐ (strong yen)
えん だか

6. ☐校 (high school)
コウ コウ

7. 草☐ (grassy plain)
くさ はら

8. ☐子 (atom)
ゲン シ

9. 社☐ (company employee)
シャ イン

10. ☐屋 (fish shop)
さかな や

11. 金☐ (goldfish)
キン ギョ

12. ☐字 (in the black)
くろ ジ

13. ☐板 (blackboad)
コク バン

14. ☐身 (egg yolk)
き み

15. ☐務 (duty)
セキ ム

16. ☐医者 (dentist)
は イ シャ

17. ☐形文字 (pictorial Kanji)
ショウ ケイ モ ジ

18. ☐げ (ivory)
ゾウ

READING EXERCISE

Read the following sentences, and write the correct *furigana* (pronunciation of Kanji written in Hiragana regardless of whether the reading of the Kanji is On or Kun) below the underlined Kanji.

1. このあいだはじめて<u>馬券</u>を買いました。

   (I bought a horse race betting ticket for the first time the other day.)

2. あの柔道せんしゅの<u>骨格</u>はすばらしいですね。
   じゅうどう

   (That jūdō champion's build is sturdy, isn't it?.)

3. <u>日本</u>の<u>高速道路</u>はいつも<u>込</u>んでいます。

   (Expressways in Japan are always crowded.)

4. ここは桜で名高い上野です。
　　　さくら　　　うえの

(This is Ueno, which is famous for cherry blossoms.)

5. 夏は涼しい高原で休みたいです。

(In the summer, I would like to vacation on a cool plateau.)

6. あなたはこのゴルフ場の会員ですか。

(Are you a member of this golf course?)

7. これは朝早く魚市場で買った新鮮な魚です。

(This is some fresh fish that I bought early this morning at the fish market.)

8. 毎日ビーチへ行って顔がまっ黒になりました。

(Because I went to the beach every day, my face became very tanned (dark).)

9. これは黒白のつけにくい事件です。

(This is an incident in which it is difficult to determine right and wrong.)

10. その黄色いバラはきれいですね。

(Those yellow roses are beautiful, aren't they?)

11. そんなにわたしを責めないでください。

(Please don't blame me (so much).)

12. それはだれの責任ですか。

(Whose responsibility is it?)

13. 彼は歯科医になりました。

(He became a dentist.)

14. はじめて日本へ行った時の印象はどうでしたか。

(What were your impressions of your first visit to Japan?)

ANALYZING AND READING EXERCISE FOR EXAMPLE KANJI

Analyze the following Kanji. Write the *furigana* below the underlined Kanji. (Some familiar Kanji are included in this exercise.)

1. 驚 ＝ [　　] ＋ [　　] ＋ [　　] ＋ [　　]
   <u>一年</u>の<u>間</u>に<u>彼</u>の<u>日本語</u>は<u>驚</u>くほど

   <u>上手</u>になりました。
   じょうず
   (His Japanese improved remarkably (surprisingly) within one year.)

2. 滑* ＝ [　　] ＋ [　　]
   このゆかは<u>滑</u>るから<u>気</u>をつけてください。
   (This floor is slippery, so please be careful.)

3. 稿* ＝ [　　] ＋ [　　]
   <u>原稿</u>はいつまでにできますか。
   (When will the manuscript be ready?)

4. 願 ＝ [　　] ＋ [　　]
   あなたの<u>幸福</u>を<u>願</u>っています。
   (I wish you happiness.)

5. 損 ＝ [　　] ＋ [　　]
   <u>株</u>が<u>下</u>がって<u>大分</u> <u>損</u>をしました。
   (I lost quite a bit [of money] because the stock went down.)

6. 鮮* ＝ [　　] ＋ [　　]
   この<u>魚</u>は<u>新鮮</u>ですね。さしみにしましょう。
   (This fish is fresh, isn't it? Let's make it into sashimi.)

7. 黙 ＝ [　　] ＋ [　　] ＋ [　　]
   この<u>事</u>はだれにも<u>黙</u>っていてください。
   (Please remain silent about this matter with everyone.)

8. 横 ＝ [　　] ＋ [　　]
   わたしの<u>横</u>に<u>青木</u>さんがいます。
   (Aoki-san is at my side.)

9. 積 = [   ] + [   ]
    <u>雪</u>はどのぐらい<u>積</u>もっていますか。

    (How much snow has accumulated?)

10. 績 = [   ] + [   ]
    <u>今度</u>のテストの<u>成績</u>はどうでしたか。

    (What was your grade on this [last] test?)

11. 齢* = [   ] + [   ]
    <u>父</u>の<u>年齢</u>は<u>六十五才</u>です。

    (My father's age is 65.)

12. 像 = [   ] + [   ]
    <u>百年後</u>の<u>世界</u>を<u>想像</u>できますか。
        ご

    (Can you imagine the world 100 years from now?)

Exercise Answers

Part I

p. viii

bird, bamboo, eye, ricefield, person, rain

three, below, above

p. ix

cliff, cry, flame

p. x

1. HAN, HAN, HAN

2. 休 yasu·mu

p. 4

1. ahiru	2. yoko sen, magari
3. nanamekagi, naname sen	4. naname sen, ahiru
5. ten, magari	6. naname sen, yoko sen, tate sen
7. tate sen, nanamekagi, naname sen	8. tate sen, kado kagi, yoko sen
9. naname sen, naname kagi, ten	10. kado kagi, naname sen, yoko sen
11. tate sen, yoko sen, kado kagi, ten	12. tate sen, kado kagi, yoko sen, naname sen

p.8

1. (1) a. (2) a. (3) b. (4) a. (5) b. (6) a. (7) b. (8) a.

p. 10
1.

1. 3	2. 2	3. 2	4. 4	5. 3	6. 5	7. 5
8. 3	9. 3	10. 4	11. 4	12. 5	13. 3	14. 3
15. 4	16. 5	17. 4	18. 5	19. 3	20. 2	21. 4
22. 4	23. 3	24. 5	25. 5	26. 6	27. 6	28. 6

p.11
2.

1. 4	2. 8	3. 4	4. 8	5. 3	6. 7	7. 3	8. 5
9. 4	10. 4	11. 3	12. 2	13. 4	14. 1	15. 2	16. 5
17. 9	18. 9	19. 6	20. 7	21. 8	22. 4	23. 5	24. 3

3.

7 strokes: (1) and (4)   8 strokes: (3) and (6)

p.24
1.

1. 1, 3   2. 13, 15   3. 4, 10   4. 8, 9   5. 7, 11

2.

1. kuruma-hen	2. te-hen	3. gyō-nim-ben
4. kozato-hen	5. me-hen	6. yumi-hen
7. shimesu-hen	8. kane-hen	9. onna-hen
10. ni-sui	11. hi-hen	12. tsuchi-hen
13. nogi-hen	14. koromo-hen	15. ki-hen

p.28
1.

1, 3 ,4, 6, 7, 9, 11, 12, 14, 15, 16, 18

2.

1. 2, 9   2. 1, 12   3. 6, 13   4. 4, 10   5. 5, 11

p. 31
1.

1, 3, 5, 6, 10, 12, 15, 16

2.

1. 5, 8   2. 1, 14   3. 9, 11   4. 2, 12   5. 3, 6

3

1. ana-kammuri	2. u-kammuri	3. ame-kammuri
4. nabebuta	5. take-kammuri	6. wa-kammuri
7. kusa-kammuri	8. hito-gashira	9. ana-kammuri

p. 35
1.

1, 3, 5, 6, 8, 9, 12, 16

2.

1. 8, 15   2. 2, 10   3. 1, 13   4. 5, 11   5. 4, 6

p. 37
1.

2, 5, 8, 10, 11, 14, 15

2.

1. 5, 8   2. 2, 6   3. 12, 15

p. 39
1.

2, 5, 6, 8, 10, 11, 12, 13, 17, 19

2.

1. 5, 6, 12, 13, 17

2. 8, 10, 19

3. 2, 11

p. 42
1.

1, 2, 4, 11, 12, 13, 15, 18, 19, 21, 23, 25

2.

1. 6, 9, 13   2. 2, 4, 11   3. 7, 10, 15

p. 43
1.
a.

1. 7   2. 1   3. 5   4. 3   5. 4   6. 2   7. 6

b.

1. 1   2. 2   3. 2   4. 6   5. 2   6. 3   7. 1   8. 1 or 2

9. 4   10. 1   11. 6   12. 3   13. 3   14. 7   15. 6   16. 1

17. 7   18. 3   19. 7   20. 2   21. 5   22. 5   23. 1   24. 7

25. 1   26. 5   27. 4   28. 5   29. 7   30. 3   31. 4   32. 1

p. 44
c.

1. 1, 7   2. 6, 3   3. 2, 4   4. 1, 5

5. 1, 3   6. 4, 5   7. 3, 6   8. 3, 8

9. 5, 3   10. 7, 3   11. 2, 9   12. 3, 5

2.

a. 8   b. 1   c. 5   d. 11   e. 15   f. 3   g. 7

h. 6   i. 14   j. 12

p. 45
3.

a. 2   b. 4   c. 19   d. 12   e. 1   f. 13   g. 3

h. 20   i. 14   j. 15   k. 7   l. 18   m. 8   n. 5

o. 16   p. 6   q. 11   r. 9   s. 10   t. 17

4.

a. san-zui   b. nim-ben   c. te-hen   d. gyō-nim-ben

e. kusa-kammuri   f. nogi-hen   g. mon-gamae   h. shin-nyū

i. ame-kammuri   j. take-kammuri   k. risshim-ben   l. gom-ben

p. 46
5.

a. ki-hen, nogi-hen   b. shin-nyū, en-nyō

   c. nim-ben, gyō-nim-ben   d. u-kammuri, wa-kammuri

   e. shimesu-hen, koromo-hen   f. gan-dare, ma-dare

   g. ni-sui, san-zui   h. kozato-hen, ōzato

   i. te-hen, ushi-hen   j. boku-zukuri, ka-keru

   k. shikabane, to-dare   l. kai-hen, ōgai

p. 54
2.

1. g   2. e   3. a   4. j   5. c   6. f   7. h   8. i   9. b   10. d

p. 58
1.

1. variation of katakana リ + katakana ヨ + katakana ワ + haba

2. varation of 小 + katakana ワ + kuchi=mouth + kai=shell

3. u-kammuri + fuyu-gashira + kuchi=mouth

4. take-kammuri + me=eye + nijū-ashi

5. katakana ツ + katakana ワ + chikara=strength

6. hi-hen/nichi-hen + katakana ヨ + furutori

7. katakana ソ plus Kanji 一 + tsuki=moon + rittō=sword

8. tsuchi-hen + 也

p. 59
2.

1. d   2. e   3. b   4. h   5. f   6. i   7. j   8. a   9. g   10. c

p. 63
2.

1. c   2. f   3. h   4. i   5. d   6. g   7. b   8. a   9. e   10. j

p. 68
2.

1. d   2. f   3. g   4. a   5. b   6. c   7. e

p. 75
2.

1. n   2. d   3. e   4. b   5. a   6. c   7. i   8. j
9. l   10. g   11. m   12. f   13. h   14. k   15. o   16. p

p. 81

1. d   2. i   3. g   4. a   5. h   6. b   7. k   8. j
9. c   10. f   11. l   12. e

p. 85
2.

1. h   2. f   3. e   4. a   5. c   6. i   7. d   8. j
9. g   10. b

Part II

p. 93

1. 一　　2. 乙　3. 二　4. 七　5. 八, 八　6. 九, 七

7. 十, 十　8. 十　9. 人　10. 人　11. 入　12. 入

13. 刀　14. 刀　15. 力　16. 力　17. 力　18. 丁

p. 94

1. ひと（つ）, ふた（つ）　　2. に, か（う）　　3. しちがつ, なのか

4. やっ（つ）　　5. くがつ, ここのか　6. きゅうふん

7. ひと, じん　　8. い（り）ぐち　9. はい（る）

10. ななちょうめ

p. 95

1. もの, かわ（く）　　2. げんき　　　3. けんきゅう

4. まいあさ, はや（く）, お（きる）　5. にほん, にく, たか（い）　6. こ（む）

7. こがたな, き（れる）, たいせつ　8. に, なな／しち, くわ（える）, きゅう

9. いもうと, まち　　10. ねんしゅう

p. 101

1. 三　2. 三十人　3. 千　4. 干　5. 干　6. 十万　7. 万　8. 大　9. 大

10. 小　11. 小　12. 上　13. 上　14. 上下　15. 下　16. 下　17. 下　18. 山

19. 山　20. 小川　21. 川　22. 土　23. 土　24. 士　25. 女, 子　26. 子　27. 女

p. 102

1. さんがつ, みっか　　2. まど, みっ（つ）　　3. たなか, ちば

4. さんぜん　　5. まんいち, あめ, いえ　6. いえ, おお（きい）

7. ちい（さい）, くるま, か（う）　8. しょうせつ　9. つくえ, うえ

10. ようふく, いろ, じょうひん　11. ちかてつ, こ（む）　12. やまのぼ（り）

13. ふじさん, かざん　　14. どようび　　15. こ, じょしだい, にゅうがく

p. 103

1. こ（ども）, とも（だち）, した, だ（す）　2. げんいん　　3. あめ, すく（ない）

4. とうげ, むら　　5. やま, いわ　　6. にほん, しまぐに

7. かんじ, おん, くん, よ（み）　8. かんじ, か（く）, とき, ひつじゅん, し（る）, たいせつ

9. こがた, くるま, か（う）　10. まいにち, かいしゃ, しごと

11. みせ, う（る）　12. こえ　　13. やす（い）, か（う）

14. だいす（き）

p. 108

1. ロ　2. ロ　3. 夕　4. 弓　5. エ

6. 大工　7. オ　8. 丸　9. 丸　10. 久

11. 己　12. 己　13. 一寸　14. 亡　15. 与

p. 109

1. こ, くちごた（え）　　　　2. じんこう

3. こんばん, ゆうはん, た（べる）

4. いっちょういっせき, かいけつ, もんだい

5. いま, くに, じんこう, う（ち）あ（げる）

6. いま, さんじゅうに, さい

7. ひ, まる, にほん, はた

8. ひさ（しぶり）, げんき

9. ようふく, すんぽう

10. ちち, にねん, まえ, な（くなる）

11. こ（ども）, かね, あた（える）

12. かれ, およ（ぶ）

p. 110

1. なまえ

2. とうきょう, じんこう, おお（い）

3. ゆうがた, そと

4. にほん, みち, ひだり, はし（る）

5. いろ, くちべに, す（き）

6. こ（ども）, ざい, のこ（す）

7. りょうり, ざいりょう

8. すこ（し）, ねつ

9. はんじゅく, す（き）

10. ゆうかん

11. かいがん

12. まいにち, にっき, か（く）

13. まいあさ, じ, お（きる）

14. てら

15. わす（れる）

16. ちか（ごろ）, いそが（しい）

17. かいしゃ, やく, にじっぷん

18. うつ（す）, しゃ

19. どうきゅうせい

20. ちか（ごろ）, す（う）, ひと, すく（ない）

p. 117

1. 五　　2. 六人　3. 日　　4. 月, 日　5. 月　　6. 火　　7. 火, 日　8. 水

9. 水, 日　10. 木　　11. 木, 日　12. 天　　13. 天　14. 夫　　15. 午　　16. 牛

17. 牛　　18. 中　　19. 中　　20. 内　　21. 内　22. 手　　23. 手　　24. 毛

p. 118

1. いつ（つ）, むっ（つ）

2. ごがつ, いつか, きゅうじつ

3. ろくがつ, むいか, にほん, い（く）

4. こんど, にちようび

5. せんじつ

6. つきひ, はや（い）

7. じゅうにがつ, にじゅうごにち

8. にほん, かざん, おお（い）, くに

9. みずいろ, ふく

10. すいえい, しゅ

11. てんき

12. おっと, だいす（き）

13. すく（ない）, くふう

14. ごご, かいもの, い（く）

15. ぎゅうにく, つく（る）

16. ちゅうりつこく

17. うちきん

18. みぎて, も（つ）

19. せんげつ, め, しゅじゅつ

20. もうふ

p. 119

1. ご, はな（す）

2. こんばん, ほし

3. あか（るい）

4. あき, やま, うつく（しい）

5. せんろ

6. にほん, けい, さか（える）

7. かんが（え）, さんせい

8. ゆる（す）

9.

10. じけん, かいけつ

11. やまだ, たなか, なか

12. にほん, ぜいきん, さんがつ, じゅうごにち, おさ（める）

13. あ（げる）

14. おながどり, し（る）

p. 126

1. 方   2. 方   3. 文   4. 文   5. 父   6. 今   7. 分   8. 九, 五, 分

9. 分   10. 公   11. 友   12. 友   13. 反   14. 戸   15. 戸   16. 尺

17. 化   18. 化   19. 比   20. 王   21. 円   22. 円   23. 止   24. 止

p. 127

1. つく（り）, かた, し（る）

2. にほん, ぶんか, し（る）

3. ふぼ, いま

4. ことし, あめ, おお（い）

5. やっ（つ）, わ（ける）

6. だいぶ

7. こうえん, こ（ども）

8. ゆうじん, ほん

9. はんたい

10. いえ, と

11. こ（ども）, ば（ける）, はなし, す（き）

12. きょうと, とうきょう, くら（べる）, まち

13. いま, えん, つよ（い）

14. あめ, ちゅうし

p. 128

1. とも, たず（ねる）

2. とり, はな（す）

3. いえ, もん, もん

4. がっこう

5. こむぎこ

6. まず（しい）, いえ

7. いま, そうり

8. は, ぬ（く）, た（べる）

9. ゆうはん, じ

10. ところ, うみ, ちか（く）

11. にほんご, ぶん, ご, やく（し）

12. えき, じっぷん

13. むかし, くら（べる）, か, さ（がる）

14. にかい

15. ひひょう

16. せいしょ, よ（む）

17. まいにち, ある（く）, がっこう

18. にほん, れきし

p. 135

1. 元   2. 元   3. 予   4. 二十三区   5. 氏

6. 片方   7. 心   8. 心   9. 犬   10. 不

11. 支   12. 少   13. 欠   14. 斗   15. 井

16. 井   17. 一升   18. 介

1. がんじつ, おんな, ひと, きもの, き（る）

2. よやく

3. はな, くべつ

4. にほん, かたみち

5. こころづよ（い）

6. げんき, あんしん

7. あきたけん, ばんけん

8. ことし, あめ, すく（なく）, みず, ふそく

9. ささ（える）

10. しじ

11. すこ（し）, さむ（い）

12. しょうすう, ひと, き（く）

13. ちゃ, すこ（し）, か（ける）

14. けってん, き, みじか（い）

15. むかし, ます, こめ

16. じゅうねん, はは, かいほう

p. 137

1. だいがくいん, がく

2. かね, あず（ける）

3. おうしゅう

4. かみ, しめい, か（く）

5. ちか（い）, ほん, しゅっぱん

6. ほん, おも（う）

7. あい

8. びょうじょう

9. かんが（え）, ひてい

10. まつ, き, えだ, すこ（し）, き（る）

11. ぎじゅつ, すす（む）

12. すな, こ（ども）

13. まいにち, みず, の（む）

14. つぎ, でんしゃ, じ

15. ないか

16. きょうと, やま, かこ（む）, まち

17. ちか（く）, や

18. せかい, いちばん, たか（い）, やま

p. 143

1. 白　2. 白　3. 目　4. 目　5. 田　6. 田

7. 由　8. 申　9. 正　10. 正　11. 正　12. 石

13. 石　14. 石　15. 立　16. 立　17. 出　18. 出

19. 四　20. 生　21. 生　22. 生　23. 主　24. 主

25. 矢　26. 失　27. 白

p. 144

1. しろくろ

2. こと, めいはく

3. にほんご, なら（う）, もくてき

4. ゆでん

5. しごと, やす（む）, りゆう

6. もう（しわけ）

7. ぜいきん, しんこく

8. まさ（に）

9. こうせい, と（り）, ひ（き）

10. むかし, だ（す）

11. こんばん, がいしゅつ

12. しがつ, よっか

13. いま, よじ, よんぷん

14. ながい（き）

15. う（まれる）, からだ

16. も（ち）ぬし

17. にほん, こめ, しゅしょく

18. いえ, ざいさん, うしな（う）, ひと　19. しつれい

20. しっぱい, せいこう

p. 146

1. よっ（つ）, とき, なら（う）

2. てそう, み（る）

3. ゆび, ほそ（い）

4. あぶら, い（る）

5. うちゅう, かがく, けんきゅう, たいせつ

6. かみ, しん（じる）

7. しょうけん, がいしゃ, つと（める）

8. すこ（し）, つくえ, うえ, せいり

9. せいかい

10. こ（ども）, おお（きい）, こえ, な（く）

11. にほん, どうわ

12. せいかく, す（かれる）

13. さんち, ゆうめい

14. いま, す（む）

15. くるま, ちゅうい

16. しょう, ひと, うたが（う）

17. てつ

p. 152

1. 母　2. 母　3. 半　4. 平　5. 平　6. 古　7. 古

8. 兄　9. 兄　10. 史　11. 央　12. 皮　13. 皮　14. 世

15. 世　16. 世　17. 去　18. 皿　19. 以　20. 必　21. 必

p. 153

1. ふぼ, す（き）

2. こんげつ, なか（ば）, とうきょう, い（く）

3. はんにち, しごと, やす（む）

4. いえ, ひらや

5. ちち, のこ（す）, かね, きょうだい, こうへい, わ（ける）

6. だんじょ, びょうどう, あつか（う）

7. ちゅうこ, か（う）

8. こだい, ぶんか, けんきゅう

9. せんげつ, しじょう

10. かれ, ひにく, い (う)

11. いま, せかい, じんこう

12. かこ

13. はいざら

14. きゅうじゅうど, いじょう

15. にく, いがい

16. がくせい, ひつどく, ほん

p. 154

1. じょせい, はんじ, すく (ない)

2. えいが, ひょうばん

3. ひろ (い) , いま

4. ふじさん, おお (きい) , みずうみ

5. こんばん, こ, いわ (い)

6. せいとう, しじ

7. じびき, つか (う)

8. とも (だち) , えいが, み (る) , い (き)

9. かのじょ, えいご, にほんご

10. なみ

11. わか (い) , ひと, やぶ (れる)

12. こ (の) , は

13. かれ, だいがく, ほうか, はい (る)

14. いま, せかい, くに, かめい

15. に (る)

16.

17. あいだ, ひみつ

p. 161

1. 広   2. 広   3. 司   4. 可   5. 句   6. 包   7. 包   8. 示   9. 永

10. 穴   11. 穴   12. 用   13. 民   14. 台   15. 北   16. 北   17. 市   18. 市

1. えきまえ, ひろば, ひと

2. こうだい, うちゅう, けんきゅう

3. じょうし

4. ちち, きょか, だいがく, はい (る)

5. つつ (み) , がみ

6. ほうちょう, き (れる)

7. こ (ども) , しめ (す)

8. えいじゅう

9. おおあな, あ (てる)

10. ほん, ごさつ, か (う)

11. たんざく, はいく, か (く)

12. しゃよう, とうきょう, い (く)

13. じゆう, びょうどう, みんしゅしゅぎ, せいしん

14. あたら (しい) , くるま, いちだい, か (う)

15. きたぐに, はる

16. ほくせい, かぜ, つよ (い)

17. しじょう, で (る) , あたら (しい)

p. 163

1. かいしゃ, かくだい

2. ちち, こうざん

3. うた, かし

4. こんばん, なに

5. にほんじん, ひと, けいご

6. けいかん, しごと

7. あか, だ (く)

8. がっこう, きんし

9. なつ, まいにち, およ (ぐ)

10. まど, あ (ける)

11. まいにち, はなや, まえ, とお (る) , がっこう, い (く)

12. さくばん, すこ (し) , あたま, いた (い)

13. こ (ども) , ねむ (る)

14. にほんご, べんきょう, はじ (める)

15. せ, たか (い)

16. あね, しょうがっこう, こうちょう

p. 168

1. 代   2. 代   3. 代   4. 加   5. 未   6. 末   7. 末   8. 令   9. 冬

10. 冬   11. 付   12. 付   13. 召   14. 占   15. 占   16. 丙   17. 甘   18. 矛

p. 169

1. か（わり），で（る）
2. いもうと，こうたい，さら
3. いち，に，くわ（える），さん
4. せかい，じんこう，まいねん，ぞうか
5. よてい，みてい
6. ごがつ，すえ，にほん，い（く）
7. ふゆやすみ，い（く）
8. ちか（ごろ），はやし，つ（き），あ（い）
9. なに，め（し），あ（がる）
10. ほしうらな（い）
11. かれ，どくせんよく，つよ（い）
12. かれ，か（つ），べんきょう
13. かれ，むじゅん

p. 170

1. とも（だち），か（す）
2. ねんがじょう，か（く）
3. あじ
4. いもうと，いま，じゅうご
5. て，つめ（たい）
6. ねん，にほん，せんりょう
7. しごと，お（わる）
8. とうきょう，にほん，しゅふ
9. とうきょう，きっぷ，か（う）
10. まね（く）
11. とも，しょうかい
12. みせ
13. びょうき
14. くみあい，かにゅう
15. そせん
16. にほん，おとこ，ひと，こん，き（る）
17. かれ，じゅうどう
18. かいぎ，つと（める）

p. 176

1. 糸　　2. 糸　　3. 耳　　4. 耳　　5. 虫　　6. 虫　　7. 羽
8. 羽　　9. 竹　　10. 米　　11. 米　　12. 色　　13. 色　　14. 羊
15. 肉　　16. 血　　17. 舌　　18. 寺　　19. 衣　　20. 衣　　21. 米

p. 177

1. けいと
2. みみ，はい（る）
3. むし，じ，よ（める）
4. ことり，いちわ
5. かれ，ちくば，とも
6. にほん，べいか，おお（きな）
7. えいが，とくしょく，おんがく
8. ぎゅうにく，とりにく，す（き）
9. ちか（ごろ），けっしょく
10. かれ，どくぜつ
11. きょうと，じいん
12. いしょくじゅう，せいかつ，たいせつ

p. 178

1. にほんご，さんそ
2. むらさき，ようふく
3. かれ，はなし，き（く）
4. しちがつ，よっか，べいこく，どくりつ
5. あめ，よくじつ
6. こた（える）
7. とも（だち），たず（ねる），とき，みち，まよ（う）
8. かれ，だいがく，で（る），ちち，みせ，つ（ぐ）
9. かれ，た（える）
10. いま，たいへいよう，うえ
11. さかな，しんせん
12. ふ，す（き）
13. こうしゅう，でんわ
14. とうきょう，せいかつひ
15. ま（たせる）
16. かれ，しじん
17. あたら（しい），せいひん

p. 183

1. 百　　2. 兆　　3. 光　　4. 光　　5. 先　　6. 先　　7. 毎年　8. 年　　9. 合

10. 合　　11. 各　　12. 自　　13. 同　　14. 曲　　15. 曲　　16. 西　　17. 西　　18. 両

p. 184

1. ほん, さんびゃくえん
2. き, め, で (る) , はる, きざ (し) , み (える)
3. ぜんちょう
4. ほし, ひか (る)
5. なつ, たいよう, つよ (い)
6. さき, しつれい
7. かれ, まいばん, の (む)
8. ねんまつ, い (く)
9. たなか, むかし, し (り) , あ (い)
10. がっしゅうこく, こくみん
11. かくち, はな
12. はは, じぶん, じぶん, い (う)
13. かれ, どうそうせい
14. こんばん, きょくもく, なん
15. なつ, にしび
16. せいよう, りょうり, す (き)
17. つう (じて) , とうざい, ぶんか
18. りょうほう, き (く) , き (める)

p. 185

1. まいにち, しゅく
2. いぬ, に (げる)
3. くるま, あら (う) , あめ
4. うめ, はな, はる
5. みち, かね, ひろ (う)
6. まいつき, げつまつ, きゅうりょう
7. だんじょ, かくさ
8. さか, のぼ (る) , いき, くる (しい)
9. いぬ, はな
10. かのじょ, どう
11. いちねん, ゆた
12. のうか, ひと

p. 190

1. 州　　2. 共　　3. 共　　4. 行　　5. 成, 行

6. 成　　7. 式　　8. 交　　9. 交　　10. 因

11. 至　　12. 至　　13. 舟　　14. 吉　　15. 充

1. きゅうしゅう, ほんしゅう
2. ちか (ごろ) , わか (い) , ひと, なん
3. かれ, い (く) , さき, い (う) , いえ, で (る)
4. いちぎょう, か (く)
5. こ (ども) , せいちょう, はや (い)
6. にほん, よっ (つ) , しま, な (り) , た (つ)
7. にほんじん, けいしき
8. ようしき, わしき
9. とも (だち) , まじ (わる)
10. せかい, かっこく, ぶんか, こうりゅう
11. かれ, びょうき, よ (る)
12. しじょう, めいれい
13. じんじゃ, だいきち
14. にほん, か, しゅにく, はん
15. かね, ほんだい, あ (てる)
16. すこ (し) , じゅうぶん

p. 192

1. ほうしゅう
2. なつ, いじょう
3. くるま, きょうきゅう, お (う)
4. えら (ぶ)
5. ごばんがい, ある (く)
6. かれ, ひと, せいい
7. にほん, しろ
8. にほん, いま, さか (ん)
9. しけん
10. ひかく, ぶんがく, けんきゅう
11. ふぼ, おん, やま, たか (く) , うみ
12. きょうしつ, がくせい, にじゅうにん

13. や, ほんや

14. ふね, せかい, りょこう

15. かれ, こうくう, がいしゃ, つと (める)

16. むす (ぶ)

17. いま, ぎんこうかぶ, か (う)

18. おな (じ) , いろ, とういつ, ほう

p. 199

1. 見　2. 見　3. 貝　4. 足　5. 足　6. 走　7. 走　8. 車
9. 車　10. 里　11. 里　12. 言　13. 言　14. 言　15. 豆　16. 豆
17. 谷　18. 角　19. 角　20. 身　21. 身　22. 良　23. 臣　24. 兵

p. 200

1. みほん, み (せる)

2. たいりく, はっけん, い (われる)

3. あかがい, だいす (き)

4. ほん, か (う) , かね, た (りる)

5. いっそく, か (う)

6. こんど, か (う) , しんしゃ, なん

7. いえ, で (る) , なが (い) , さとごころ

8. きょうり

9. かた, げんごがく, べんきょう

10. なに, でんごん

11. かのじょ, たにま, ひと

12. よ (つ) , かど, ひだり, ま (がる) , てん, み (える)

13. なかみ, なん

14. どくしん

15. くるま, まいとし, かいりょう

16. やまだ, よ (い) , とも (だち)

p. 201

1. こ, ちちおや, に (る)

2. かんじ, にじゅう, おぼ (える)

3. かれ, ま (ける)

4. で (る) , しょうひん

5. かのじょ, か (す) , かね, そく

6. いま, にほんご, せいと, なんにん

7. こ (ども) , つ (れる) , こうえん, い (く)

8. かれ, くうぐん

9. のはら, こ (ども)

10. かのじょ, りょうり

11. い (う) , しん (じる)

12. かれ, あたま

13. みじか (い)

14. ほん, ないよう

15. せわ, ひと, かんしゃ

16. むすめ, いま, だいがくせい

17. らん

18. すなはま, こ (ども)

p. 207

1. 求　2. 束　3. 束　4. 来　5. 来　6. 余　7. 赤　8. 赤　9. 我
10. 我　11. 君　12. 君　13. 告　14. 告　15. 系　16. 図　17. 麦　18. 卵

1. せかい, へいわ, もと (める)

2. きゅうじん, こうこく, しんぶん, で (る)

3. ひとたば, か (う)

4. やまだ, き (ます) , ことし, こ (な)

5. あま (り) , た (べ) , す (ぎ) , いた (く)

6. ひとり, よけい

7. あか, か (う)

8. かれ, せきじゅうじ, びょういん, にゅういん

9. は, いた (く) , が (まん)

10. なかむら, くん, とも (だち)

11. かのじょ, きも (ち) , こくはく

12. けい, じんこう

13. まいにち, としょかん, べんきょう

14. らんおう, おお (い)

p. 209

1. にほん, やきゅう

2. しんかんせん, はや (い)

3. かえ (る) , とちゅう, ほんや

4. にちようび, のぞ (く) , かれ, いえ

5. かれ, おんしゃ, つみ   6. かれ, ぎろん, す (き)

7. にほんご, ぐん   8. かれ, ぞうせん, がいしゃ, つと (める)

9. かいしゃ, がかり   10. まご, ごにん

p. 214

1. 青   2. 青   3. 金   4. 金   5. 雨   6. 雨

7. 東   8. 東   9. 京   10. 長   11. 長   12. 表

13. 表   14. 門   15. 表門   16. 並   17. 幸   18. 幸

1. あおぞら, しろ (い) , くも   2. せいしゅん, にど

3. いま, かね   4. げんきん, も (つ) , ほう

5. おおあめ, しごと, やす (む)   6. うてん, とき, しあい, ちゅうし

7. えき, ひがしぐち, ま (つ)   8. いま, ちゅうとう, へいわ, おお (き)

9. こんど, じょうきょう   10. しゃちょう, いま, がいしゅつちゅう

11. じぶん, きも (ち) , ひょうげん, ほう   12. かどで, いわ (い)

13. かれ, せんもん, なん   14. ひとな (み) , せいかつ

15. さいわ (い) , てんき   16. けんこう, こうふく, せいかつ

p. 216

1. そら, は (れる)   2. たにがわ, みず, きよ (く)

3. しず (かな) , うみ, み (る) , こころ, やす (む)   4. とも (だち) , ぎん

5. みず, も (れる)   6. まいにち, れんしゅう

7. れいとう, す (き)   8. まど, うつく (しい) , やま, ふうけい, み (る) , す (き)

9. ことし, なつ, すず (しい)   10. かれ, じぶん, いけん, つよ (く) , しゅちょう

11. てちょう   12. ほん, と (じる)

13. じけん, かんけい   14. しけん, もんだい

15. きょく, がくふ   16. じょうほう, はい (る)

p. 221

1. 者   2. 者   3. 昔   4. 果   5. 果   6. 非

7. 直   8. 周   9. 固   10. 官   11. 垂直   12. 免

1. とうきょう, わかもの, まち   2. しょうせつ, さくしゃ

3. かのじょ, むかし   4. かれ, せきじつ

5. わかもの, は (て) , ひろ (がる)   6. けっか

7. えいが, ひじょう   8. ただ (ち) , びょういん, い (く)

9. じ, なお (す)   10. ちょくつう, でんわ

11. いえ, まわ (り)   12. かのじょ, せかい, いっしゅう, たび, で (かける)

13. かれ, きょうこ, ひと   14. すいどう, みず, た (れる)

15. くるま, まぬか (れる)   16. にほん, りょこうしゃ, めんぜいひんてん, い (く)

p. 223

1. あつ (い)   2. きょうと, ふる (い) , みやこ

3. とも (だち) , か (りる) , ほん   4. ふく, お (しい)

5. こくせき   6. いま, はっか, なら (う)

7. かし

9. つみ

11. お（く）

13. せんしゅう, ほん, か（う）

15. かのじょ, こじん, もんだい

17. すいどうかん

19.

8. し（め）, いぬ, かんが（える）, かな（しい）

10. はいく, じゅうしち, あらわ, みじか, し

12. か（い）ね

14. もんだい, しら（べる）

16. としょかん, ちか（く）

18. ゆうびん, き（ました）

20. まいばん, べんきょう

p. 230

1. 南　2. 南　3. 風　4. 風　5. 音　6. 音　7. 食　8. 品
9. 品　10. 首　11. 首　12. 重　13. 重　14. 相　15. 相　16. 則
17. 革　18. 革　19. 面　20. 面　21. 単　22. 軍　23. 飛　24. 乗

1. ちか（い）, とうなん, りょこう

3. にほん, くがつ, たいふう, きせつ

5. かのじょ, ねいろ

7. ゆうはん, わしょく, ようしょく

9. かんじ, なら（う）, ぶしゅ, し（る）, たいせつ

11. ことし, じゅうだい, なん

13. かれ, かくしん, せいとう

15. かれ, たんどく, のぼ（る）

17. じょうきゃく

2. いま, そと, おおかぜ

4. なに, ものおと

6. はつおん

8. いま, しなぎ（れ）

10. つくえ, うえ, ほん, かさ（ねる）

12. なつ, そうとう, あつ（く）

14. びょういん, めんかい, じかん

16. あつ（い）, と（び）, こ（み）

18. ぜひ, き

p.232

1. まいつき, てら, けんきん

3. ことば, いみ, し（る）

5. かれ, たいそう, せんせい

7. うご（く）, ま（つ）

9. かんそう, き（く）

11. いえ, みち, ひだりがわ

13. まいにち, うんどう, はこ（ぶ）

15. とうきょう, じんこう, かじょう, す（む）

2. よる, みち, くら（い）

4. いま, さんにん, こ（ども）, やしな（う）

6. かれ, どう

8. かのじょ, あさ, ばん, はたら（く）

10. はこ, なか, なに

12. せんそう, せかい

14. しきしゃ

17. まいにち, しゅくだい, ていしゅつ

p.238

1. 馬　2. 馬　3. 骨　4. 骨　5. 高　6. 高　7. 原　8. 原　9. 員
10. 魚　11. 魚　12. 黒　13. 黒　14. 黄　15. 責　16. 歯　17. 象　18. 象

1. ばけん, か（う）

3. にほん, こうそくどうろ, こ（む）

5. なつ, すず（しい）, こうげん, やす（む）

7. あさ, はや（く）, うおいちば, か（う）, しんせん, さかな

9. こくびゃく, じけん

11. せ（める）

13. かれ, しかい

2. こっかく

4. なだか（い）

6. じょう, かいいん

8. まいにち, い（く）, かお, くろ

10. きいろ（い）

12. せきにん

14. にほん, い（く）, とき, いんしょう

p. 240

1. いちねん, あいだ, かれ, にほんご, おどろ (く)
2. すべ (る), き
3. げんこう
4. こうふく, ねが (う)
5. かぶ, さ (がる) , だいぶ, そん
6. さかな, しんせん
7. こと, だま (る)
8. よこ, あおき
9. ゆき, つ (もる)
10. こんど, せいせき
11. ちち, ねんれい, ろくじゅうごさい
12. ひゃくねん, せかい, そうぞう

<ruby>漢<rt>かん</rt></ruby><ruby>字<rt>じ</rt></ruby>を<ruby>勉<rt>べん</rt></ruby><ruby>強<rt>きょう</rt></ruby>しましょう
Let's Learn Kanji

1997年10月　第 1 刷発行
2010年 6 月　第11刷発行

著　者　　ジョイス・ユミ・ミタムラ
　　　　　ヤスコ・コサカ・ミタムラ
発行者　　廣田浩二
発行所　　講談社インターナショナル株式会社
　　　　　〒112-8652 東京都文京区音羽1-17-14
　　　　　電話　03-3944-6493 （編集部）
　　　　　　　　03-3944-6492 （マーケティング部・業務部）
　　　　　ホームページ　www.kodansha-intl.com

印刷・製本所　大日本印刷株式会社